Understanding Kubrick's *2001: A Space Odyssey*

Understanding Kubrick's *2001: A Space Odyssey*
Representation and Interpretation

Edited by James Fenwick

intellect Bristol, UK / Chicago, USA

Published in the UK in 2020 by
Intellect, The Mill, Parnall Road, Fishponds, Bristol, BS16 3JG, UK

Published in the USA in 2020 by
Intellect, The University of Chicago Press, 1427 E. 60th Street,
Chicago, IL 60637, USA

Copyright © 2020 Intellect Ltd.
First edition published in 2018

All rights reserved. No part of this publication may be reproduced, stored in a retrieval system, or transmitted, in any form or by any means, electronic, mechanical, photocopying, recording, or otherwise, without written permission.

A catalogue record for this book is available from the British Library.

Copy-editor: MPS Technologies
Cover designer: Aleksandra Szumlas
Production manager: Matthew Floyd
Typesetting: Contentra Technologies

Hardback ISBN: 978-1-78320-863-0
ePDF ISBN: 978-1-78320-865-4
ePUB ISBN: 978-1-78320-864-7
Paperback ISBN: 978-1-78938-212-9

Printed and bound by TJ International, UK.

This is a peer-reviewed publication.

For Marlie,
At the start of your own odyssey

Contents

List of Illustrations		ix
Notes on Contributors		xi
Acknowledgements		xv
Notes on the Text		xvii
Introduction:	Forging new perspectives James Fenwick	1

Part One: Narrative and Adaptation — 13

Chapter One:	'God, it'll be hard topping the H-bomb': Kubrick's search for a new obsession in the path from *Dr. Strangelove* to *2001: A Space Odyssey* Simone Odino	17
Chapter Two:	*2001: A Space Odyssey*: A transcendental trans-locution Suparno Banerjee	33
Chapter Three:	Four-colour Kubrick: Jack Kirby's *2001: A Space Odyssey* as adaptation and extension Dru Jeffries	45

Part Two: Performance — 59

Chapter Four:	Performing the man-ape in 'The Dawn of Man': Daniel Richter and The American Mime Theatre James Fenwick	63
Chapter Five:	Life functions terminated: Actors' performances and the aesthetics of distanced subjectivity in *2001: A Space Odyssey* Vincent Jaunas	79

Part Three: Technology		**95**
Chapter Six:	From technical to cinematographic objects in *2001: A Space Odyssey* Antoine Balga-Prévost	99
Chapter Seven:	*Homo machinus*: Kubrick's two HALs and the evolution of monstrous machines Cynthia J. Miller and A. Bowdoin Van Riper	115
Part Four: Masculinity and the Astronaut		**129**
Chapter Eight:	Clarke and Kubrick's *2001*: A queer odyssey Dominic Janes	133
Chapter Nine:	'But as to whether or not he has feelings is something I don't think anyone can truthfully answer': The image of the astronaut in *2001: A Space Odyssey* and its lasting impact Nils Daniel Peiler	151
Part Five: Visual Spectacle		**163**
Chapter Ten:	Negative/Positive: Metaphors of photography in *2001: A Space Odyssey* Caterina Martino	167
Chapter Eleven:	The sublime in *2001: A Space Odyssey* Rachel Walisko	181
Part Six: Production		**197**
Chapter Twelve:	*2001*: A comprehensive chronology Filippo Ulivieri	201
Appendix One:	Stanley Kubrick filmography	225
Appendix Two:	*2001: A Space Odyssey* film credits	227
Notes		229
Bibliography		239
Index		261

List of Illustrations

Figure 1: Daniel Richter dressed in a test man-ape costume. From the collection of Daniel Richter.

Figure 2: Dan Richter's choreography notes for *2001: A Space Odyssey*'s 'The Dawn of Man'. From the collection of Daniel Richter.

Figure 3: United Nations Secretariat Building under construction, New York. Photograph by Eugene Kodani, c.1951. Courtesy of Environmental Design Visual Resources Center, University of California, Berkeley.

Figure 4: Anita Steckel and the Skyline Painting (1974), by permission of the artist. Steckel photographed in front of one of her works which she had included in the exhibition at Rockland Community College (part of the State University of New York, located 25 miles northwest of Manhattan).

Notes on Contributors

Antoine Balga-Prévost is completing a two-year technical degree in audiovisual production at the Institut National de l'Audiovisuel (Ina, France). He completed a Masters in audiovisual and cinema studies at the Sorbonne-Nouvelle Paris III University, University of Montreal, and Goethe-University Frankfurt am Main, with a thesis entitled, 'Kubrick, McLuhan, and Simondon: A philosophical reading of the machine in *2001: A Space Odyssey*'. His research interests include media theory, the philosophy of technology, new media practices and the aesthetics of cinema.

Suparno Banerjee is associate professor of English at Texas State University, San Marcos, specializing in science-fiction and postcolonial studies. His scholarship has appeared in many academic journals including *Science Fiction Studies*; *Journal of the Fantastic in the Arts*; *Extrapolation*; *Journal of Commonwealth and Postcolonial Studies*; and *South Asian Popular Culture* and in multiple anthologies of critical works on science-fiction including *SF 101: A Guide to Teaching and Studying Science Fiction* published by SFRA.

James Fenwick has written about the British Eady Levy for *The Routledge Companion to British Cinema History* (2017a) and he has also written several articles on Stanley Kubrick including '"Freddie, can you talk?": The Ethics of Betrayal in Frederic Raphael's Memoir *Eyes Wide Open* (1999)' (2017b) and 'Curating Kubrick: Constructing "new perspective" Narratives in Stanley Kubrick Exhibitions' (2017c). His research interests include American cinema, the role of the producer, unmade cinema, and the films of Bob Dylan.

Dominic Janes is professor of modern history at Keele University. A cultural historian, his research focus is on texts and visual images relating to Britain in its local and international contexts since the eighteenth century. His interests are centred on gender, sexuality and religion and he is the author of several books, including *Picturing the Closet: Male Secrecy and Homosexual Visibility in Britain* (2015); *Visions of Queer Martyrdom from John Henry Newman to Derek Jarman* (2015); and *Oscar Wilde Prefigured* (2016).

Vincent Jaunas passed the Agrégation in 2015, with a specialty in English Literature, before starting his Ph.D. at the Université Bordeaux-Montaigne under the direction of Professor Jean-François Baillon. His thesis focuses on subjectivity in the work of Stanley Kubrick.

Dru Jeffries is postdoctoral fellow at the University of Toronto's Cinema Studies Institute. His current research project, 'Kubrick's afterlife: Cultural reverberations and the legacy of a filmmaker', explores the role of paratexts in constructing auteurs in contemporary popular culture. He received his Ph.D. in film and moving image studies from Concordia University in 2014. He is currently completing work on his first book, *Comic Book Film Style: Cinema at 24 Panels Per Second*, and has been recently published in *Porn Studies* (forthcoming); *Cinephile*; and *Quarterly Review of Film and Video*.

Caterina Martino received her Ph.D. from the University of Calabria (Italy) for her thesis 'Photographic Archives: From the Documentation of Cultural Heritage to the Formation of a Visual Culture'. During the Ph.D., she was a visiting research student at the Photography and the Archive Research Centre (London College of Communication) and worked as a volunteer at the Stanley Kubrick Archive. She is now continuing her research in Italy alongside her work as a member of the editorial staff of the academic journal *Fata Morgana*. Her research focuses on photography and its relationship with other fields such as philosophy, art, cinema, etc. She is also a member of the Laboratory of Photography 'Saverio Marra' (University of Calabria) and international volunteer for the Renaissance Photography Prize.

Cynthia J. Miller is cultural anthropologist, specializing in popular culture and visual media. She is the editor or co-editor of ten scholarly volumes, including the award-winning *Steaming into a Victorian Future: A Steampunk Anthology* (2012, with Julie Anne Taddeo); *The Silence of the Lambs: Critical Essays on Clarice, a Cannibal, and a Nice Chianti* (2016); and *What's Eating You?: Food and Horror on Screen* (2017, with A. Bowdoin Van Riper). She also serves as the series editor for Rowman & Littlefield's Film and History book series, and as editorial board member for the *Journal of Popular Television* and Bloomsbury's Guide to Contemporary Directors series.

Simone Odino is public librarian and archivist in Bologna. For the last five years he has been actively researching *2001: A Space Odyssey*, conducting interviews with cast and crew and visiting archives in the United Kingdom, the United States and Italy. He runs the website http://www.2001italia.it.

Nils Daniel Peiler is Ph.D. candidate at Heidelberg University with a project about the artistic resonance of Stanley Kubrick's *2001: A Space Odyssey*. His research interests include filmic reception, filmic paratexts, and film dubbing. He is the co-editor on the first German anthology on film dubbing *Film im Transferprozess* (2015).

Filippo Ulivieri is a writer and a teacher of film theory. He is the leading expert on Stanley Kubrick in Italy with over fifteen years of research on the subject. His features on the director's career have appeared in several international newspapers and magazines. He is the author of *Stanley Kubrick and Me*, the biography of Kubrick's personal assistant Emilio D'Alessandro ([Il Saggiatore, 2012] Arcade Publishing, 2016); and co-scenarist of Alex Infascelli's documentary *S Is for Stanley* (2015).

A. Bowdoin Van Riper is an historian who specializes in depictions of science and technology in popular culture. His publications include *Imagining Flight: Aviation in Popular Culture* (2003); *A Biographical Encyclopaedia of Scientists and Inventors in American Film and Television* (2011); and *Teaching History with Science Fiction Films* (2017). Additionally, he is editor or co-editor of seven scholarly volumes, including *Learning from Mickey, Donald, and Walt: Essays on Disney's Edutainment Films* (2011); *1950s "Rocketman" TV Series and Their Fans: Cadets, Rangers, and Junior Space Men* (2012, with Cynthia J. Miller); and *Horrors of War: The Undead on the Battlefield* (2015, with Cynthia J. Miller).

Rachel Walisko completed her MSc at the University of Edinburgh with a thesis titled '"Projecting the past into the present": The aesthetic representation of history in *12 Years a Slave*, *Django Unchained*, and *Lincoln* as a catalyst for political consciousness'. Her work is forthcoming in *Mise-en-scène: The Journal of Film & Visual Narration*. She has previously held internships at the Smithsonian Institution, National Geographic Channel and WETA Television. Her research interests include aesthetics, adaptation, genre and female authorship.

Acknowledgements

I would like to thank the contributors to this volume, with their shared passion for *2001: A Space Odyssey* making this project possible. I would especially like to thank those who attended the *Stanley Kubrick: A Retrospective* conference at De Montfort University, Leicester, in May 2016. Thanks also to Professor Ian Hunter for convening the Kubrick conference. I would like to give special thanks to Jan Harlan, who supported both the conference and the simultaneous Kubrick exhibition, *Stanley Kubrick: Cult Auteur*, held at De Montfort University's Heritage Centre in May 2016, from the very beginning. He patiently sat through the entirety of the three-day conference and made the event a truly special occasion. Special thanks also to The American Mime Theatre, Jean Barbour and Daniel Richter for their feedback, advice and patient responses to my questions. I must also thank De Montfort University, who awarded me the Vice-Chancellor's High Flyers Scholarship in 2014 that has funded my research into Stanley Kubrick and provided me with the invaluable opportunity to make many a regular visit to the Stanley Kubrick Archive. Thanks also to Kieran Foster, Dru Jeffries, Simone Odino, Elisa Pezzotta, Antoine Balga-Prévost, Nash Sibanda, Filippo Ulivieri and Rachel Walisko for their valued feedback. Thanks to the International Association for the Fantastic in the Arts for allowing us to republish '*2001: A Space Odyssey*: A transcendental trans-locution', originally published in 2008, volume 19, issue 1 of *Journal of the Fantastic in the Arts*. And thanks also to Liverpool University Press for allowing us to republish 'Clarke and Kubrick's *2001*: A Queer Odyssey', originally published in *Science Fiction Film and Television*, 2011, volume 4, issue 1.

Notes on the Text

The full title of *2001: A Space Odyssey* has been shortened to *2001* throughout the chapters for ease of reading. The same applies to Arthur C. Clarke's novel of the same name. Also, the years of release for Kubrick's films are mentioned only once and are not repeated in subsequent chapters. Details for all of Kubrick's films can be found in the appendix rather than in the bibliography. Where possible, character names have followed either Clarke's novel or Kubrick and Clarke's screenplay: both Moon-Watcher and Star-Child are with hyphen, apart from where quoted sources differ.

Introduction

Forging new perspectives

James Fenwick

By the beginning of the 1960s, the Space Race – that Cold War competition for space supremacy between the United States and the USSR – had gained momentum following President John F. Kennedy's inauguration. He had set the greatest challenge of human endeavour in his address before a Joint Session of Congress on 25 May 1961, declaring that he wanted the United States to land a man on the Moon and return him safely to Earth by the end of the decade. Yet Kennedy's target would be beaten by a year by film director and producer Stanley Kubrick – albeit with fictional astronauts digging up alien artefacts. Kennedy had emphasized how difficult it would be to land a man on the Moon, saying, 'We choose to go to the Moon in this decade and do the other things, not because they are easy, but because they are hard' (Kennedy 1962). Maybe the same could be said of Kubrick, a film director who would not settle for an easy life, but instead preferred to set challenges and to be challenged, to innovate and to push the boundaries of what was considered possible. Up until the mid-1960s, the majority of science-fiction films had largely been low-budget fare, with unconvincing and often unintentionally cringe-worthy special effects (Kolker 2017a: 142–44). Kubrick did not want his film to be like all that had gone before. He wanted to make something special. Something mysterious. A Space Odyssey.

The American fascination with the Space Race grew throughout the 1960s; the technological innovation NASA's Apollo Program (1961–72) brought and the collective global spirit it momentarily wrought were in stark contrast to the social and cultural divisions that were tearing apart the United States and the West. The potential to explore the Final Frontier, and the prospect of encountering alien life, were tantalizing. Kennedy himself summed this up when he said, 'The vast stretches of the unknown and the unanswered and the unfinished still far outstrip our collective comprehension' (Kennedy 1962). It was certainly not undue that the Apollo Program came to be viewed as, 'the single greatest technological achievement of all time' (Garber 2002) when Neil Armstrong finally set foot on the Moon on 21 July 1969.

The technological challenges faced by Kubrick in producing his science-fiction epic, *2001: A Space Odyssey* (1968), (the film will be henceforth referred to in this volume as *2001*) were by no means similar to those faced by NASA. But Kubrick certainly did face a challenge in overcoming cinematic technology in order to create a realistic and authentic portrayal of space travel and of the Moon. He was critical of the majority of science-fiction films, 'always noting the poor quality of the design and special effects and the puerility of the scripts' (Frayling 2014: 20). What he was aiming for, initially at least, was a film that was 'based on the latest discoveries; a fictional semi-documentary' (2014: 18). He no doubt kept abreast of the developments of the Space Race, of the Apollo Program and of the latest NASA research. Indeed, his pursuit of scientific accuracy led him to recruiting the services of two NASA employees, Frederick I. Ordway III and Harry Lange; Ordway was a communications specialist and Lange an illustrator, designing spacecrafts. On meeting the pair, and studying Lange's drawings, Kubrick is reputed to have said to them, 'I can get better illustrators in New York City a dime a dozen, but they don't have your NASA background, your combination. That's what I need' (Frayling 2014: 20). In order to successfully realize his ambition in creating *2001*, Kubrick understood that he needed to combine his own artistic vision with the technological enterprise of NASA.

Kubrick amassed a wealth of research material on space, astronautics and technology throughout the conception and filming of *2001*. Prior to my first ever visit to the Stanley Kubrick Archive at the University of Arts London (UAL), I believed I would write a comprehensive biography of the film. How quickly my foolhardy dreams were scuppered upon seeing the Archive; the indexed letters files of the Archive's *2001* section alone consists of 47 boxes, with hundreds more boxes for the film catalogued into various categories and subcategories, including 'Space Research', 'Commercial Tie-Ups', 'Pre-Production Artwork' and much more besides. The daunting task facing any researcher soon became apparent. More startling is the estimated size of the whole Stanley Kubrick Archive at UAL, approximately 873 linear metres. I sat afterwards in an Elephant and Castle pub pondering the impossible task facing anyone who ever wanted to write a comprehensive history of *2001* based on the Archive. It would be an endeavour as perilous as the production of the film itself.

I distinctly recall the first time I watched Kubrick's science-fiction odyssey: age fourteen, a rainy spring morning in Sheffield. The year was (coincidentally) 2001 and I sat perplexed watching as a band of monkeys – surely, men in monkey suits, I wondered, or maybe they are real? – screeched at each other and threw bones. Then silence, as they foraged for food in an ancient landscape. I had no idea that the film was by Stanley Kubrick until I bought the DVD several days later; a cardboard case, stark white border around a futuristic image of a spacecraft: *2001: A Space Odyssey*. I quickly removed the DVD disc and spent the rest of the evening watching the film, confused, startled, bored, but most of all, enthralled. So it was that I came to be introduced to the films of the now legendary producer-director Stanley Kubrick. What started as sheer befuddlement at a group of men in monkey suits hitting each other ended up as a love affair with the films of this great director, and of the whole of cinema. Schmaltzy, I know, but *2001* is a film that has embedded itself into our culture and our cultural consciousness. One does not even need to have seen the film to get the references – countless commercials use the musical cues from *2001*, with slow-motion space walks or waltzing spacecraft so commonplace as to have become clichéd. It has been endlessly referenced and parodied in *The Simpsons* (1989–present), most memorably in the episode 'Deep Space Homer' (1994), which features a scene of Homer floating weightlessly through the air, eating crisps in synchronization to Strauss's *An der schönen blauen Donau* (*The Blue Danube*) (1866). Marvel Comics had the audacity to adapt the film into a comic in 1976, followed by a ten-part sequel series between 1976 and 1977, whilst Arthur C. Clarke continued the Odyssey in his sequel novels, *2010: Odyssey Two* (1982); *2061: Odyssey Three* (1987); and *3001: The Final Odyssey* (1997). The first of these was adapted into a feature film by Peter Hyams, *2010: The Year We Make Contact* (1984) acting as an unofficial sequel to *2001*. By the mid-1990s, Pink Floyd fans claimed that the band's 'Echoes' – a twenty-three minute prog epic from their album *Meddle* (1971) – 'synched' perfectly with *2001*'s Star Gate sequence, the sparse lyrics revealing hidden meanings to Bowman's journey through space, time and reality. The odyssey continued, spurred on in part by a desire to see the mysteries of Kubrick's film answered, to understand the elusive nature of the impenetrable monolith and of the omnipresent Star-Child, and to give clarity to what on earth it all meant.

Of course, no one has ever truly revealed what *2001* 'means'; academics, philosophers, theologians and artists have all attempted to interpret the film to their own whims and ideologies. And so it is that I have the nerve to throw my own hat into the ring with this edited collection, a work that sees its contributors, myself included, expound their own ideas and interpretations of the film. But this is not to rob *2001* of its subtlety, or to impose some definitive solution to the whole thing; rather it arises both out of a passion and respect for the film as a cinephile, and because of the film's stature within cinematic history, the way it broke drastically with the discursive classical Hollywood narrative, and pushed the envelope of film technology.

Science-fiction's reputation in the mid-1960s was still one of an inferior genre, despite its increasing art house pretentions with the success of films such as *Alphaville* (Godard, 1965). Film producers were said to want to avoid the genre for its '"stigma" as being low-budget, made quickly, and for being so-called "kiddie-fare"' (Moskowitz 1965: 7). Kubrick himself commented to Arthur C. Clarke that he wanted to make the 'proverbial "really good" science-fiction movie' (Kubrick 1964b). Clarke responded that this was long overdue and that only two films qualified as such: *The Day the Earth Stood Still* (Wise, 1951) and *The Forbidden Planet* (Wilcox, 1956) (Clarke 1964). The former had been directed by Robert Wise, later to helm *Star Trek: The Motion Picture* (1979), one film amongst many that owed clear influences to *2001*.[1] Of course, there had been well-made, intelligent and challenging science-fiction films prior to *2001*, with the 1950s now seen as a golden era of the genre. The post-Second World War socio-political contexts and the ever-present 'threat' of invasion in the United States by the USSR, or from a communist enemy within, often served as a metaphorical undercurrent to the genre (Bliss 2014: ix–x). The early 1960s saw a significant decrease in the number of science-fiction films being produced (Cornea 2007: 76), though there were (failed) attempts to put into production multi-million dollar science-fiction pictures, such as Ray Bradbury's *The Martian Chronicles* (1950), which was to be directed by Alan Pakula for Universal until the project fell through. There was a turn to science-fiction on television, most notably *Star Trek* (1966–69), whilst British film saw a string of cult classics being produced, including *Quatermass and the Pit* (Ward Baker, 1967). The genre largely remained within these confines – art film, European cinema, Hollywood B-movie, low budget realism, British – making it quite remarkable that in the spring of 1965, MGM announced they were to be financing Kubrick's then titled *Journey Beyond the Stars* for six million dollars.[2] Peter Krämer (2010, 2015a) has situated the decision by MGM within the industrial contexts of Hollywood's economic circumstances and the view of the project at the time as a family film. And it goes without saying that the political and social contexts of the 1960s Space Race began to increasingly excite and enthuse the American population – not to mention the world as a whole – as the Apollo Program got ever closer to achieving Kennedy's goal of landing a man on the Moon by 1969. The Final Frontier had seized the imagination of humanity.

Stanley Kubrick before *2001: A Space Odyssey*

Born 26 July 1928 and raised in the Bronx, Kubrick's fascination with photography and film began at an early age, when his father gave him a Graflex camera (LoBrutto 1997: 10). His fascination soon developed into a professional career, working as a photographer in the 1940s for *Look* magazine. By the early 1950s, Kubrick set out on his filmmaking career, producing and directing three short films: *Day of the Fight* (1951), *Flying Padre* (1951) and *The Seafarers* (1953). Thomas Pryor commented on Kubrick's early filmmaking achievements in the *New York Times* in 1951:

> Stanley Kubrick is a young man from the Bronx with a passionate interest in photography and a determination to make a name for himself in the movie world […] At the age of twenty-two he can look back on four and a half years as a top-flight magazine still photographer and, since last spring, he has directed, photographed and produced two one-reel films which RKO Pathé News will distribute. Now he is aiming at making a feature length picture, which he has budgeted at the astonishingly low cost of $50,000.
> (Pryor 1951: 5)

The feature length picture Pryor considered to be astonishingly low cost was *Fear and Desire* (1953), produced in a guerrilla mode, with Kubrick undertaking many of the crew roles himself. A similar situation unfolded on *Killer's Kiss* (1955), both films seeing Kubrick contribute to a burgeoning modern American independent cinema. *Killer's Kiss* saw Kubrick raising funds, and deferring fees, before successfully selling the picture to United Artists (UA). So impressed were UA that they partially financed Kubrick's next feature, *The Killing* (1956), an urban-thriller based on Lionel White's novel *Clean Break* (1955).

By this point, Kubrick had formed a business partnership with producer James B. Harris, together incorporating the company Harris-Kubrick Pictures Corporation. The duo would create a maverick image about them, one that challenged the conventional thinking of the industry. Their focus was on retaining as much power over their productions as possible, a belief that was solidified following their collaborations with Kirk Douglas. Harris-Kubrick entered a multi-picture contract with Douglas's Bryna Productions in 1957, which would see them as Douglas's employees following the completion of *Paths of Glory* (1957). The deal with Bryna took Harris-Kubrick into the heart of Hollywood, where Kubrick's reputation was boosted radically by his direction of Douglas's *Spartacus* (1960), a multi-million dollar historical epic with a stellar cast. Kubrick was not intimidated by fame or stature, his confidence in his own directorial abilities supreme.[3] Such confidence would allow him to take on the moral defenders of western decency throughout his career, showing no fear as he adapted Vladimir Nabokov's scandalous novel *Lolita* (1962), building on the notoriety of the book's themes of transgressive love with a teenage girl by giving the film the tagline, 'How did they ever make a film of *Lolita*?'

Kubrick continued to be held in high esteem in the mid-1960s following the release of his comedy about nuclear Armageddon, *Dr. Strangelove or: How I Learned to Stop Worrying and Love the Bomb* (1964). He was beginning to be viewed as a major artist, one that transcended Hollywood, as demonstrated by the Museum of Modern Art's Kubrick retrospective in the summer of 1965 (Anon. 1965a: E3). He had developed a reputation that preceded him; he was the director and producer that studios and stars wanted to work with, producing innovative, controversial and vital films that chimed with the booming youth culture of the 1960s. By the end of the decade, Kubrick had created a power house for himself in the United Kingdom, surrounded by a team of technicians and administrators that were some of the best in the business and, more importantly, loyal to him (Anon. 1968g). Though battles were still fought with Hollywood – MGM were often disgruntled with Kubrick and the secrecy that surrounded *2001* throughout its production (Caras 1965a) – his stature as a master filmmaker largely freed him from interference and gave him what he most desired: time to experiment.

Kubrick studies, old and new

Fifty years after its initial release in April 1968, *2001*'s place in cinematic history is assured, with a body of academic work as testimony to that fact. The film has profoundly changed the view of science-fiction and, arguably, paved the way for a new breed of super-producer in the mid-1970s: George Lucas and Steven Spielberg can be seen as high-concept directors that were heavily indebted to the technological path forged by Kubrick in their films *Star Wars* (Lucas, 1977) and *Close Encounters of the Third Kind* (Spielberg, 1977). But beyond its towering technological innovations and its mainstreaming of science-fiction, *2001* was a seminal American/British film – arguably, more British given its production at Borehamwood Studios and its largely British cast and crew, alongside the subsidy it qualified for with the British Film Fund Agency (Anon. 1968g). Wallace Coyle understatedly wrote that *2001* represented 'a major contribution to the development of film as a medium of expression' (1980: 23), though he picks up on the key critical element of the film: the need to view it as a purely visual experience, something Kubrick was keen to emphasize himself in interviews, telling Joseph Gelmis that, '[*2001*] is basically a visual, non-verbal experience' (Gelmis 1974: 394). In the same interview, as in others, Kubrick commented, and seemingly took pride in the fact that there were approximately 40 minutes of dialogue in a film with a running time of two hours and 40 minutes. This heavy emphasis on the visual experience led to an academic discourse focused on the formal composition of the film, its narrative construction and its aesthetic design. Such scholarly analysis has become a tradition with regards to *2001*, given the film's drastic break with conventional Hollywood storytelling. After all, here was a film funded by MGM, one of classic Hollywood's grandest studios, that opens with an overture of the haunting strains of György Ligeti's *Atmosphères* (1961) (Ligeti's composition itself challenged convention, utilizing his micro polyphony technique to create tone clusters and opaque sonic textures).[4] The film more closely resembled a European art house movie, not a ten million dollar Hollywood epic. And as has been well documented, initial reviews were mixed, with some condemning the film as an incoherent mess that would end Kubrick's career (Kaplan 2007). The more damning reviews largely came from high-profile New York critics (Krämer 2010: 92), with a number of other critics being much more positive. The film was invariably described as an 'overwhelming visual experience' (Watters 1968: 10) and 'the most exciting event to happen in movies in a long, long while' (Anon. 1968h: 52). The youth movement of the late 1960s and early 1970s responded enthusiastically to the picture and it continued to enjoy box office success throughout the 1970s, with multiple rereleases and a new marketing campaign by Mike Kaplan – he devised the now iconic 'Ultimate Trip/Star-Child' poster campaign. Though some audiences were undoubtedly perplexed, even bored by the film (Anon. 1968i: 29) (an inherent aesthetic quality of Kubrick's films), many more were excited by it, as Peter Krämer's research into fan reaction demonstrates: 'Irrespective of its close association with youth and the counterculture, *2001: A Space Odyssey* was a massive hit with mainstream audiences' (2009: 254). Fan reaction was positive, with many commenting that they saw the film as an ultimately optimistic portrait of humanity (Krämer 2010: 86–88).

Fans wanted to expand their interaction and understanding of the film and engaged with various paratexts. With its post-classical breaking of formal narrative structures and frustratingly ambiguous storyline, particularly towards the end, *2001* left its fictional universe open to expansion through new entry points in other forms of media, such as the comic book adaptation by Marvel. If audiences were originally pushed towards extra-textual objects such as Clarke's book *2001: A Space Odyssey* (1968) (Hunter 2013), then this process continued in the years subsequent to its release and growing popularity. Even Clarke himself was not averse to creating new texts to widen the narrative experience, doing so with *The Lost Worlds of 2001* (1972) and the sequels to the original novel, the second of which was adapted into Hyams's *2010*. Hyams's film sees the return of characters from *2001*, including HAL and Bowman; *2010* was even subsequently adapted into a two-part limited Marvel comic series. Making of books were published, including Jerome Agel's *The Making of Kubrick's 2001* (1970), furthering fan interaction and understanding of the film, whilst other merchandising tie-ins coordinated by Kubrick's Polaris Productions included the Parker Brothers' pentomino board game, *Universe* (1967).

Equally, Kubrick scholars have continued to offer new interpretations of *2001*. As Film Studies saw the burgeoning of the New Film History in the 1980s, new contexts were sought to understand the film. By the mid-2000s, following the opening of the Stanley Kubrick Archive, empirical historical inquiry became the key to understanding *2001*.[5] Krämer's *2001: A Space Odyssey* (2010) placed the film within wider production contexts in order to understand the motivations behind the making of the film and of its marketing as a family picture. The Stanley Kubrick Archive has since come to dominate Kubrick Studies, leading Robert Kolker to issue the following caution:

> There are scholars who believe no serious work on Kubrick can be done without the appropriate archival research, that criticism and analysis must be tethered to the known facts that exist on the archived paper records. But does that mean that textual analysis – readings of the films as self-contained entities – is no longer valid? Not every film scholar will have the opportunity to make it to London.
>
> (Kolker 2017b)

But even though these new historical and empirical methodologies have progressed our understanding of Kubrick's operations as a film director, they do not fully resolve the intellectual, formal and aesthetic codes that underpin his films, works made 'with a complexity of perception and execution – a formal integration of style and meaning [...] works filled with vision and intellectual passion' (Kolker 2011: 183–84). Kubrick's was a modernist cinema, one that pushed the cinematic technological envelope towards complex representations and interpretations. This was particularly evident in *2001*, a film in which Kubrick utilized experimentation and collaboration in order to create a vision of technical mastery but also sublime philosophical and technological poetry. *2001* continues to generate debate as to its meaning, largely as a result of its ambiguous narrative and aesthetic construct.

2001's production and release coincided with the rise of Film Studies in universities, and more importantly the widening acceptance of auteur theory, brought to prominence in the United States by Andrew Sarris; works such as 'Notes on the Auteur Theory in 1962' (Sarris 1962) and *The American Cinema: Directors and Directions 1929–1968* (Sarris [1968] 1996) contributed to the critical analysis of American directors as artists. Sarris did, however, patronisingly dismiss Kubrick and in particular *2001*, saying the film 'confirms Kubrick's inability to tell a story on the screen with coherence and a consistent point of view' (Sarris [1968] 1996: 196). Sarris would be one of several critics forced to re-evaluate their opinion of Kubrick and *2001* as the critical and commercial esteem for the film grew. Kubrick came to be viewed in scholarly studies as representative of auteur theory; brand management contributed in part to such a view, with MGM purposely devising a publicity strategy that placed Kubrick at the heart of the creation of *2001*, contributing to the cult-auteur status that he garnered in his subsequent years.[6] A fascination with Kubrick – the man and the myth – was building, with numerous auteurist works critiquing him in the 1970s, including Alexander Walker's *Kubrick Directs* (1972) and Joseph Gelmis's *The Film Director As Superstar* (1970). Gelmis described Kubrick as concentrating 'all control in his own hands […] he originates, writes, researches, directs, edits, and even guides the publicity campaigns for his films' (Gelmis 1974: 383). Such language and reverence perpetuated the belief that Kubrick was the sole author of his films. Yet, such a narrow view is detrimental to understanding the sheer scope and scale of *2001* as a project, one that saw Kubrick supervising over 1000 personnel during the course of the production at a cost of close to £2 million (Anon. 1968g), and a budget that ballooned to over $10 million, 'of which an estimated $6.5 million was spent on "artefacts and sets and camerawork and special effects photography"' (Frayling 2014: 24).[7]

The lengthy production of *2001*, the technological challenges set by Kubrick and the desire to achieve a realistic and scientifically accurate representation of space travel meant it was inevitably a collaboration between a range of artists, managers and technicians. Yet Kubrick's was the only name on the single Academy Award the film received for Best Visual Effects – a sore point for those who had worked for years on the special effects of the film, as Brian Johnson noted:

> I don't think that Stanley deserved to get the Academy Award for Special Effects on *2001* though. I think that that should have went [sic] to Douglas Trumbull. There were many people that worked on *2001* that didn't [get] credit for their work.
>
> (Bozung 2014)

Kubrick Studies in the aftermath of *2001*'s release approached the study of the film from semiotic, structuralist and formalist frameworks. This approach is part of what I term the 'old' Kubrick Studies, a movement that became increasingly constricted in its research focus and of its portrayal of Kubrick as a cold, misanthropic pessimist. Robert Sklar took issue with these methodologies in his historical overview of Kubrick, 'Stanley Kubrick and the American Film Industry' (1988). Sklar laid out new methodologies that needed to be taken up in the study of Kubrick in order to better understand his position within cinematic history, and his influence on industrial contexts. Sklar's challenges did not find immediate answers, and the old Kubrick Studies continued unabated, albeit with a growing parallel subfield of scholarly concern in Adaptation Studies. Comparative analyses of the source texts of Kubrick's films were made by the likes of Richard Corliss (*Lolita*, 1994) and Greg Jenkins (*Stanley Kubrick and the Art of Adaptation: Three Novels, Three Films*, 1997). But *2001* remained a monolithic work in Kubrick's oeuvre, revered as a cinematic landmark of unrivalled aesthetic sophistication and philosophical depth. As such, Robert Kolker's (2006) edited collection on the film sought to bring together the various theories of formalism, structuralism and philosophy to date.

The research questions laid out by Sklar (1988) finally began to be addressed following the opening of the Stanley Kubrick Archive in 2007; in the decade since, empirical inquiry via the Archive has seen issues such as collaboration, authorial agency, adaptation and production contexts gain relevance within Kubrick Studies, becoming the prevailing method of interpreting his life and work. This new wave of scholarly interest in Kubrick is what I term the 'new' Kubrick Studies, led by the likes of Peter Krämer – with turns to reception studies (2009, 2011), authorship (2010, 2012, 2014) and socio-political contexts (2014) – and Nathan Abrams, who emphasizes a psychohistory of Kubrick via Jewish Studies and the cultural contexts of his living in the Bohemian Greenwich Village in the 1940s and 1950s (2015a).

And yet, though the Stanley Kubrick Archive has undoubtedly provided a much broader picture of the modes of production on a Kubrick picture, it does not resolve the integration of intellectual and aesthetic concerns at the root of them, and *2001* in particular. This collection seeks to bring to light the impact of the 'new' Kubrick Studies upon the 'old' Kubrick Studies and collate together original insights, as well as textual and interpretative analyses of *2001*. By revising the textual approaches in Kubrick Studies and conflating them with new empirical approaches, we can arrive at a broader understanding of the means in which Kubrick's methods as a director were developed to create a unique aesthetic that radically changed the language of cinema. The idea for this collection stemmed from an academic conference entitled *Stanley Kubrick: A Retrospective*, convened at De Montfort University by I.Q. Hunter and myself in 2016.[8] The conference instigated conversations between researchers that led to the conviction that there was still a need to challenge and revise our understanding of a seminal cinematic work. Each text makes use of a combination of archival evidence and theoretical ideas, working towards a revision and scrutiny of *2001*. The objective of this book will be to offer a 'third way', as it were, of understanding Kubrick and *2001*, and to begin to arrive at a more rounded and complete scholarly perspective. Fifty years after its premiere, the time is now ripe for us to begin to bring together the numerous perspectives on *2001*. The more traditional approaches have investigated *2001* from a variety of representative standpoints, from semiotics to philosophy, while the more recent methodologies have interpreted historical fact within political and cultural contexts. The volume brings these two scholarly approaches together and, as a result, works towards – to borrow a phrase that has gained traction in Kubrick Studies in recent years – 'new perspectives' so as to allow us to further understand *2001*.

These chapters offer new and interpretative approaches that examine aesthetics, performance, technological design, philosophical discourse, genre and authorial agency in *2001*. Each chapter is linked by the exploration of Kubrick's intellectual concerns as an auteur and the historicism and aesthetic representation of *2001*, with the ultimate aim of bringing together a range of new scholarly perspectives from the full spectrum of Kubrick Studies. The chapters are grouped into six parts: Narrative and Adaptation, Performance, Technology, Masculinity and the Astronaut, Visual Spectacle and Production. Each part opens with an introduction to guide the reader through the key ideas under discussion, and with reference to further reading. Taken together, this volume represents a wide-ranging examination from a number of standpoints about one of the most important and influential films in cinema history.

Part One

Narrative and Adaptation

Adaptation has remained a cornerstone of Kubrick Studies; not surprising given that eleven out of Kubrick's thirteen films were adaptations of one kind or another. He often turned to obscure literary material, though not exclusively: Stephen King's *The Shining* (1977) was a number one bestseller, while Vladimir Nabokov's *Lolita* (1955) attracted controversy for its subject matter. Still, Kubrick preferred to work with novels and novelists and, in that regard, can be seen as what I.Q. Hunter calls an, 'auteur of adaptation', in that for Kubrick, 'collaborative adaptation was crucial to realising his personal vision' (2015: 278). The first three chapters in this volume are linked by their exploration of adaptation and narrative.

Simone Odino explores the genesis of *2001*, using both textual analysis and archival evidence to understand what he calls Kubrick's 'search for a new obsession'. Odino locates the themes and motivations for *2001* in the aftermath of *Dr. Strangelove*, and uncovers Kubrick's working methods in developing new projects. Odino documents the sometimes-uneasy development of a new Kubrick project and the various science-fiction ideas that were muted along the way to the eventual creation of *2001*.

Suparno Banerjee's chapter focuses on the adaptation relationship between Arthur C. Clarke's book, the Kubrick/Clarke screenplay and Kubrick's film. Revisiting existing comparative analyses of the book and film, Banerjee argues that rather than the book being an explanation of the film, the two are wholly independent of each other; instead the adaptation relationship should be seen as one of trans-locution – how the telling of the story is transformed by each of the mediums and the artists' own creative ideologies.

Dru Jeffries offers an overdue case study of Marvel's comic book adaptation of *2001*, situating the adaptation and subsequent ten-part sequel series by comics' illustrator Jack Kirby as a paratextual narrative extension of the *2001* universe. The comic books have largely been ignored or forgotten, and so Jeffries's positioning of the adaptation in historical and industrial contexts is a welcome scholarly insight. The comic series eventually morphed towards the superhero genre, expanding upon Kubrick's interest in artificial intelligence and sentient machines by introducing the character of Machine Man. Jeffries sees this as part of the sublime present not only in Kubrick but also characteristic of Kirby's work, and furthers the analysis of the relationship between technology and humans beyond the film itself.

Further Reading

I.Q. Hunter's guest edited special issue of the *Adaptation* journal, titled 'Kubrick and adaptation' (8:3, 2015), features seven essays exploring varying aspects of Kubrick's adaptation process. The issue includes an essay by Peter Krämer (2015), 'Adaptation as exploration: Stanley Kubrick, literature, and *A.I. Artificial Intelligence*' (pp. 372–82), which offers a detailed argument as to Kubrick's exploratory writing methods. Elisa Pezzotta's (2013) chapter 'A history of Kubrick adaptations', in her book *Stanley Kubrick: Adapting the Sublime* (pp. 15–33), provides a comprehensive account of the various adaptations Kubrick approached throughout his career.

Chapter One

'God, it'll be hard topping the H-bomb': Kubrick's search for a new obsession in the path from *Dr. Strangelove* to *2001: A Space Odyssey*

Simone Odino

When *Dr. Strangelove* was released in the United States on 29 January 1964, Stanley Kubrick was already considered one of the most interesting directors in the film industry. Regarded by the press as author of controversial, unconventional films, his nightmare comedy had garnered considerable attention for its original approach on the topic of nuclear war. In the round of publicity interviews surrounding the release of the film, therefore, many of the questions revolved around his creative process and what his next project would be. On one of these occasions Kubrick answered,

> I haven't found anything I can get so obsessed with. It takes me two years: that's too big a commitment for something that may suddenly go flat [...] there's no reason to do it my way unless you are, as I said, obsessed. You must be obsessed.
> (McGrady 1964: 3c)

Kubrick was referring to his distinctive authorial style, which made him the prototype of the 'total filmmaker'. As he said, 'making a film starts with the germ of an idea and continues through script, rehearsing, shooting, cutting music projection, and tax-accountants' (Southern 1962: 343). The problem to find a so-called obsession was therefore related to the considerable effort needed to put a story on screen. The director often claimed it was never easy for him to find something that would prove to be interesting in the long run, and to better illustrate this crucial point he used to employ a romantic (and fatalistic) comparison: 'Finding a story which will make a film is a little like finding the right girl. It's very hard to say how you do it, or when you're going to do it. Some stories just come from a chance thing' (Bean 1963: 12).

Kubrick had first hinted at what his new love interest would be in an interview on 3 February 1964 that revealed how he was 'fascinated by outer space, which he thinks is inhabited, and he is reading and reading and reading about it' (Anon. 1964a: 80). Tackling a topic by researching it exhaustively was already the method of choice for the director; for *Dr. Strangelove*, he had immersed himself in years of research into the topic of nuclear warfare, a long-time obsession of his, reading in the process 'almost every available book on the nuclear situation' (Southern 1963: 29).

Kubrick's mention of outer space immediately led to speculation by the trade press, and the April 1964 issue of *Show Magazine* attached the director's name to an 'untitled story of extra-terrestrial life' (Anon. 1964b). Still, it would take until December 1964 for Kubrick to officially go on the record, in an interview with journalist and friend Alexander Walker:

> His next film will have what he admitted (with obvious feat that he was saying too much) is a 'futuristic plot'. He is co-scripting it with Arthur C. Clarke, the scientist explorer […]. His coal-black eye twinkled, then he said with almost presidential gravity: 'But God, it'll be hard topping the H-bomb'.
>
> (Walker 1964)

The caution he used and the solemn tone of the last sentence suggest a sort of performance anxiety not usually associated with Kubrick's public persona. However, one should be aware that by December 1964 the director had spent the best part of the previous eight months in daily brainstorming sessions with Arthur C. Clarke, struggling to produce a completely original plot,[1] an effort that he had not undertaken since *Killer's Kiss*. Kubrick's career up to that point had been characterized by a series of rejections from major studios and continual difficulties in having his projects green-lighted, as the director himself recalled years later:

> Up until *A Clockwork Orange*, there wasn't a single producer who was prepared to produce my films. For example, MGM only took on *2001* at the last minute; no one wanted it. […] The same thing for *Dr. Strangelove*, it was turned down by all the studios.
>
> (Heymann 1987: 478)

It is against this complicated background that the director started his path towards *2001*, whose starting point is traditionally identified in a chance encounter with Roger Caras on 17 February 1964, a lunch during which Kubrick revealed his intention to follow *Dr. Strangelove* with 'something about extraterrestrials' (McAleer 1992: 190–91), to which Caras suggested the director contact his friend Arthur C. Clarke.

I think that a small step back is needed, though, to better understand the artistic decisions taken in the conception and production of the movie that would, eventually, 'top the H-bomb'. The period between the post-production of *Dr. Strangelove* (late 1963) and the director's commitment with Clarke (the two signed a deal on 20 May 1964 (McAleer 1992: 195–97) has, to date, received scarce scholarly attention. Such neglect is surprising given that in the relatively short space between late 1963 and spring 1964, the director was apparently offered a movie project about overpopulation, was nearly co-opted onto a United Nations-funded TV-series, and optioned the rights of a science-fiction radio drama about an invasion of alien lizards.

Making use of materials from the Stanley Kubrick Archive and from rare interviews, I will argue that these lesser-known entries in the long list of Kubrick's unrealized projects are not only further examples of his story-seeking difficulties, but they also make good case studies of his overriding interests and concerns of the period, whilst providing an insight into his peculiar attitude towards science-fiction. All in all they suggest a degree of social responsibility usually overlooked when Kubrick's *weltanschauung* is discussed, and that seems to have directly informed the creative process that led to *2001*.

Sex, bombs and overpopulation

When asked what was the method he used to pick the subjects of his movies, Kubrick said in 1964, 'I don't know how you can gauge anything except through your interests. That has to be the yardstick' (Alpert 1964: 34). Indeed, Kubrick was a man of catholic tastes,[2] a voracious reader gifted with a remarkable intellectual curiosity, and this open-mindedness might have been one of the reasons behind his undeniable ability at what has been called 'surfing the zeitgeist' (Murray and Schuler 2007: 134); that is, to produce movies that captured brilliantly the spirit of the era in which they were produced, a goal that he had stated as early as 1960:

> I know I would like to make a film that gave a feeling of the times, psychologically, sexually, politically, personally. I would like to make that more than anything else. And it's probably going to be the hardest film to make.
> (Anon 1960: 21)

Kubrick explicitly expressed his interests in such topics in a letter written to Terry Southern during the post-production of *Dr. Strangelove*, on 1 August 1963: 'I haven't come up with any brilliances yet for a new story [...] if you see anything you think might be good, let me know! Atomic warfare, science-fiction, mad sex relationships [...] something along those lines – possibly all three might be fun!' (Tully 2010: 135). He was still of the opinion in February 1964, when asked by McCall's magazine about his future projects:

> One likely subject he would like to tackle, now or soon – woman's place – and her displacement – in the modern world. (To Kubrick, the 'gap' between the sexes now ranks with the bomb, population explosion, and racial problems as a major world crisis).
> (Anon. 1964c)

Some of the topics Kubrick was considering had already been, or would be, the subject of one or more of his movies; the director's interest about the 'gap between the sexes' is evident not only in *Lolita*, a movie he referred to as a 'comment on the social scene' (Dundy 1963: 14), but also in several other projects he tried to develop before and after it.[3] Moreover, even *Dr. Strangelove* – Kubrick's take on *the* major political crisis of the time, the Cold War – notoriously contained many sexual innuendos, and one could argue that the displacement of women in the modern world is suggested in *2001* as well, a film where female characters are less prominent than in any other film of Kubrick's career.[4]

One interesting issue that Kubrick rated as a major world crisis was overpopulation, a growing concern in American public opinion, particularly following the publication of *The Population Bomb* (Ehrlich 1954), a pamphlet distributed in a million copies that sparked a renewed interest in the topic.[5] *Newsweek* compared the threat to that of nuclear war, noting that India's population explosion was 'of hydrogen-bomb size' (Bereday and Lauwerys 1965: 388). Many prominent science-fiction authors – among them Robert Heinlein, Frederik Pohl and Isaac Asimov – had already published stories where uncontrolled population growth was depicted as a threat to mankind, and it's plausible that the director's interest on the topic could have been aroused by these works,[6] as we know that by the time of his first meeting with Clarke, Kubrick had already absorbed an 'immense amount of science fact and science fiction' (Clarke 1972: 29). Anthony Burgess, author of *A Clockwork Orange* (1962), wrote an interesting and provocative novel about overpopulation, *The Wanting Seed* (1962), which was reportedly suggested to Kubrick by cinematographer Robert Gaffney in 1969 as a possible source for a movie (Lobrutto 1998: 330; Booker 2005: 37–39). Brian Aldiss wrote several stories in which overpopulation was featured within a science-fiction context (see Heise 2003: 74–77, 2008: 71). One in particular, *Supertoys Last All Summer Long* (Aldiss 1968) was set 'in an overpopulated future society where pregnancy is allowed only if you win the weekly lottery' (Watson 2000). According to Ian Watson, though, when he worked with Kubrick in 1990 on the adaptation of *Supertoys*, overpopulation was neither the focus of the story nor what Kubrick was interested in. By then 'his primary interest was in creating a "fairy story" for the future, a technological version of Pinocchio […]. Thus the population aspect only served as a pretext for a world where population might be controlled and a substitute robot boy might be plausible'.[7]

Kubrick publicly expressed interest in the issue in a *Newsweek* interview from 3 February 1964: 'I can always do a story about overpopulation. Do you realize that in 2020 there will be no room on earth for all the people to stand? The really sophisticated worriers are worried about that' (Anon. 1964a: 80). Eight days later, Kubrick was offered a related movie by an unknown company/producer: 'He is in no rush to tackle the next project, though he has been offered a challenging idea based on the population explosion' (McGrady 1964: 3c). This project has no further archival sources to support it, but the undeniable fascination Kubrick felt for the topic continued, as demonstrated by a conversation between him and his contemporary, Joseph Heller:

> On one hand you've got someone saying, if we don't get ourselves straightened we're going to blow up the whole world and kill everybody. On the other hand, somebody's saying that by the year 2000, if we don't stop the birthrate, there won't be room to stand on the surface of the Earth. This sense of paradoxes makes it very enjoyable to an audience to take a seemingly serious or important situation and then allow the reality to intrude.
> (Heller 1964)

This suggests that, besides being personally concerned by overpopulation as a world crisis, Kubrick was intrigued by the cinematic potential of the inherent paradox of the current state of affairs. The director had already commented on the usefulness of exposing contrasts for dramatic purposes as a narrative device that gave him the opportunity to 'contrast an individual of our contemporary society with a solid framework of accepted value, which the audience becomes fully aware of, and which can be used as a counterpoint to a human, individual, emotional situation' (Stang 1958), and had just exploited the paradoxes of nuclear strategy in *Dr. Strangelove* (Southern 1963; Bernstein 1966a). It's significant, therefore, to notice that Kubrick would not overlook this dialectical relationship when working on his extraterrestrial project. Rather, the issue was present right from the start of its development.

For example, here's how the narrator in the initial film treatment for *2001*, titled *Journey Beyond the Stars* (December 1964), illustrates the state of the world at the beginning of the twenty-first century: 'The two great problems facing the world in the year 2001 had an ominously ironic convergence – overpopulation, and the cancerous spread of nuclear weapons' (Kubrick and Clarke 1964). This passage comes right after the 'The Dawn of Man' section, as a prologue to the part of the movie set in the twenty-first century; Kubrick and Clarke presumably intended to use overpopulation in relation to the threat of extinction that loomed upon the primordial man-apes, extensively depicted as hopelessly starving before the timely intervention of the monolith. The paradox lies in the fact that humans were once starving because they had not yet learned how to hunt and kill; and now that they can (and worryingly so, thanks to the H-bomb), starvation is brought about by overpopulation. The reasons are different, but the bleak human outlook remains the same.

The relationship between these two themes appeared in later scripts as well, like the following from October–December 1965 – again mentioned by the narrator at the beginning of the part of the movie set in space: 'By the year 2001, overpopulation had replaced the problem of starvation, but this was ominously offset by the absolute and utter perfection of the weapon' (Kubrick and Clarke 1965a). In this version there's apparently a shift in focus in favour of overpopulation, but famine will come back to haunt the unfortunate citizens of the twenty-first century in the eventual novel by Clarke:

> Since the 1970s, the world had been dominated by two problems which, ironically, tended to cancel each other out […] the population of the world was now six billion […]. As a result, food was short in every country; even the United States had meatless days, and widespread famine was predicted within fifteen years, despite heroic efforts to farm the sea and to develop synthetic foods.
>
> (Clarke 2012: 424)

Such references, and others that clarified how the nuclear threat would loom heavily on the twenty-first century, were ultimately discarded; Kubrick commented that he wanted a 'non-specific result' (Krämer 2010: 47) for the film and removed the narrator altogether in the late stages of the editing. It would be up to Clarke to make clear in his book that after the famous match cut of Moon-Watcher's bone turning into a satellite, what we are presented with is a series of nuclear bombs put in orbit by some of the 38 existing nuclear powers,[8] and that the spaceship Discovery One is propelled by a series of explosions of atomic bombs behind the spacecraft in a way that echoes the US Air Force's Project Orion from the 1960s.[9] Despite the ambiguity of the movie, Kubrick did admit that there was a 'contrast in the story between giant orbiting bombs, which you might say is the negative use of nuclear energy and this particular spaceship, which leads to great, fantastic accomplishments, which is also another, the good use of nuclear energy' (Bernstein 1966a).

All in all, the director's interest in the relationship between overpopulation, starvation and nuclear weapons appears to provide an interesting insight into the extent and the artistic relevance of Kubrick's socially related concerns and their influence on the thematic richness that underpins *2001*. It also hints towards a rather pessimistic view of the early twenty-first century that is often overlooked when referring to *2001*, commonly presented as the most optimistic film of Kubrick's oeuvre, and offers a significant connection to the dystopian future later seen in *A Clockwork Orange* (Kubrick, 1971). Yet, the director did not find a true 'love interest' in overpopulation, and as the mysterious movie offer about it faded, other intriguing suggestions seemed to be on the horizon.

'Nothing has clicked yet': Kubrick and the United Nations

On 6 April 1964 Kubrick sent a telegram to movie executive Harold Mirisch, turning down the proposal to helm the project of adapting an unnamed book: 'I have to decline for the most subjective of reasons, namely that I am presently at work on two ideas that have more fascination to me' (Kubrick 1964a). As it is most likely that the first of such ideas was his extraterrestrial project, about which he had first written to Arthur C. Clarke on 31 March (Kubrick 1964b), the second idea could refer either to the previously mentioned overpopulation movie or to the second project Kubrick was involved with by early 1964: a TV-movie project with the United Nations.

Three days after Kubrick's telegram to Mirisch, the American press announced that on the occasion of the 25th anniversary of the United Nations, the Xerox Corporation would produce a series of television dramas that would revolve around the activities of the intergovernmental organization (Adams 1964a). Kubrick was mentioned as one of the high profile filmmakers involved, along other directors like Joseph Mankiewicz and Otto Preminger, as well as actors Marlon Brando and Paul Newman; basically the most respectable names in Hollywood seemed to have gathered to 'waive fees' in order to gain the prestige associated in working with the United Nations (Patureau 1964). The directors involved would have had the chance to choose a script or a story to their liking; it was explicitly mentioned that Kubrick would write the script for his film.

Kubrick's involvement with the United Nations seems to have been originated by Peter Hollander, an old New York acquaintance of Kubrick, who by then was at the executive level in the film department of the United Nations.[10] The Stanley Kubrick Archive holds material related to the contacts between the director and Edgar Rosenberg – the executive producer of TELSUN, the company in charge of the United Nations TV effort – that seem to have begun in March 1964 (Anon. 1964d). In a letter to Rosenberg dated 16 April, Kubrick mentions taking part in an 'extremely impressive' United Nations luncheon; once again, Kubrick seized the opportunity to state how important it was, for him, to first find a suitable and interesting story. Explaining to Rosenberg how it has never been a 'particular gift of mine to find stories that interest me, even when the unlimited choice of subject matter for general films is the spectrum of choice' (Kubrick 1964c), Kubrick said this problem was exacerbated by having to limit himself to narratives relevant to the United Nations. He insisted, however, that he was 'doing my level best to find something, and that as soon as I have anything approaching a good germ of an idea I will then call upon your services to hire any appropriate people to develop the idea' (Kubrick 1964c).

The indisputable uneasiness that transpires from the letter to Rosenberg is connected to Kubrick's recurring story-related struggles and, evidently, also to the fact that the director's name was leaked to the press before it was sensible to do so. Despite all this, Kubrick kept the United Nations option open, as elsewhere in the letter he asks Rosenberg to be sent materials and ideas from the other writers that had worked with TELSUN on the United Nations project by then. Three months later, Kubrick wrote the last note to Rosenberg to be found in the Archive: 'I am still looking, thinking and hoping. Unfortunately, nothing has clicked yet. This is very difficult' (Kubrick 1964d). The press announced Kubrick's withdrawal from the project a month later, on 18 August (Adams 1964b).

Perhaps by early April Kubrick had not foreseen the extent of his future commitment with Clarke; the two had first met on 22 April and had quickly established a fruitful intellectual relationship.[11] Because of things moving so fast Kubrick might have needed to move the search of a story suited to the United Nations to the background; and then, by the summer, he was so involved in his science-fiction project that he had to withdraw from the United Nations assignment. Still, an intriguing question arises, one most likely destined to remain unanswered: what would have become of *2001* had the director found a story that 'clicked'?

Without Kubrick, and after the defection of other tentative artists, the TELSUN project would sink without leaving significant traces in TV history, among financial troubles, assorted controversies and the opposition of the American networks – if not for a movie, *A Carol for Another Christmas* (Mankiewicz 1964), broadcast on 28 December 1964. Its main actors were the two leads from *Dr. Strangelove*, Peter Sellers and Sterling Hayden; their involvement (Sellers even got to do the Texan accent he supposedly claimed he couldn't master for Kubrick) and the plot, a post-atomic take of the Dickens' classic *A Christmas Carol* (1843), leaves a sense of déjà vu.[12] But speculation aside, the evidence of Kubrick's involvement in what was essentially a propaganda vehicle for the United Nations is an interesting addition to the director's record of stances on contemporary issues, especially if we consider that, in the wake of the heating debate that followed *Dr. Strangelove*, he had avoided making public statements or appearances that would associate him and his films with a particular political position, turning down invitations from several political groups (Krämer 2014: 98–99; Broderick 2017: 7).

Shadow on the Sun (1961)

Kubrick had indeed found one story that 'clicked' before *2001*, and it was, no less, a science-fiction story; it proved to be a chance encounter whose influence lasted for almost 30 years. In late 1961 the director was in England to put the finishing touches to *Lolita* and start research for *Dr. Strangelove*. He regularly listened to BBC radio (Bull 1965: 112) and it was whilst listening to the 'Light Programme' that he discovered *Shadow on the Sun*, a radio drama broadcast in thirteen episodes between October and December 1961 and written by Gavin Blakeney, an experienced theatre, radio, and TV writer (Ronson 2016: 177–78).

What was in the plot that could have fascinated Kubrick? The titular 'Shadow' is a weapon apparently engineered by a race of twelve-feet-tall lizards from Jupiter's moon Europa,[13] which are discovered by the main characters in a state of suspension in a spaceship in Antarctica. The Shadow is causing the decrease of the Sun's heat output in order – humans think – to drop the temperature of the Earth to make it suitable to the unusual metabolism of the lizards before they can launch a full-fledged invasion. As if that were not enough, a virus is spread on Earth that immunizes those it infects from cold weather; many humans, therefore, start to demand infusions of infected blood, basically turning themselves into the invaders. Halfway in the series, after a rocket hastily assembled by an international consortium destroys the Shadow and victory seems to be at hand, comes the plot twist: the lizards' bodies are analysed and it is discovered that their brain would be too small to allow them to fly their own spaceships, let alone build them. The real Europans are then identified, in horror, as the inhabitants of the hovercraft-like machines that are now appearing in force on Earth: 'Metal outside… and this… this brain, this fleshy thing inside!' – they are discovered to be using the lizards as slaves and as frozen food, and are most probably about to use the humans for the same purpose; hence the decrease of the temperature caused by the Shadow on the Sun. Eventually, our heroes prevail, finding a cure for the virus and jamming the machines by turning their energy against them.

Intriguingly, before the happy ending, *Shadow on the Sun* takes a Strangelovian turn when one of the surviving British politicians suggests, as last resort against the Europans, to carpet-bomb the United Kingdom with H-bombs: 'some [humans] will survive – enough to start again, build the world again. In six months or a year […] some in America, some here in other parts'. Then, addressing one female character: 'you're young and healthy – and you're a woman […]. We shall need you afterwards'. Males would not, though, have been as lucky as the survivors in Kubrick's nightmare comedy: in order to be spared 'man will probably have to draw lots' (Blakeney 1961). Although the similarities with *Dr. Strangelove* are too evident to be ignored, it is to be stated that the gestation of the ending of the movie was so complex that evidence of a direct influence cannot be conclusive.

It is highly probable that Kubrick recalled this radio-drama – with a story that is reminiscent of the plot twist in Clarke's *Childhood's End* (1953a)[14] – a couple of years later, while in the early stages of planning his outer space movie. In December 1963 his associate producer Victor Lyndon got in contact with the representatives of the BBC author Gavin

Blakeney and the rights for *Shadow* were acquired in October 1964, for the relatively low sum of £200 (Kavanagh 1964; Lovejoy 1964). While the purchase of rights or options for an intellectual property is a standard Hollywood procedure and does not necessarily mean that a film will ever be developed, let alone produced, the fascination Kubrick felt for *Shadow* led him to suggest it to Clarke as a basis for their science-fiction movie, as the writer himself recalled 30 years later:

> He had also acquired rights to a property with the intriguing title *Shadow on the Sun*; I remember nothing whatsoever about it, and have even forgotten the author's names, [...]. Whoever he was, I hope he never knows that I sabotaged his career, because Kubrick was promptly informed that Clarke was *not* interested in developing other people's ideas.
>
> (Clarke 2012: 116)

As the rights of *Shadow* were purchased only in October, by which time Kubrick and Clarke had already been working for five months on the novel-length treatment they eventually used to sell the project to MGM, it's hard to think that the radio-drama could have ever been a serious contender to Clarke's input. Clarke noted the rejection of Kubrick's proposal only ten days after their first meeting: '2 May. S. scrapped "Shadow on the Sun" and agreed on "Sentinel" as basis for movie' (Clarke n.d.). Still, the fiercely competitive and intellectually proud writer (whose affectionate, self-appointed nickname was 'Ego') would never mention, in his many recollections about his involvement in *2001*, any other rival work in his contribution to Kubrick's science-fiction movie. But the above suggests that Kubrick's choice of 'The Sentinel' as the source material for *2001*, something that Clarke had suggested as early as 9 April 1964 in his second letter to the director (Clarke 1964), was not so straightforward as is thought.

The director's longtime interest in *Shadow on the Sun* can be read, I suggest, from the perspective of a commentary on contemporary society, capturing a feeling of the times. After all, Kubrick noted that the best science-fiction movies, by then, had mostly been 'social quests in disguise' (Renaud 1968: 45). In *Shadow* there is a distinctive focus on the different reactions of several levels of the society to the alien invasion – politicians, clergyman, the military, women, scientists. The shifting alliances and the resulting tension between these groups is perhaps the most compelling part of the drama, and alien actions and intentions are mostly in the background, or as a source of speculation for the human characters – just like they would be in *2001*.[15]

In 1965 one of the voice actors of *Shadow on the Sun*, Californian-born William Sylvester, was cast as Dr Heywood Floyd in *2001*, but this is not the last trace of the radio-drama in Kubrick's career. After being shelved for more than twenty years, it would reappear in the late 1980s, when Kubrick was again interested in a new science-fiction project. Browsing in his archive in search of ideas, Kubrick found his old notes about *Shadow* and swiftly dispatched his collaborator Anthony Frewin to fetch the original script from the BBC archives, buying again the rights from Blakeney in 1988 for £1500 (Ronson 2016: 177–78; Church 2004: 12), because 'Stanley's interest in a project might lapse for years on end but as soon as it re-awakened things must happen instantly' (Watson 2000). Kubrick reportedly worked on and off the project for several years, only to abandon it (again) to focus on Aldiss's *Super-Toys Last All Summer Long*, arguably a less dated story that dealt with a theme Kubrick had been keenly interested in ever since his research about it during the pre-production of *2001*: artificial intelligence.[16]

'I'm a bit more of a science-fiction addict that you might have suspected'

Why did Kubrick ultimately choose an original story about extraterrestrials, instead of adapting a science-fiction story like *Shadow on the Sun*, or one of the many books he had reportedly read? Perhaps the answer is in his difficult relationship with a genre he was 'impatient with, as he liked the ideas but he found the writing jejune and the characterization deplorable' (Frewin 2005a: 378). Kubrick had indeed been interested in science-fiction for a long time, at least since the 1930s, when as a child he read pulp magazines like *Amazing Stories* and *Astounding Stories*.[17] Speaking in the documentary *The Last Movie: Stanley Kubrick and Eyes Wide Shut* (Joyce 2008), Kubrick's wife, Christiane, stated that both her and Kubrick were no less than a couple of science-fiction buffs: 'I read it all the time. I read Arthur C. Clarke and I was complete science-fiction mad. And Stanley more so even. Both constantly, you know, exchanging books'. The director himself confessed, 'I'm a bit more of a science-fiction addict than you might have suspected' when replying to a fan letter that had contained suggestions for possible inspiration among famous science-fiction authors (Kubrick 1964e).

Still, in public Kubrick refrained from presenting himself as a science-fiction fan. In an interview with Charlie Köhler he said, 'I've never been a science-fiction buff' (Köhler 1968: 246); and in the drafts for Alexander Walker's *Stanley Kubrick Directs* (1972), composed with Kubrick's active assistance, he originally stated, 'I had always been a science fiction fan', before crossing out the sentence to ensure that it did not appear in the published version (Lippi 2008: 204). In all the interviews given during and after the production of *2001*, Kubrick explicitly distanced himself and his movie from the stigma that was attached to the genre and its stereotypes (ray-guns, mad scientists, scantily-clad girls), defining his movie either as 'a speculative story' (Archerd 1965a: 2), 'a romance' (Oakes 1965: 15) or 'science-fact' (Lightman 1968: 412) rather than science-fiction.

As a matter of fact, Kubrick had chosen to tackle the genre from another perspective. Being interested in socially relevant events, he couldn't possibly ignore the other great story of his times – the Space Race – but, as described by his daughter Katharina, his need was 'for blinding stories about the human condition' (Glintenkamp 2013a), and a traditional yet technically accurate story of space exploration couldn't meet such criteria; this was, after all, a filmmaker who had just turned down the suggestion to adapt a popular book, *The*

Slaves, because it was 'of dubious social value today' (Kubrick 1964f). Instead, the story he eventually picked revolved around 'the reasons for believing in the existence of intelligent extraterrestrial life' and especially 'the impact [...] such discovery would have on Earth', as he described it in his first letter to Clarke on 31 March 1964 (McAleer 1992: 192; Krämer 2010: 18). Indeed, when commenting on what prompted him to make a science-fiction movie, he answered:

> I was reading a book published by the Rand Corporation which listed the number of planets habitable by man [...] incredibly it ran to something like 100,000 earth-type planets. I started to think about it, and finally I thought why haven't I been excited about this before?
>
> (Oakes 1965: 15)[18]

The origins of *Dr. Strangelove* provide us with another clue, once again connected to Kubrick's own interests and concerns. In the early sixties, being extremely concerned about the risk of nuclear holocaust and irritated by the 'stupefying reverence' (Weiler 1962) the subject had been met with in the past, Kubrick stated that he explicitly felt the need to 'do something about it' (Southern 1963: 29) to focus the public opinion on the issue.[19] Regarding the potential influence of movies, Kubrick said that it was 'interesting to think about ways of influencing people in a medium such as mine' (Archer 1964), and even explicitly advocated a sort of moral renovation of society:[20]

> The arms race is not likely to produce an everlasting peace [...] if not accompanied by a profound moral change in nations and men [...]. The only solution and defense lies in the minds and hearts of men.
>
> (Weiler 1962)

> Unless we learn to create a new system of law and morality between nations, then we will surely exterminate ourselves.
>
> (Fay 1963: 5)

The audience reaction to *Dr. Strangelove* leads us to believe that the effect on the public was just what Kubrick hoped; various people stated that such a film was needed and it was the kind of artistic work that could help bring about a 'more sensitive and sensible society' (Krämer 2016: 47). It is arguable that the director might have felt inspired by this reaction to use the same perspective with *2001*; after all, his wife Christiane has stated that 'it was not his intention to lose [*Dr. Strangelove*'s] inferences completely' (Bizony 2014: 505). The 'first contact' between mankind and aliens surely had dramatic cinematic potential, but it was apparently its social value – and the importance of a sustained effort to explore space and maximize the chances of their possible detection – that Kubrick valued the most.

Significantly, a press release for *Journey Beyond the Stars* from February 1965, drafted by Kubrick himself, reads as a passionate appraisal of the transformative potential of space exploration, comparing it to 'the voyages of the Renaissance that brought about the end of the Dark Ages' (Bizony 2014: 544–45). In a contemporary interview, Kubrick was said to have been:

> [...] increasingly disturbed by the barrier between scientific knowledge and the general public [...] Mr. Clarke and Mr. Kubrick said that they hoped their film would give people a real understanding of the facts and of the overwhelming implications that the facts have for the human race.
>
> (Bernstein 1965: 38)

In light of this goal, Kubrick could not have chosen a better collaborator than Arthur C. Clarke, one of the most ardent popularizers and supporters of space exploration, who was at least as concerned as Kubrick about mankind's ultimate destiny and also shared his attitude towards the role of science-fiction; that is, to prepare people to accept the future and to encourage a flexibility of mind: 'Politicians should read science fiction, not westerns and detective stories' (Agel 1970: 300).

Conclusion

While critics and academics tend to see *2001* as the middle chapter of a science-fiction trilogy comprising *Dr. Strangelove* and *A Clockwork Orange*, I think that those movies, as well as the other projects Kubrick didn't realize, may be better understood as significant examples of the director's attention to stories that revolved around the urgent state of affairs in contemporary society. If good science-fiction channels the anxieties of the age in which it was produced, the evidence suggests that what may have set Kubrick apart was his deeply personal stance in the subjects he chose to tackle, and the sheer ambition of his goals.

In the pivotal moment of his career the director came to elaborate that, to be proverbially 'really good' (Kubrick 1964b), a movie had to actively stimulate the audience on thinking about a major issue. With *2001*, Kubrick tried literally to 'top the H-bomb', that is to overcome his very own fears about nuclear annihilation and, in the process, arouse a response in the audience, 'of wonder, awe [...] even, if appropriate, terror' (Clarke 1972: 29). After 50 years, the lasting legacy of *2001* on cinema history and popular culture in general is a testament of the value of his intuition, and the ambiguity of the storytelling devices he employed to achieve his goal of 'a majestic visual experience' (Alpert 1966: 34) did not diminish the message – it may be argued that it might have even helped to convey it to the public.

Despite his explicit artistic and social goals, Kubrick's attitude was that of a concerned filmmaker, not a political activist. In a 1968 interview he was said to be 'mildly impatient with film-makers who forget their primary mission is to entertain, not lecture [...] his only philosophy (he says) is to make good pictures' (Musel 1968: 19). Kubrick was also aware that he worked in an industry whose goal was to produce profitable products, once remarking to Brian Aldiss, 'how can I make a movie that would gross as much as *Star Wars* and yet allow me to retain my reputation for social responsibility?' (Joyce 2008). It was a self-confessed half-joke that summarizes the inevitable tension between artistic and social responsibilities and the need to make a commercially and critically successful film.

Kubrick's attitude was illustrated in an interview to an Italian news magazine published in that fateful April 1964, and which reads like the perfect summary of the unmistakable blend of disenchanted, yet concerned social commitment and esthetic concerns that characterized Kubrick's whole career:

> Insofar as we believe that good movies can educate the masses, we must believe that bad movies can make them worse.
>
> (Marcelli 1964: 57)

Chapter Two

2001: A Space Odyssey: A transcendental trans-locution

Suparno Banerjee

Stanley Kubrick's *2001: A Space Odyssey* has invited an army of commentators and probably encouraged the publication of Arthur C. Clarke's more discursive novel of the same name shortly after the movie release in April 1968. However, the existing critical discourse on *2001* rarely foregrounds the importance of Clarke's novel as an independent work with inherent differences from the movie. In fact, major science-fiction film scholars such as Vivian Sobchack (1987), Scott Bukatman (1993) and J. P. Telotte (1995) do not even mention Clarke's novel in their discussions about the film. Both the movie and the novel originated in Clarke's short story 'The Sentinel' (1951), but 'The Sentinel' merely foreshadows the complex conceptual scopes of the works that later emerged from it. The general critical stance regarding *2001* is a somewhat linear one – from 'The Sentinel' to Kubrick's film and then to the novelization of the film by Clarke. Early commentators such as Jeremy Bernstein, Stanley Kauffmann and Jerome Agel even regarded Clarke's novel as an explanation of the film, a view which is echoed to some extent by critics like Robert Kolker in 2006.[1] Again, commentators like David Patterson and Zoe Sofia seem to acknowledge the difference between the novel and the film and yet end up appropriating the novel to explain the film.[2]

A closer comparative examination of the novel and the film, however, will clearly show that Clarke's novel is neither an explanation nor a novelization of the film, but a work existing independently, entrenched in its formal and methodological specificities. While Clarke's novel is rooted directly in the tradition of hard-core science-fiction, Kubrick's film subverts all the norms of traditional films to create something unique. On the one hand, Clarke exploits the conventional devices of science-fiction discourse to contemplate the existence of higher forms of intelligence in the universe. On the other hand, Kubrick employs a method similar to what Paul Schrader calls the 'transcendental style' to bring about an ineffable quality that gives the film a quasi-religious air of mystery. I contend that, although dealing with the same theme, the film and the novel are products of two completely different media and should be seen as such. Unlike most screen adaptations or novelizations, the film and the novel were created simultaneously; they both function independently of one another, each with its own unique structures, themes and significances.

In *Novels into Films*, George Bluestone observes that 'novel and film are both organic – in the sense that aesthetic judgments are based on total ensembles, which include both formal and thematic conventions' (1957: 137). But he also points out that novel and film are two completely different media, with limits and advantages peculiar to their forms. The aim of a successful film adaptation should not be merely to turn a novel into a moving version of words on the pages; rather, this is precisely the thing that can never be done. A film and a literary text operate in two distinctly different ways. Later adaptation theorists such as Keith Cohen (1979), Brian McFarlane (1996), James Naremore (2000) and Mireia Aragay (2005) challenge such medium-specific and formalistic approaches by focusing more on ideological, contextual and intertextual approaches that do not look for fidelity in adaptation. Yet Jakob Lothe, drawing on Russian Formalism, reiterates some of Bluestone's basic principles of difference between the visual and linguistic modes of narration, namely the 'strikingly visual quality' of film (Lothe 2000: 11). Despite claims of the similar qualities of literary and cinematic symbolism and the sequential nature of both mediums, the material differences between literary art and cinematic art is ignored at one's own peril, especially in case of such a 'non-verbal' film as *2001* and its relationship to a highly discursive, yet eponymous, novel. As Lothe asserts, 'although film communication clearly has points of contact with verbal communication, the film medium is very different from the verbal form of communication we meet in narrative texts' (Lothe: 13).

I have argued elsewhere that a film is primarily a 'photo text', in which auditory and linguistic components are subordinated to the visual image, while literature works with language that sometimes evokes images through the processes of signification, but not in the cinematic sense (Banerjee 2001: 154). Such media as television ('far sight'), video (from Latin 'I see'), and cinema (from Greek 'kinemat' or 'movement') all share the same primary visual quality, audio and linguistic properties being secondary. We can have silent cinema, or cinema with no language (written or spoken) in it, as Charles Chaplin has so effectively shown, but not a cinema sans visuals.

On the contrary, literature is a linguistic art. As Ferdinand de Saussure (2001) argues, language is a self-contained system, functioning through a differential relationship of signs, not leading to any actual sensory external reality: that is, meaning is constructed through relationships between the words, not by comparing the words with actual physical objects that they purportedly signify. Literature, which functions only through the operations of linguistic conventions, then can only be an extra-sensory experience. The eye, in context of literature, acts as an instrument that sends the optical impressions of the lexical symbols on the paper to the brain where the real experience takes place through the process of signification. The letters that combine into words, which then form paragraphs and so on, are really sequences of significations: forming images, denoting actions, characters, relationships and so on. The words on the page raise connotative impressions in the brain that then works out their meanings and suggestions. In spite of Jacques Derrida's (2001) argument to the contrary (i.e., writing is not a mere system of substitution for the spoken language), substituting the eye/sight with the ear/hearing (spoken words as opposed to written) or the hand/touch (braille) will not lead to an experience that is qualitatively vastly different in this context.

A film (although it is, like language, a sequential medium), however, is primarily a sensory experience, the eye and the ear serving their uniquely different purposes, in which sound and language are supplements to the image, not substitutes. The images create an immediate and almost tangible reality on which the viewers build their comprehension of the narrative. This immediate palpability of the image is at once films' advantage and its limitation, while the intangible conceptual quality, literatures. The presentational nature of film limits its access to the discursive power of the novel, and so restricts its ability to portray concepts and abstractions. Obviously, a film can engage in discourse through language/dialogue, but dialogue is rather a supplemental element, enhancing the effects of the primary visual object. And even dialogues are unlikely to render the whole world of abstraction on screen, especially when that abstraction is related to an experiential quality or to purely conceptual realms, beyond human senses. As Bluestone says, 'the rendition of the mental states – memory, dream, imagination – cannot be as adequately represented by film as by language [...]. Conceptual imaging, by definition, has no existence in space' (1957: 140). However, film utilizes its own narrative strategies to counter the challenges posed by its formal constraints – deployment of the devices of ambiguity, irony, symbolism, metaphor, etc. Indeed, the scant visual suggestions and cleverly employed visual symbolisms often create an effect not achieved by the discursive excesses of the novel. Lothe argues, 'since film (through directors such as Luis Buñuel and Alain Resnais) may represent the unreal and logically impossible, one may equally claim that film is best suited to showing, for instance, dreams and fantasies' (2000: 13). This is especially so because memories, dreams and fantasies are often visual (rather than linguistic) in nature. In many places such is the case with *2001*.

Reaction to Kubrick's *2001*'s unconventional style of narrative ranges from 'incoherent' and 'boring' to bewildered acclaim. The film relies heavily on its visual force to drag the viewer through long stretches of aural inactivity and deliberately slow pace. The visual repetitiveness gives *2001* a mythic structure ultimately connecting the film to its epic ancestor, Homer's *The Odyssey*. Kubrick urges the viewer to look for the experiential quality of the film, taking in the 'sensual, emotional, and subconscious elements coupled with a resistance to categorization' (Man 1994: 50). In Kubrick's own words:

> *2001* is a non-verbal experience; out of two hours and 19 minutes of film, there are only a little less than 40 minutes of dialog. I tried to create a visual experience, one that bypasses verbalized pigeonholing and directly penetrates the subconscious with an emotional and philosophic content [...]. I don't want to spell out a verbal road map for *2001* that every viewer will feel obligated to pursue or else fear he's missed the point.
>
> (Man 1994: 50)

Clearly, Kubrick did not intend to follow the narrative of the book entirely; neither did Clarke follow Kubrick's lead to make his novel less discursive in its exploration of the realms imaginable only in theoretical astrophysics and in speculations of the causes debated by evolutionists and theologians alike. Clarke and Kubrick chose to follow their own paths appropriate to their respective modes of expression.

Clarke's novel is painstaking in its commentary, precise in its reasoning, and detailed in its analysis. Kubrick's movie is suggestive in operation, deliberately intuitive in its function, and mystically vague in the end. The novel focuses on a main character in every part: Moon-Watcher in 'Primeval Night', Heywood Floyd in 'TMA-1' and David Bowman in the remaining sections. The novel covers four million years in a leap from the ape to the man, and traces humanity's evolution back to an alien origin: human intelligence – a result of an alien experimentation. The omniscient narrator pushes the reader through the petty politics of mechanized man to the vastness of space, then on a quest to Saturn following the crumbs thrown by the black monolith on the Moon, and finally beyond the limits of time and space to the transformation into a new existence. Though the reader is not told what that new existence is, the birth and return of the Star-Child/David Bowman to normal space and time clearly points to a new stage in the evolutionary chain, in the evolution of the cosmic existence and cosmic intelligence itself – earthly childhood's end and initiation into a cosmic maturity (the same theme is also explored in *Childhood's End* (1953), probably Clarke's best known novel).

Kubrick explores the same theme but in a completely different manner. He cuts the linear connections between the different parts of the novel and leaves gaps and obscure images. The viewer is to discern the pattern running through all the sections of the movie in an effort to circumnavigate the farthest shores of the universe to the point of origin, the Earth, to complete the odyssey. The opening shot of the Earth rising over the Moon and the Sun coming up from behind the Earth, and the concluding shot of the Star-Child's bemused beholding of the globe are almost identical in composition. Kubrick's use of music at critical points also acts as an aural aid to highlight the focal points in the movie: György Ligeti's eerie resonances of the black monolith hint at its otherworldliness, Richard Strauss's *Also Sprach Zarathustra* (1896) triumphantly announces new movements of the plot (generally accompanied by some precise stellar alignment), and Johann Strauss's *The Blue Danubes* (1866) waltz during the movement of the space station confirms the faith in man's rationality and self-confidence. For Kubrick, the story acts as another tool to create a 'receptive mood for a vision that is basically beyond narrative' (Geduld 1973: 30). For Clarke, the narrative is a serious meditation on the scientific and philosophical speculations on alien life forms and their role in human evolution.

Kubrick's reliance on visual symbolism contributes the most to the film's formalism. He admits the influence of Jungian symbolism on *2001*. He explains that in this order of symbols, 'a circle divided into four quadrants represents inner wholeness and a rectangular form, the conscious realization of this wholeness (in short, greater intelligence)' (Geduld 1973: 30). That explains the repeated juxtaposition of the rectangular shapes (the black monolith) with the round spherical forms (the celestial bodies). The monolith acts as the central symbol of the movie – the symbol of a higher intelligence and perhaps a higher order of existence. This symbolism is always reinforced by musical accompaniment.

The monolith appears at four critical moments in the movie, every time signifying a momentous change. It first appears to the man-apes, igniting the first sparks of intelligence in them (which is also the first stage of the alien experiment on Earth). The second appearance on the Moon as 'TMA-1' trumpets the human initiation into the Space Age. The third time the monolith acts as a star gate to push the human representative beyond the limits of time and space. The fourth monolith accompanies the birth of the Star-Child. Each appearance of a monolith is accompanied by a magical arrangement in the stellar bodies. In the first instance the Sun comes up exactly on the top of the monolith with the man-apes running around in bewilderment. The second time the rising Sun sets off the alarm; the position of the Sun and the monolith are the same as they were in the first section, with only the Earth and the Moon exchanging places. The third time, Jupiter and its satellites line up in expectation of Bowman's ritual of passage through the star gate. And the last monolith's appearance in the middle of the Louis XVI bedroom is immediately followed first by the orb of the Star-Child, and then by the peculiar positioning of the Moon, the Earth and the Star-Child in its orb-like womb, itself now a being of pure energy. Thus, a set of related images refers the viewer back to the very first shot of the film: the alignment of the Moon, the Earth and the Sun, only now the Sun has been replaced by the Star-Child, not so subtly suggesting a new dawn for humanity. This repetitious structure of the film can be seen to foreground its evolutionary and transcendental themes:

> The human has been taken to its evolutionary limit […] but death is only a prelude to the triumphant rebirth heralded by the same Richard Strauss theme that was heard earlier as the ape picked up a bone to use as a tool […]. The passage from humanoid to human is thus recapitulated in the finale of *2001* by a passage from human to more-than-human.
> (Bukatman 1993: 283)

Consequently, the association of images and sounds used in a circular pattern in *2001* suggests the evolutionary process while displacing the concept of a linear time. This circularity works in other ways too. As Carolyn Geduld mentions, Kubrick seems to be fascinated by the number four: the movie is divided into four parts, has four heroes and is dominated by the four-sided monolith that appears four times in the movie, signifying four leaps in human evolution. Geduld charts out a four-level interpretation in context of the symbolic and mythic association of the monolith:

> As a symbol of alien technology, technology in general, and the 'robotized' aspects of human nature, […] a symbol of predestined fate, […] a Jungian symbol of consciousness (intelligence) […] as a box, a Freudian symbol of the womb.
> (1973: 68)

The first aspect points towards the cold, dry and inscrutable logic of the universe; by analogy with the Frankenstein myth (more pronounced in the novel), technology is portrayed as the monster created by man that ultimately turns to his own destruction (HAL being analogous to the monster). The second aspect suggests the removal of the agency of self-determination for man through a form of predestination by the mysterious forces whatever that may be – an 'alien life-form, a cosmic mind, or God'; it is 'abstract and evil (black) in the sense that it turns life into passive clockwork' (Geduld 1973: 68). The third interpretation pits the force of life against a deterministic universe. Geduld comments, 'Parallels to *Odyssey* belong in this category. HAL is the one-eyed Cyclops the film's Ulysses must fight on the round-about voyage that brings him back home as a Star-Child and King – a being of greater consciousness and self-control' (1973: 68). And the fourth category brings all the erotic foetal imageries of the film together.

Geduld's interpretation connects the symbolism of *2001* with Kubrick's other films, especially the image of the robotized clockwork of a man portrayed in a different but more violent manner in *A Clockwork Orange* and man as a war machine in *Full Metal Jacket* (Kubrick 1987). The mythical, religious and psychological interpretations hint at the film's tendency to delve deep into the conceptual realm. The methodology of this multi-layered interpretation also makes the viewer cognizant of the cinematic tools employed by Kubrick: the lack of dialogue or voiceover narration, use of transitional jump-cuts, juxtaposition of images imbued with metaphorical and symbolic qualities, bleeding over of music and scenes (especially in the later parts), and inexorably slow progress.

But all these tools prove insufficient when Bowman enters the star gate and the realm 'Beyond the Infinite'. The problem that Kubrick encounters here is embedded in human cognitive faculty. The human cognitive abilities are bound by two limiting factors: space and time. In the human three-dimensional sensory input system, the movements of space and time are not necessarily mutually entwined. The arrow of experiential time is always forward and sequential: nothing can move it backwards. Spatial movement, however, suffers no such constraint. The universe, though, is not bound by three dimensions only; it is a warped whole of space-time continuum extending beyond human kind. Human beings exist only on the fringes, like two-dimensional shadows trying to measure the distance between two facing walls in the three-dimensional world. Nevertheless, human beings can filter out the principles of nature and life on a cosmic scale through the ability to engage knowledge beyond the experiential and to think beyond the empirical. This intuitive or speculative reasoning, however, pushes the boundaries of human semiotic capacity, discursive ability being the main instrument for such exercises. And the power of discourse is absent almost by definition in the film medium.

In his discussion of chronological and psychological time in novel and film, Bluestone (1957) asserts that the formative principle in the novel is time, and in film, space:

> Where the novel takes its space for granted and forms its narrative in a complex of time values, the film takes its time for granted and forms a narrative in arrangements of space. Both film and novel create the illusion of psychologically distorted time and space, but neither destroys time or space. The novel renders the illusion of space by going point to point in time; the film renders time by going from point to point in space.
>
> (1957: 148)

To put it another way: language, the medium of novel, by its nature works in linear time. The linguistic symbols come one after the other to signify their meanings. The whole sense cannot be present together at any given point in time. The sense of space can only be constructed by going from point to point in time. Conversely, any visual art such as cinema needs a space to construct its image. Film can create its meaning on any specific presentational space at any given point in time. Thus, a movie can construct a sense of temporal variation by employing various techniques in combining a series of visual images on any presentational space. However, both the novelist and the filmmaker will encounter fundamental difficulties when trying to present something radically different from normal space and time. That is precisely the situation with *2001*. While Clarke had recourse to the discursive power of language to create the conceptual vision in the reader's mind, Kubrick had to show something that is barely even imaginable on a confined space (the screen). At the time of Bowman's passage through the star gate, the kaleidoscopic spray of light rushing towards the viewer coupled with the blurred and frozen face of Bowman act as an unsatisfactory symbolic representation of something exterior to the scope of representation.

But surely Kubrick cannot discuss the scientific theories that would explain Bowman's journey solely through the medium of sight and sound. Bowman moves through a kind of hyperspace, which poses a number of problems for film that creates its illusion of time by going from point to point in space. The problems are many: while the concept of time within the star gate is an illusion, a film is experienced over a certain amount of time, which is occupied by the viewer's focus on the screen; the events that occur inside the star gate and thereafter do not occur in a space definable in three-dimensional terms, although this 'space' must be projected on to a two-dimensional space creating illusion of three-dimensional objects if it is to be experienced by the viewer. In effect, Kubrick had to create an illusion of an illusion about an experience of an uncertain spatio-temporal nature through a medium possessing clearly defined spatio-temporal properties. Kubrick does this by using the kaleidoscopic effect as a visual metaphor for hyperspace and the frozen frames of Bowman's face as a metaphorical representation of distorted time. The same can be said about the Louis XVI bedroom. The juxtaposition of images, Bowman at two different ages in a sequence shot, works to suggest something more than simple blending of scenes: these shots represent the metaphorical progression and regression that Bowman is made subject to; this sequence also functions as a technique of implying the twisted nature of space-time. The obvious symbols – Bowman's last supper, the breaking of the glass, his transformation from a vegetative state into a Star-Child and the sudden appearance of the monolith in the room – add to Kubrick's unique way of handling the problem.

This 'unique way' is probably the closest that one can get to what Paul Schrader calls the transcendental style in film. Though Schrader associates this style specifically with presenting the holy or the religious in film, this style can very well be applied to any attempt to present 'the ineffable and invisible' (1972: 3). Schrader specifically mentions that, 'although transcendental style, like any form of transcendental art, strives toward the ineffable and invisible, it is neither ineffable nor invisible itself' (1972: 3). The dictionary meanings of the word 'transcendental' are related not only to religion but also to anything beyond experience, from Kant's philosophical system to mathematical connotations – numbers impossible to express as integers. Schrader observes: 'The Transcendent is beyond normal sense experience, and that which it transcends is by definition, immanent [...]. Human works, accordingly, cannot inform one about the Transcendent, they can only be expressive of the Transcendent' (1972: 5). Although Schrader tries to restrict its stylistic implications within the field of religious expression, the 'transcendental style' lends itself well enough to other interpretations: 'Transcendental style seeks to maximize the mystery of existence; it eschews all conventional interpretations of reality: realism, naturalism, psychologism, romanticism, expressionism, impressionism, and, finally, rationalism' (Schrader 1972: 10). While *2001* does not deal explicitly with religion or the sacred, the film takes on topics that are beyond human experience and logic and is akin to the mystical and the religious. Though it sounds contradictory, Kubrick's presentation of theoretical astrophysics (more specifically, Einstein's special theory of relativity) is closer to mystical than scientific; thus the term 'transcendental style' may very well be applied to his way of presenting the ineffable through the film medium. This is very different from Clarke's treatment of the same topic.

Clarke's novel deviates at various points from the Kubrick movie. In *The Lost Worlds of 2001* (1979), Clarke recounts the various endings proposed for the movie. The one Kubrick selected is known to everyone. However, in the novel Clarke decided to choose his own alternative. The plot of the novel differs from the film in many ways. In the novel, Heywood Floyd's wife is dead. In the space station, Floyd is accosted not by a group of cardboard Russian scientists but by his friend Dr. Dmitri Moisevitch of the USSR Academy of Science. The biggest discrepancy, however, is in the mission of Discovery One. There is no Jupiter mission. The target is Saturn, and the third monolith is found not in space but on Saturn's satellite Japetus (Iapetus). Yet when Clarke decided to write a sequel to *2001, 2010: Odyssey Two*, for some reason he thought that the Jupiter mission would be a better choice to follow and picked up the threads from where the movie left them. In a sense this can be marked as a case of reverse influence, wherein a novel follows (though not in the exact sense) the plot of the movie version of the novel's predecessor.[4] Besides these deviations in plot, Clarke uses a tool that Kubrick didn't have: discourse. Although at times the explanatory passages become too drawn out, the narrative discourse has the power to evoke concepts and images far beyond their possibilities of physical depiction. The movie is superior in terms of its special effects – the slowly rotating planets, the graceful movement of Discovery One through space, the tossed bone transforming into an orbiting satellite – and in its mysterious experiential quality. But the film lacks the descriptive specificities of the novel. The film also lacks the analytic discourse that allows Clarke to draw on his scientific resources to capture the readers' attention and engage their intellect. The movie functions through omission, the novel through explication.

In the first section of the novel, Clarke provides a detailed view of the nature of the experiment (the chapters 'The New Rock' through 'Ascent of Man'). This discussion provides him an opportunity to expound his own theory of evolution. Kubrick deliberately keeps this part vague, cutting out many of Clarke's details. Kubrick also lacked the power of philosophical musing by the virtue of using film as his medium of expression. In the second section the movie could outsmart the novel through its depiction of zero-gravity travel and its grand descriptive shots, but it completely cuts out scientific explanations and even the transitional elements between the sections. In the third section, the novel provides an impressive genealogy for HAL that would be tedious in the movie. The fourth section is the most problematic. Here both the author and the filmmaker struggle with the limitations of their respective mediums. Kubrick struggles with the physical properties of his representational space; Clarke struggles with language's inherent self-referentiality that always creates slippages of meanings and associations. Clarke describes the 'nonlinear' expansion of space in this section: 'the stars at the centre hardly seemed to move, while those toward the edge accelerated more and more swiftly, until they became streaks of light just before they vanished from view' (Clarke 1968: 196). Although Clarke clearly struggles to render this scenario, he probably evokes an extra-sensory vista in his reader's mind more successfully than Kubrick's actual light show on screen. Clarke is also more effective in his rendering of warped time:

> Normally, the numbers in the tenths-of-a-second window flickered past so quickly that it was almost impossible to read them; now they were appearing and disappearing at discrete intervals, and he could count them off one by one without difficulty. The seconds themselves were passing with incredible slowness, as if time itself were coming to a stop.
> (1968: 196)

The farther the reader proceeds from this point, the stranger, the more abstract the incidents and concepts become. Although language depicts space through the manipulation of temporal points, it does not have the disadvantage of a visual medium when the demarcation of space and time dissolves; because language works through signification, the stimulation of images and emotions takes place inside the brain, rather than through sensory depiction on an actual physical space. Therefore, all of Kubrick's light-play and symbolic presentation of the events inside the hotel room falls short of Clarke's evocative language and the vistas that they create in the mind. The flow of pure energy in the giant red star, the sense of draining memory into a better receptacle, and ultimately Bowman's transformation into a being of pure energy are not translatable onto the silver screen as direct visual objects. The novel's meditation on the mathematical significances of the structure of the monolith gives a hint towards its basic symbolism: 'How obvious – how necessary – was the mathematical ratio of its sides, the quadratic sequence 1:4:9! And how naïve to have imagined that the series ended at this point, in only three dimensions!' (Clarke 1968: 219). The consciousness of the Star-Child carries the narrative flow through further, more unimaginable cosmic vistas, giving the reader the sense of a new birth, of a childish wonder in its new existence, without the realization of its own being, its ascendancy over all earthly powers.[5] The novel re-joins the film only when the Star-Child is watching the Earth with its great big eyes.

The novel and the movie both work on several allegorical levels. While the symbols and metaphors are more explicit in the movie, the novel as a whole becomes allegory of the evolution of human consciousness. In spite of its technical brilliance, the movie is often mystical and obscure. Often pedestrian in its narrative flow, the novel excels in its expository quality. Its discourses on the conceptual realm render the novel a more 'scientific' work than the movie, which relies more on mythical associations and the transcendental style. For every phenomenon Clarke, a traditional science-fiction writer, looks for rational explanations. He seeks to engage his readers in the age-old question: 'are we alone in the universe?' Kubrick, a convention-breaker in the film industry, tries to present to his viewer a revolutionary idea of the transcendental existence. To Clarke, human evolution is an experiment on a cosmic scale.[6] To Kubrick, it is a mysterious process overseen by some higher existence, with obvious religious undertones. Both Clarke and Kubrick strive to speculate about the fate of life and intelligence in this inconceivably complex multidimensional universe in their own ways. Clarke's work is not a novelization of Kubrick's film; neither is Kubrick's work a direct adaptation of Clarke's plot on to the screen. The theme that they dwell on transcends the boundaries of their mediums. Rather than one being a translation of the other into a different medium, the novel and the film are 'trans-locutions' of the same original artistic impulse.

Acknowledgements

This article was originally published in 2008, volume 19, issue 1 of *Journal of the Fantastic in the Arts*, pp. 39–50, and is updated and revised for this collection with the kind permission of the International Association for the Fantastic in the Arts.

Chapter Three

Four-colour Kubrick: Jack Kirby's *2001: A Space Odyssey* as adaptation and extension

Dru Jeffries

Chapter Three

> The comic couldn't feel more out of sync with *2001*. It's all Kirby, no Kubrick or Clarke. It's mind-boggling. It's just not right.
> – Julian Darius, *The Weirdest Sci-Fi Comic Ever Made* (2013)

With ten out of his thirteen feature films being adaptations of pre-existing literary works, it's appropriate to label Stanley Kubrick as 'an inveterate adapter' (Jenkins 1997: 24). *2001* is an uncharacteristic work in this regard, as the screenplay and Arthur C. Clarke's novel were written collaboratively and simultaneously.[1] As such, the film cannot be accurately characterized as an adaptation of the novel, and nor can the novel be described as a novelization of the film. On the flip side of the adaptation coin, Kubrick's films have also been the *subject* of many adaptations, with *2001* arguably having the richest intertextual afterlife of his films, boasting 'no fewer than nineteen sequels involving four different authors' (Westfahl 2011: 135). Among these nineteen sequels, one text is both a true adaptation and novelization of *2001*: Marvel Comics' *2001: A Space Odyssey*, written and drawn by Jack Kirby and published in the company's large-scale 'Marvel Treasury Special' format in 1976. Preceding Clarke's own sequel *2010: Odyssey Two* by 8 years, Kirby's comic book version of Kubrick's self-proclaimed 'proverbial good science-fiction movie' (Clarke 1972: 17) has been called no less than 'the weirdest sci-fi comic ever made' (Darius 2013: Penn, Kindle loc. 1490), and itself spawned a sequel series, published between December 1976 and September 1977, that accounts for another ten of the film's nineteen sequels.[2] The 'weirdness' of Kirby's *2001*, however, has perhaps been overstated in the admittedly scant critical attention these comics have received since their initial publication; as the epigraph that precedes this chapter suggests, the dismissive attitude towards Kirby's adaptation and later narrative extension of *2001* emerges primarily out of the cartoonist's supposed failure to accurately reproduce key aspects of Kubrick's film in comic form, as well as his inclusion of material that is judged to be incompatible with the film's tone and narrative approach. In other words, Kirby's *2001* is not 'weird' in and of itself, but rather insofar as it is perceived to be tonally oppositional to Kubrick; it is 'not right' only insofar as it is gets Kubrick's film 'wrong'. By this standard, if Kubrick's *2001* is, as Robert Kolker so wonderfully describes it, 'a Helvetica film' (2000: 134), Kirby's *2001* might be aptly characterized as Comic Sans, that most childlike, consistently derided and perhaps misunderstood of typefaces.[3]

The negative assessment of Kirby's adaptation fails to recognize the ways in which the cartoonist deliberately distances his adaptation from traditional novelization practice and the expectation of textual fidelity in particular. Indeed, Kirby's primary goal in adapting *2001* seems not to have been to produce a 'faithful' adaptation but rather to render the film's narrative in a comprehensible and utterly unambiguous way; in stripping the story of ambiguity – one of the film's defining features – Kirby's comic functions less as a traditional novelization and more as an active act of interpretation, using distinctive textual and visual strategies to assign clear and concrete meaning to the narrative at many junctures where the film resists or refuses to do so. Following Nicolas Labarre's comparative analysis of the film *Alien* (Scott, 1979) and its own graphic novelization, *Alien: The Illustrated Story* (1979), I am also interested in how the change in medium from film to comics effects the generic affiliation of the narrative; in the case of *2001*, Kirby's adaptation doesn't so much recast the narrative within the superhero genre as it reveals the latent affinities that already existed between Kubrick's film and superhero narratives.

Under any other name, I do not believe that these comics would rank among the strangest ever produced – but since adaptations are 'inherently "palimpsestuous" works, haunted at all times by their adapted texts' (Hutcheon 2006: 6), we cannot help but to read Kirby's *2001* in relation to its filmic source. The fact that it is not merely an adaptation but a *novelization* – a graphic novelization, to be precise – further increases the already strong likelihood that readers will assess the work against the original text on which it is based in terms of narrative, visual style and tone.[4] Jan Baetens compares novelizations and other kinds of adaptations thusly: 'novelizations are opposed to cinematic adaptations of literary texts by their apparent lack of freedom. In the case of a cinematic adaptation, once the adaptation rights are bought, the director can freely transform the source text' (2010: 65); the novelization, by contrast, is generally 'conceived with faithfulness in mind' (Labarre 2014: 90) to such an extent that it does not 'so much aspire to become the movie's *other* as it wants to be its *double*' (Baetens 2005: 50, italics in original). While adaptation studies has rightly (though often unsuccessfully) attempted to distance itself from fidelity as a qualitative metric (Leitch 2008: 63), the topic remains central to novelization readers seeking a prose-based cinematic surrogate. As Labarre suggests, 'Fidelity to a source may not be a relevant criterion for academic studies of adaptation […] but it is a factor for tie-in products, in the mind of their producers, creators and consumers' (2014: 90). In this case, however, the expectation of fidelity short-circuits attempts to assess Kirby's *2001* as precisely that – *Kirby's*, not Kubrick and Clarke's. Before turning our attention to the text, then, it behoves us to briefly identify the ways in which Marvel's *2001: A Space Odyssey* falls in line with certain aspects of traditional novelization practice while challenging others.

Film novelizations – like comic books in general – are not afforded the same level of respect as original works of literary fiction: at best, novelizations are thought to be 'mere tools of film advertising' (Mahlknecht 2012: 137) and at worse they are dismissed 'as routinely commissioned, worthless by-products of the film whose release they accompany' (2012: 139). Neither of these claims can be convincingly applied to Kirby's graphic novelization: while Kubrick's film undoubtedly had a longer-than-average theatrical life, the comic was released eight years after the film's premiere and was not specifically timed to coincide with any particular revival of the film. The temporal separation between the film's initial marketing blitz and the publication of Kirby's graphic novelization opens up the possibility for an increased sense of prestige compared to the average tie-in novelization; per Baetens:

> […] 'serious' writers do not novelize a film to coincide with its release and serve its marketing policy. Instead, such writers remember the films they liked when they started going to the movies, and their ambition is less to reproduce faithfully the film's story, as traditional novelizers are obliged to do, than to shape as carefully and originally as possible a personal viewpoint on the world of the cinematic images.
>
> (2010: 55)

As such, Marvel's *2001* may function less as a marketing paratext for the film than as Kirby's own recollection and creative interpretation of what made the film significant. The book even ends with a ten-page illustrated retrospective essay about the film, including its reception and legacy on the science-fiction genre (Kraft 1976), which reinforces the relationship between the graphic novelization with acts of personal retrospection and criticism.

Baeten's quotation also suggests another key difference between *2001* and typical novelization practice. Since most novelizations are released in time to market a film during its theatrical run, they are most often written based on screenplays – often not even the final draft, if on-set rewrites occur – and tend to be cagey when it comes to describing the film's visual design, necessarily favouring simile and comparison over concrete description (Van Parys 2011: 293). Labarre cites Alan Dean Foster's novelization of *Alien*, which 'was written without the writer having had access to the film's visual effects, leading to a novel which differs markedly from the movie' (2014: 81). By contrast, the writer and cartoonist behind the same film's graphic novelization were given access to the set and even screened an early cut of the movie so that they could accurately capture its iconic visuals (2014: 80). To an even greater extent than *Alien*, the eight-year delay between the release of *2001* and the publication of Kirby's graphic novelization allow for the kind of visual specificity that is usually impossible in prose novelizations.

The saga of *2001*: A cartoonist's odyssey

Though it may seem wildly counterintuitive, Stanley Kubrick and Jack Kirby were extremely comparable artists, perhaps even roughly analogous in their respective spheres. Both worked across a variety of popular narrative genres while developing and maintaining distinct visual styles, and each is credited not just with the creation of culturally significant artworks but also aesthetic innovations that would have immeasurable impacts on their medium of choice and later generations of artists. Their lives even began in similar circumstances: both Kubrick and Kirby were born in New York City to Jewish families of Austrian descent just nine years apart (in 1928 and 1917, respectively). In 1976, however, at the sole juncture at which their artistic paths definitively cross, the circumstances in which the two found themselves could hardly have been more different. Kubrick's past successes, including *2001* and *A Clockwork Orange*, had afforded him a practically unprecedented degree of artistic autonomy, giving him the freedom to work on whatever projects he wanted without the pressure of chasing trends or meeting studio-mandated release dates; Kirby, similarly, enjoyed great success throughout the 1960s, co-creating many of the most popular, recognizable and enduring fictional characters of the twentieth century – including the Fantastic Four, Hulk, Iron Man and the X-Men, all for Marvel Comics – simultaneously accumulating a devoted following among comics readers and setting the aesthetic template for what came to be known as the 'Silver Age' of American superhero comics. The autonomy that Kubrick enjoyed, however, was not forthcoming for Kirby at Marvel; thus, in 1969 he defected to rival publisher DC Comics, where he hoped for greater creative freedom. It did not quite work out as he had hoped: Kirby's increasingly ambitious and heady attempts at science-fiction world-building, collectively known as the Fourth World, were mostly met with ambivalence and lacklustre sales. This prompted a return to Marvel, where he would slog away at his drawing board at the unforgiving rate of thirteen pages per week and for the measly payment of $85 per page (Howe 2012: Kindle loc. 2858). As Charles Hatfield summarizes in his definitive account of Kirby's career, *Hand of Fire: The Comics Art of Jack Kirby*:

> The story of Kirby at Marvel, in sum, is that of so many singular artists who toiled in popular media under conditions of heteronomy: artists whose primary job, and goal, was to make sales for the sake of studio, publishing house, or brand. Consider the great filmmakers who worked, often chafed, under the studio system during Hollywood's peak years – or, in comics, the many artists and writers who have bridled against the terms of corporate-owned, work-for-hire production.
>
> (2012: Kindle loc. 1965)

While Kubrick avoided becoming a cog in the Hollywood studio machine, Kirby was very much at the mercy of the comic book industry's equivalent[5] – and as Kubrick's career continued its ascension in the 1970s, Kirby's return to Marvel marked a new low for the innovative cartoonist. Coincidentally, the publisher's acquisition of the *2001* adaptation rights coincided with Kirby's return;[6] given his pursuit of increasingly cerebral science-fiction at DC, the project seemed like an ideal fit for the cartoonist.

This all seems clear enough from various historical accounts, but more difficult to parse is whether Kirby sought out or even *wanted* the assignment of adapting Kubrick's film. According to Baetens, novelizations are most often commissioned works: 'a movie producer will contact a book publisher, who will contact an editor, who will contact a writer' (2010: 69). While Kirby's *2001* differs in many respects from traditional novelizations, this is most likely one area in which it adheres to the norm. Per Ronin Ro, the assignment was simply handed to Kirby, who would have been in no position to negotiate (2004: 183); indeed,

Ro elaborates that the cartoonist 'wasn't thrilled' with the assignment (2004: 184).[7] In his authoritative history of Marvel Comics, however, Sean Howe implies that Kirby did negotiate what projects he would work on after returning to Marvel, declining titles like *Fantastic Four* and *Thor* in favour of *Captain America*, *2001* and a new original series, *The Eternals* (2012: Kindle loc. 2858). Writing for *The Jack Kirby Collector*, a fanzine dedicated to celebrating and analysing Kirby's work, John P. Alexander makes the bolder claim that 'Kirby did it [*2001*] because it was something he wanted to do, even though there was no market demand for it' (2001: 57). This explanation is less convincing: it portrays Kirby's inclination to adapt *2001* in direct opposition to Marvel's financial interests, and ignores the larger context that the publisher was omnivorously purchasing adaptation rights for a variety of existing intellectual properties at this time. Moreover, it seems that Alexander is massively overestimating Marvel's willingness to indulge Kirby at this time, given his recent defection to DC. In another issue of *The Jack Kirby Collector*, Jon B. Cooke suggests that 'Jack must have taken on the assignment of producing the [*2001*] comic book with some satisfaction' (1997: 38). This claim also seems to be based entirely on the author's supposition, though he does provide support in the form of an excerpt from a 1969 interview with Kirby in which he was asked if he'd seen Kubrick's film. His reply: 'I loved it! I loved the music and the concept was terrific' (quoted in Cooke 1997: 38).

The cartoonist's affection for the film is unsurprising, given that he had been exploring similar ideas in his own comics, albeit from within the more bombastic confines of the superhero genre, for years. Take, for instance, the Negative Zone – a separate dimension that makes its first appearance in *Fantastic Four* #51 (1966) – that Howe describes thusly:

> Two years before *2001: A Space Odyssey*, before the cinema could hope to approach the psychedelic imagination, the Human Torch emerged from an epiphanic trip in the laser-light show that was the Negative Zone, the Ultimate Nullifier finally in hand, but stricken with something like cosmic trauma, stammering in shock: 'I traveled through worlds… so big… so big… there… there aren't words! We're like ants… just ants… ants!!!'
> (2012: Kindle loc. 1277)[8]

While the Torch's interstellar experience seems to anticipate Bowman's journey beyond the infinite, later Kirby comics would bear more direct traces of the film's influence. As Hatfield observes, *New Gods* #7 (Kirby 1972) cites the monolith by substituting a typical anthropomorphic god with an '"ageless, inscrutable" presence' represented as 'a bare wall of rugged whitish stone standing in the middle of nowhere' (2012: Kindle loc. 4338). There are also conceptual similarities between *2001* and Kirby's *The Eternals*, which he was producing concurrently with his *2001* comics. The series is introduced with an expository caption that strongly recalls the film's premise:

> *Is man alone in the universe? Every myth and legend to emerge from the distant past points to a strange visitation from the stars!!* **Beings of great power have been on this**

earth – and then departed! **Who** *were they?* **What** *did they do here?* **Where** *have they gone? These awesome questions create the background for this exciting new saga of a day which lies ahead... the day of* **answers***... the day of the gods.*

(Kirby 1976b: 1, original emphasis)[9]

This admittedly generic premise is later sketched in with details that reinforce its similarity to *2001*. In the first issue, Kirby reveals that human beings are one of three races to descend from 'the dawn ape', a Moon-Watcher-esque representative of a primitive ancestral species that was experimented upon by an alien race known as the Celestials, closely echoing the monolith's intervention in human evolution.[10] Such parallels, whether intentional or not, suggest that Kirby's comics were at least conceptually similar to Kubrick's film, making him a natural choice to produce Marvel's adaptation.

Adapting Kubrick the Marvel way

Christopher Priest[11] has described the overarching task and goals of the novelizer as follows:

> In general, what you try to do is produce a book that will run parallel to the film. It should try to have the same effect on the reader as the film will have on its audience. It should tell the same story, have the same characters, have the same general 'feel'. But a book requires many more words than a screenplay, so you have the opportunity to embellish a little: work in some back-story, fill out the background, describe the locations, and so on.
>
> (Baetens 2010: 67)

While Kirby's *2001: A Space Odyssey* bucks many tendencies associated with novelizations, it nevertheless adheres to Priest's description fairly well, with one significant exception: Kirby's version does not have the same 'general "feel"' as Kubrick's film. While certain attributes can transfer from one medium to another intact, there are medium-specific differences between film and comics that render them fundamentally different kinds of aesthetic experiences. For instance, the fact that comics cannot incorporate a soundtrack means that the film's evocative use of silence, sound effects, and especially music, cannot migrate to the graphic novelization as sonic experiences of any kind; diegetic aural phenomena can only be rendered in a comic via text, whether in a dialogue balloon, caption box or as graphic onomatopoeia. Similarly, the languid pacing of the film relies largely on the duration of its individual shots; while cartoonists can attempt to control the reader's pace (e.g., by manipulating panel size, filling panels with text or visual details that prolong the reading experience or demand close inspection), comics simply do not have a pre-determined duration in the same way that films do. Since the 'feel' of Kubrick's film is so bound up with these kinds of medium-specific qualities, it is unfair to criticize Kirby for failing to replicate them in comics form. It is more productive to analyse the specific creative choices that he makes and what kinds of transformative effects they have on the narrative.

While readers will surely be familiar with the plot of *2001*, it is helpful to refer to Kubrick's own synopsis to compare how differently the narrative is represented in the comic. To concisely convey the extent to which the film cloaks its narrative in ambiguity, I have added italics to indicate story details that are not explicitly represented in the film:

> You begin with an artifact left on earth four million years ago *by extraterrestrial explorers who observed the behavior of the man-apes of the time and decided to influence their evolutionary progression.* Then you have a second artifact buried on the lunar surface *and programmed to signal word of man's first baby steps into the universe – a kind of cosmic burglar alarm.* And finally there's a third artifact placed in orbit around Jupiter *and waiting for the time when man has reached the outer rim of his own solar system.* When the surviving astronaut, Bowman, ultimately reaches Jupiter, *this artifact sweeps him* into a force field or star gate that hurls him on a journey through inner and outer space and finally transports him to another part of the galaxy, where he's placed *in a human zoo approximating a hospital [sic] terrestrial environment drawn out of his own dreams and imagination. In a timeless state,* his life passes from middle age to senescence to death. He is reborn, an enhanced being, a star child, *an angel, a superman, if you like, and returns to earth prepared for the next leap forward of man's evolutionary destiny.*
> (Rowe 2013: 55–56, emphasis added)

By this (admittedly subjective) estimation, roughly half of the material that Kubrick himself identifies as the 'lowest level' of meaning conveyed by the film is left to audiences' imagination. As a result of these and other ambiguities, *2001* has sustained a vast array of interpretations since its release. Leonard F. Wheat's *Kubrick's 2001: A Triple Allegory*, for instance, presents three separate interpretations of the film, each of which sharpens up what he calls the 'fuzzy areas of the narrative' (e.g., the precise nature and meaning of the monolith[s]) in distinct ways (2000: 29). While Kirby does not seem particularly interested in delving into the allegorical or symptomatic meanings to be mined from *2001*'s mysteries, his articulation of the literal plot in explicit, unambiguous detail should be considered as an interpretive effort in the same vein as Wheat's work. In the interest of concision, the analysis to follow will focus primarily on Kirby's understanding and representation of the monoliths.

As Christopher Rowe points out, assigning meaning to the monolith – 'be it that of an extra-terrestrial intelligence, a universal totem, or even the image or idea of God' – is necessary 'to sustain the film's narrative integrity' (2013: 59). Each of Wheat's allegorical readings revolves in part around the meaning of the monoliths, and the same is true of Kirby's adaptation. The very first page of his *2001: A Space Odyssey* provides some telling indicators of Kirby's approach to adapting the film, and the centrality of the monoliths in his interpretation. The comic opens with a splash page – that is, a page that is entirely occupied with a single panel, rather than a grid of sequential images – depicting astronauts in the year 2001 dramatically confronting a monolith on the moon. The monolith is centred in the composition, represented as a floating black slab emanating radiant beams of light from its core. Five astronauts, seen at the bottom of the page, raise their hands and reach their arms towards the object, either in awe or reverence. The page also features two captions: one at the top right, reading '*With the **monolith begins the journey of man!***', and one at the bottom right, reading '*The universe **communicates** with man ... and **history's greatest adventure** is launched upon the eternal roads of time and space! This is a trip you **mustn't** miss!! There are sights you've got to see to which you will **marvel!***' (Kirby 1976a: 3, original emphasis).

The first thing to note here is how strongly and unambiguously Kirby assigns meaning and agency to the monolith. In Kubrick's film, the monolith appears suddenly and performs its evolutionary work on the man-ape Moon-Watcher – unnamed in the film – in ways that defy understanding; the film steadfastly refuses to explain the monolith's origins, intent, or abilities. In the monolith's second appearance in the film, it (seemingly) reacts to being photographed by emitting a high-pitched sound that is painful for the humans to hear – but again, Kubrick denies us any explanation of what message, if any, is being sent through this sonic assault. By contrast, Kirby establishes the monolith not only as the central figure but also as a benevolent force in the narrative from the outset. Visually, the monolith is undoubtedly the active agent in this opening image, beaming its mysterious energy outward in all directions, while man is passive, helplessly worshipping at its altar – a reaction quite distinct from the film, in which the astronauts uniformly reel in pain at the monolith's sound. Through a dense arrangement of abstract lines – presumably representing light, energy or some other kind of cosmic power – Kirby renders the monolith's action in visual, rather than sonic, terms, while also recasting its impact on the humans in a positive light; to ensure that there is no room for ambiguity, he adds expository captions that describe the monolith's communicative intent ('*The universe communicates with man...*'). The cartoonist also explicitly establishes here that the monolith is a representative of the universe itself, of 'the infinite' (Kirby 1976a: 9), rather than the extraterrestrial race that Kubrick intended. With a turn of the page, the timeline reverses by 4 million years to focus on Moon-Watcher's encounter with a monolith. In contrast to the film, this sequence is contextualized as a flashback that readers approach already having knowledge of the monolith and its greater purpose.

This opening page is also indicative of Kirby's penchant not just for purple prose but also for verbosity in general. As a graphic novelization of Kubrick's 'cinematic tone-poem' (Kuberski 2008: 63), this stands out as an unusual choice; Kirby, however, is not interested in fidelity at the expense of narrative clarity. Accordingly, there is not a single panel across the comic book's 70 pages that is 'silent': every panel features omniscient narrative captions, dialogue balloons, or both. This has been a significant sticking point for critics of Kirby's adaptation, who regard the imposition of narration and the increased amount of dialogue in the comic compared to the film as objectively wrong-headed: as Julian Darius puts it, 'Kirby can't resist adding captions, which use many words without either propelling the plot forward or poetically teasing out implications of what we're seeing' (2013: Kindle loc. 234).

This is a choice worth unpacking in more detail, however, as it gets to the heart of Kirby's approach to novelizing Kubrick's film. To start, novelizations tend to favour narration to a greater extent than films as a general matter. As Baetens asserts:

> Novelizations emphasize narration, in the double sense of the term; the level of the story retains the attention and is at the same time often filtered by a narrative device missing in the movie (think of how the cinema is less drawn to voiceover, especially in the case of fictional movies).
>
> (Baetens 2005: 55)

While Kirby's graphic novelization does not adhere to standard novelization practice in many ways, this emphasis on verbal narration happens to align with Kirby's storytelling style, which was established – and, indeed, largely defined – the 'Silver Age' of superhero comics (1956–70). Throughout this era, convention dictated that panels be verbally narrated, regardless of how clear the visual storytelling might be without such textual interventions. While Kirby's frequent scripter Stan Lee specifically wanted the art in Marvel Comics 'to function like silent movies, to minimize the need for verbal exposition' (Howe 2012: Kindle loc. 892), he nevertheless seldom missed an opportunity to impose text upon Kirby's narrative drawings,[12] a tendency that Kirby would echo when he assumed scripting duties throughout the remainder of his career.

Regardless of whether the verbosity of Kirby's *2001* is simply a manifestation of the cartoonist's style or a concession to the dominant storytelling conventions of the time, Darius's claim that *2001*'s captions do not advance the narrative or the themes of the work is fundamentally incorrect. This assertion indicates that Darius understands the relationship between Kirby's words and images to be 'duo-specific', meaning that they communicate the same message in different ways (McCloud 1993: 153); accordingly, the words are deemed redundant additions to a narratively self-sufficient image. Taking the Moon-Watcher sequence as an example, it is clear that most of the panels are not duo-specific but are rather *word*-specific; that is, the pictures serve an illustrative function but it is the *text* that is the primary vehicle driving the narrative forward. For instance, the first panel on the second page of this sequence depicts Moon-Watcher sympathetically gazing upon a fallen ape, his hand tenderly placed upon the dead ape's chest. The caption, however, adds a great deal of narrative information that is not conveyed by the image alone, including the cause of death ('*The tribe has always been hungry, and now, it is starving*') and the relationship between Moon-Watcher and the dead ape ('*When Moonwatcher discovers the emaciated body of the "old one", his father, he feels something akin to sadness…*'). The following panel tips the balance even further towards verbal narration; while the image features only a close-up on Moon-Watcher's face, the narration gives us to access his state of mind ('*He does **not** know the 'old one' was his father, for such a relationship is beyond his understanding*') and omnisciently foreshadows the direction of the narrative and Moon-Watcher's purpose within it ('*[…] he unmistakably holds in his genes the **promise** of humanity […] the **first*** *intimation of intelligence which will not fulfill itself for another two million years*') (Kirby 1976a: 5, original emphasis). Such interventions serve to clarify aspects of the narrative that Kubrick leaves ambiguous. Kirby adheres to this strategy throughout his adaptation, explicitly depicting his own understanding of the story told in the film.

The visual style of the comic also represents a significant difference between the two works that impacts the 'feel' and perhaps even the generic affiliation of the narrative. Again, comparing how the monoliths are represented in Kubrick's 'Helvetica' film and Kirby's 'Comic Sans' graphic novelization is particularly instructive in this regard, as it speaks to the two artists' contrasting approaches towards science-fiction as a genre. For Kubrick, ambiguity is again central to his representational strategy in *2001*. As Eliza Pezzotta puts it in *Stanley Kubrick: Adapting the Sublime*, 'The aliens are not shown, and their existence is only suggested through a monolith that could be a natural, unknown element, a god's miracle, or an extraterrestrial's gift' (2013: 169); eschewing the kinds of otherworldly visuals commonly associated with science-fiction, Kubrick chooses an inert, unmoving, matte-black rectangular slab as his sole representative of extraterrestrial life. The object is relentlessly austere and fundamentally ineffable: if it communicates, it does so in ways that transcend human comprehension. Kubrick's monolith is not merely 'a confrontation with the unknowable', as Wendy Steiner describes the sublime (Hatfield 2012: Kindle loc. 3063); it is a literal 'machine in the garden', Leo Marx's definitive example of the technological sublime (Hatfield 2012: Kindle loc. 3030). Kirby shares Kubrick's interest in the technological sublime but represents it in a fundamentally opposite way. Where Kubrick's *2001* is grounded in scientific detail – represented in terms of the monolith by his reluctance to explicitly represent or even confirm the existence of an alien race – Kirby demonstrates the awesome power of the monolith (not to mention the cold vacuum of space) with wild flourishes of visual design that give literal shape (and colour) to the monolith's actions. Most spectacular in this regard is page 58 of Kirby's adaptation, which depicts the monolith orbiting Jupiter not against the inky blackness of space, as in Kubrick's film, but rather amidst a psychedelic swirl of yellow, blue and green, replete with the cartoonist's visual trademark of 'coruscating mark or dot patterns' known by fans as 'Kirby krackle' (Hatfield 2012: Kindle loc. 1437). In striking contrast to Kubrick's imagery, Kirby's splash page features more colour than blackness, visualizing the monolith's activity that is described in more concrete detail in the caption at the top left of the page ('*The monolith waits no longer – it **activates** to allow an ancient experience to **reach** its climax*') and foreshadowing the interdimensional voyage that awaits Bowman (Kirby 1976a: 58, original emphasis).

Conclusion

Nicolas Labarre's comparative analysis of *Alien* and its graphic novelization reveals how the different formal qualities of comic books recalibrate the narrative's genre 'towards a more intellectual and less visceral kind of horror' (2014: 88); by clarifying the film's ambiguous narrative and amplifying its visual flair, Kirby accomplishes something similar for *2001*, pushing its narrative away from the 'proverbial good science-fiction movie' and towards the kind of work with which Kirby is most closely associated: cosmic-scale superhero fiction.[13] Stripped to a basic outline, the story of *2001* is that of mild-mannered astronaut Dave Bowman, whose encounter with a murderous artificial intelligence puts him on a collision course with a greater destiny, culminating in his ultimate transformation into a 'superman', to use Kubrick's own word. The film's unconventional structure and style obscures this basic narrative core, more closely aligning it with art cinema, but this arc is fundamentally that of a superhero origin story. In a final narrative intervention meant to shed light on Bowman's mysterious transformation into the superhuman Star-Child, Kirby devotes his closing pages to explicitly dramatizing the metamorphosis in visual and conceptual detail. Over six panels of equal size, the aged Bowman becomes increasingly obscured by '*a membranaceous cocoon of gossamer strength*'. In the fourth panel his body is obscured entirely, but a caption informs us that '*The monolith knows this creature can **transcend** itself… The monolith knows that this is happening **beneath** the membrane…*'. In the sixth and final panel, the unmistakable outline of the Star-Child – or '*new one*' – becomes distinctly visible, accompanied by text that informs us that '*He is to be the **first** of **many** "new ones." For the monolith knows there must be **more** than one new seed to sow the harvest of a new species…*' (Kirby 1976a: 71, original emphasis). The monolith is thereby ultimately cast in an equivalent role to other agents of destiny in the superhero genre: a radioactive spider bite, a bath of cosmic rays, a genetic mutation. It is not surprising, then, that Kirby's *2001* sequel series would follow this path to its conclusion, first building towards assembling an ensemble of '*new seeds*' before introducing the humanoid artificial intelligence Mister Machine, who recasts HAL 9000 in a superheroic mould.

Kubrick's film remains a classic in the genre, widely influential, widely available in various home video editions and widely studied in books such as this one. Kirby's comics, by contrast, have fulfilled the usual destiny of the novelization: Marvel has never been reprinted them, collected them in a single volume, or made them available for digital purchase and few have taken it upon themselves to subject them to the rigors of analysis. They remain a curiosity for Kirby die-hards, though fans overwhelmingly prefer his earlier work. Jonathan Letham, representing Marvel fandom in general, summarily dismisses all of Kirby's post-DC work thusly:

> I'd be kidding if I claimed anyone much cherishes the comics of Kirby's 'return to Marvel' period – *2001, The Eternals, Machine Man*. Even for souls who take these things all too seriously, those comics have no real place in history; they define only a clumsy misstep in a dull era at Marvel.
>
> (2004: 13)

For Kubrick scholars, however, they remain worthy of investigation, if only to see how such a complex and specifically cinematic work can be translated to such a different paradigm.

part two

testimony

Kubrick's use of actors and the performances he elicited from them has remained a largely untouched aspect of Kubrick Studies. Often exaggerated – think of Jack Torrance in *The Shining* (Kubrick, 1980) or Drill Sergeant Hartman in *Full Metal Jacket* – what is most fascinating about the performances in any Kubrick movie is in what 'lies in the frequent pauses and the sustained counterpoint between calm statements and "hidden" emotions' (Naremore 2007: 149). HAL's 'death' in *2001* is a perfect example of this hidden emotion, his banal and monotonous voice-urging Bowman not to terminate him. The following two chapters explore aspects of performance in *2001* and what these reveal about the complexity of meaning in the film.

James Fenwick examines 'The Dawn of Man' and the role of Daniel Richter, the actor who portrayed Moon-Watcher. Richter's skills as a mime performer and choreographer were crucial to the successful realization of these opening scenes that had eluded Kubrick until the end of the production. Richter utilized the methods of Paul J. Curtis's American Mime Theatre to bring the man-apes to life. Drawing on the history and methodologies of American Mime, the chapter looks at the representation of the man-apes and interprets the performances of Richter in the contexts of this burgeoning performance movement in the 1950s and 1960s.

Vincent Jaunas examines the performances of the male actors that dominate *2001*. He argues that Kubrick had two methods of directing actors; one to provoke a naturalistic acting style, and another – and more commonly used – to obtain over/under-played performances. The latter was very much the case in *2001*, a result of what Jaunas sees as Kubrick's attempt to create a distance between the actors and characters from their environment, and in doing so placing emphasis on the philosophical themes.

Further Reading

While there has not been an abundance of scholarship on performance in Kubrick's films, there have been analyses of the dialogue (or lack of) in *2001*, including by James Naremore in his *On Kubrick* (2007: 146–50). Mario Falsetto does provide an introductory overview to the issue of performance in his *Stanley Kubrick: A Narrative and Stylistic Analysis* (2001: 149–67). Though he presents case studies of *A Clockwork Orange*, *Barry Lyndon* (Kubrick, 1975) and *The Shining*, his approach is applicable to Kubrick's career as a whole, arguing that performance is a 'crucial component in Kubrick's aesthetics' (2001: 149).

Chapter Four

Performing the man-ape in 'The Dawn of Man': Daniel Richter and The American Mime Theatre

James Fenwick

My first encounter with a Kubrick film was the 'The Dawn of Man', the prehistoric prologue that opens *2001*. I remember being both perplexed and engrossed; I had started watching it around five minutes into the sequence, with the man-apes aggressively screeching at one another. I could not work out if they were real or men in suits, their behaviour so convincing as to leave me verging on the belief they were real and somehow they had been trained to act for this scene. Others perhaps validate these two states of emotional reaction, such as Peter Krämer who describes 'The Dawn of Man' as being about 'ape-like creatures – or hominids – who are difficult to tell apart from each other and whose behaviour can therefore be puzzling' (2010: 9). Quite. My second state of emotional response – are these real or men in costume – was sardonically captured by Arthur C. Clarke with regards to the Academy Awards snub of the costume and makeup of *2001*, given instead to the other simian film of 1968, *Planet of the Apes* (Schaffner 1968). Clarke, indignant, said that 'to my fury, at the 1969 Academy Awards a special Oscar was presented for make-up – to *Planet of the Apes*! I wondered as loudly as possible whether the judges had passed over *2001* because they thought we used real apes' (Clarke 1972: 50).

Such initial reactions as mine may not be that uncommon then, with 'The Dawn of Man' presenting a vision of the "ape" like nothing ever seen before in Hollywood. Prior to *2001*, cinema was graced with the inauthentic vision of what Kubrick himself derisively referred to as the 'man in the monkey suit' (Richter 2002: 4), from horror films such as *Murder in the Rue Morgue* (Florey 1932), to comedies such as the less-than-funny Abbott and Costello vehicle *Africa Screams* (Barton 1949). Of course, the defining ape in Hollywood up to that point was the stop-motion animated *King Kong* (Cooper and Schoedsack 1933), but that was decidedly outdated by the 1960s and unsophisticated for what Kubrick wanted to achieve with 'The Dawn of Man'. His desire was to be technologically innovative in his creation – ironically contrasting with the way Kong himself, atop the Empire State Building, 'stands with his fist raised against technology' (Shantoff 1968: 62).

But what was it that Kubrick wanted to achieve and to create with 'The Dawn of Man'? And is the final vision for 'The Dawn of Man' solely attributable to Kubrick, as the auteur orthodoxy surrounding him often leads us to believe, or can it be more accurately prescribed to the framework of the collaborative process? These questions become pertinent when one considers the complex authorial nature of the screenplay and novel, with the overall film deriving from a number of Clarke's short stories, most obviously 'The Sentinel'(1951); 'The Dawn of Man' itself was partly inspired by yet another Clarke short story, *Expedition to Earth* (1953b). The mark of Arthur C. Clarke on the final 'The Dawn of Man' sequence is but one of many, including Kubrick, but also owing a huge amount to the creative technicians: Stuart Freeborn, who was Head of Makeup; John Alcott, who took over the role of Director of Photography from Geoffrey Unsworth for 'The Dawn of Man'; Andrew Birkin, the photographer who led a team to the Namibian desert to take the images that would be used for the front projection system developed specifically for 'The Dawn of Man', and that would allow Kubrick to film in a studio. But most important, as I will argue in this chapter, was Daniel Richter, employed by Kubrick in late 1966 as the choreographer for 'The Dawn of Man' and who would go on to portray the lead man-ape, Moon-Watcher. Each of these individuals contributed significantly to 'The Dawn of Man', often working in free creative spaces facilitated by Kubrick, rather than minutely supervised or dictated to; in fact, the creative freedom given by Kubrick is quite remarkable, with the likes of Richter filling in 'the unwritten sections in the script' (Richter 2002: 129). Richter goes further, remarking on these unwritten sections that he is providing as 'becoming some of the film's greatest moments. The creative freedom he [Kubrick] gives me is exhilarating' (2002: 129). These unwritten sections were the movements and gestures of Moon-Watcher, and the creative freedom given allowed Richter to create a unique performance.

Kubrick's greatest talent as a producer was his ability to identify innovative talent, which he then gave the creative space to experiment. Richter comments on this in his memoir, saying that Kubrick sought creative collaboration, not dictatorial control (2002: 129). Such freedom and collaboration on 'The Dawn of Man', involving a number of individuals, led to a genuinely authentic representation of hominids, one that did not conform to the generic tropes of Hollywood, with the man in the monkey suit played for laughs in comedy, or hammed up for horror films. Instead, the resultant representation plays into a Darwinian nightmare of human evolution, one that still pervades Hollywood, with its numerous and at times terrifying remakes of the *Planet of the Apes* franchise. The man-apes in 'The Dawn of Man' are, by the end of it, blood-thirsty killers, the primate group inspired by the 'murderous violence' (Krämer 2010: 16) of Moon-Watcher, the lead man-ape; these are creatures ruled by the 'harsh logic of survival' (Clarke 1968: 7). In large part, this representation came about from Kubrick's repeated failure to successfully express the man-ape on screen and, as a result, Kubrick positioned Daniel Richter at the centre of bringing them to life for the sequence.

This chapter will examine Richter's role as choreographer and the influence of his use of The American Mime Theatre's methods in the representation of the man-apes in 'The Dawn of Man'. The case study will explore Richter's use of psychologically motivated performance, combined with formalized mime in his interpretation of the man-apes, stemming from the training methods of Paul J. Curtis's American Mime, and how this led to the successful realisation of 'The Dawn of Man', and of the main character Moon-Watcher. The aim will be to position Richter as a key authorial agent in the aesthetic construct of the man-apes, as well as going a long way towards explaining why – in Arthur C. Clarke's words – Academy Award members assumed the man-apes in *2001* were real. I want to begin, however, by briefly looking at Kubrick's failure to successfully express the man-ape on screen, and then to offer an overview of the principals of Paul J. Curtis's American Mime.

Failure to represent the man-apes

Kubrick had been attempting and failing since at least May 1965 to put into production 'The Dawn of Man', collaborating with Stuart Freeborn, Head of Makeup, to ensure costumes were ready for the shoot. During a series of production meetings held in New York, based on the treatment by Clarke and Kubrick titled *Journey Beyond the Stars*, personnel had been set to work by Kubrick on bringing to life 'The Dawn of Man'. During these meetings, it was agreed that the costume department had to prepare at least thirty costumes, but the agreed requirements were vague and left open for the technical personnel to work out, with instructions such as 'different sizes and possibly detail for males, females and children. One or two miniature costumes may be required for dolls representing baby man-apes' (Anon. 1965b); the latter in the end was not required as real infant chimpanzees were used.

The production notes are revealing in confirming the complexity of 'The Dawn of Man', but also in how there was still no clear concept of exactly what the man-apes were to look like or how they would be represented, with Kubrick seemingly providing little direction. The notes show that Stuart Freeborn was asked to look at 'some form of flexible rubber or plastic masks' as the best solution to the creation of the costumes (Anon. 1965b). Freeborn was even guided towards Jean Cocteau's *La Belle et la Bete* (1946), starring Jean Marais as the eponymous Beast. But there was little progress concerning any firm ideas, with Kubrick ostensibly at a loss in how to depict the man-apes. In one instance, he had hired, in Keith Hamshere's (stills filing clerk) words, 'some skinny black teenagers made up to look like apes' (Richter 2002: 32); Kubrick's publicist, Roger Caras, along with senior figures at MGM, were quick to steer Kubrick away from a potential PR disaster (2002: 32). Backstage photographs reveal near-naked teenagers in unconvincing make-up (Anon. 1965–68), resembling creatures that were half-man and half-ape and fell, at best, into the category of bad science-fiction movies that Kubrick wanted to avoid, and at worse the racially bigoted ideas of the 'negro ape' (Lott 1999).

Casting was erratic to say the least. Keith Hamshere was at one time brought in to model as a man-ape, with Freeborn building a prototype costume for him. More bizarre was when Kubrick brought in the comedian Ronnie Corbett, again for Freeborn to make up as a man-ape; needless to say, it did not work out. Others considered were the actor Robert Shaw and the actress Penny Brahams. Worse still, Kubrick was not even sure of where the sequence would be filmed, with notions of filming in South Africa or Spain. There had even been vague attempts to find a desert in the United Kingdom, after Kubrick did not like a set built for the sequence. However unlikely this may have seemed, suggestions had been made to film in Wales (Kubrick 1966), whilst runner Andrew Birkin found a desert location outside of Liverpool, featuring shallow sand dunes behind a gasworks (Bizony 2000: 129). And yet, despite all of his attempts, Kubrick was no closer to realising 'The Dawn of Man'.

The American Mime Theatre

What is obvious from the above is that Kubrick's main problem in creating a truthful representation of the man-apes was performance; he was using actors versed in literary traditions and the spoken word, instead of performers who knew how to move. It would be the training methodology of Paul J. Curtis (1927–2012) who created the art form American Mime that would prove vital in the eventual and authentic realisation of 'The Dawn of Man'. Curtis founded The American Mime Theatre in 1952, and the American Mime School in 1953 in New York. He had previously studied Method Acting with Lee Strasberg and visited Paris to observe European mimes. Curtis graduated with a Certificate in Directing from the Dramatic Workshop of the New School for Social Research in 1949 under the tutelage of Erwin Piscator. It was at the Dramatic Workshop that he developed his ideas of American Mime, not concerned with what he referred to as commercial theatre, but intent on exploring the traditions of the theatrical form. He explained his motivations, saying, 'We explored work from the Bauhaus and from Brecht's early theatre [...] and we went out and saw everything we could. We looked at the Noh drama, the Kabuki, and the French and the Italian pantomime' (Sagolla 2007: 21). After his visit to Paris and return to New York City in 1952, Curtis went to the Actors' Equity for permission to use five actors and five dancers in a project in mime, 'that would demonstrate its potential and correct the limitations of the medium as practiced by the French'.[1] That project with this first company of actors and dancers resulted in the creation of a repertory of mime plays, produced at the 92nd Street Y, New York in 1953. Encouraged by their success, Curtis began developing his training methodology, what he called procedures 'exercises that would produce a kind of performer who had the ability to act and move at the same time [...] the main procedure is called "preparation" [...] It lasts 14 minutes and is done together silently' (Sagolla 2007: 21). Preparation involved a 'series of specifics to produce individually and collectively a performing state (physical, mental, emotional and spiritual). Preparation is done before every class, rehearsal and performance'.[2]

Curtis's American Mime was part of a growing modernist trend in mime that was also taking place across the United States and Europe;[3] his methods contrasted with the French school of Pantomime, which had come to be associated in the mid-twentieth century with Marcel Marceau. Curtis's ideas were instead closely related to the thoughts of Jacques Copeau, founder of the Théâtre du Vieux-Colombier, who also focused on the 'expressive qualities of the body, particularly in "corporeal mime", in which actors used masks to break their reliance upon the face' (Naito 2008: 395). Curtis's concentration was on the 'emotionally motivated physical extension of characterization aimed at assisting the actor's complete development as an artist' (Anon. 1966k: 16). Rather than the silent performances of pantomime and its illusion of the movement of invisible objects, American Mime aimed towards realism through the key principals of characterization, movement and motivation. The latter is of particular importance, as Curtis has explained:

In American mime, everything has to be motivated; it has to be true. And of course we don't wear white face. American mime actors perform symbolic actions and express the feelings of their characters honestly through motivated movement they call 'form'.

(Sagolla 2007: 21)

Reviews of The American Mime Theatre's performances in the 1960s commented on this motivated realism and its innovative techniques. One critic who saw Curtis and his troupe at the Lincoln Center in 1969 said:

Quite a bit of his teaching is innovative and quite unlike anything that has gone before where the art of mime is concerned. He does not, for example, hesitate to use voices where suited [...]. While traditionalists may not have approved, they would be compelled to admit that it was all fresh, vital and stimulating.

(Schulman 1969: 16)

Other reviews were similarly praising of Curtis's techniques and of his merging of acting, movement, pantomime and playwriting. Allan Charlet, watching a performance of the group's *The Unitaur* (1984), noted that the play was a success because of the use of 'silent actors playing symbolic activities in characterization expressing the feelings and desires of their characters honestly through a kind of motivated movement' (Charlet 1984: 6a). Proponents of Curtis's American Mime have insisted that characters motivated by his methods is 'in a manner which is psychologically pleasing to a modern audience', which Curtis attributed to the performers 'movement [being] stimulated organically – by thoughts, by desires, by spirits' (Gehman 1986).

Performance and mime in 'The Dawn of Man'

The methods of Curtis's American Mime were brought to Kubrick's attention via Daniel Richter, a mime artist born in 1939 in Connecticut, and who had trained and worked as the lead performer with Curtis's American Mime Theatre for four years (Richter 2002: 5).[4] The first ideas to utilize mime for 'The Dawn of Man' had been proposed by Roger Caras as early as 1965 in a memo to Kubrick and Victor Lyndon, the film's associate producer. Caras had commented that he found the character of Moon-Watcher puzzling and that 'The Dawn of Man' risked laughter from the audience. Moon-Watcher was crucial to avoid such a disastrous response and Caras realized how Moon-Watcher and the man-apes had to be played:

Moonwatcher is compelled to work in mime, so why not use the greatest mime of them all? I would suggest and urge that you consider Marcel Marceau for the character of

Moonwatcher. I cannot imagine anyone else bringing authentic character capable of arising the feelings of pathos.

(Caras 1965b)

Kubrick did not immediately follow up on Caras's suggestion. Instead, it had been a producer, Mike Wilson, who had eventually recommended Daniel Richter to work on 'The Dawn of Man'.[5] Victor Lyndon brought Richter in for an audition in front of Kubrick on 24 October 1966, during which he gave a short demonstration of a mime of a gorilla using Paul Curtis's form walks technique, whereby the character was defining the movement (Richter 2002: 5). Kubrick immediately hired Richter, appointing him as choreographer for 'The Dawn of Man' and allowing him the time and space to research not just the character of Moon-Watcher, who Richter would portray, but also an entire tribe of man-apes. Kubrick delegated a tremendous amount of creative and aesthetic freedom to Richter and over the coming months – a whole nine months, in fact, before shooting of 'The Dawn of Man' would commence – Richter immersed himself in the worlds of anthropology and primatology in order to be able to fully realize an authentic vision of the *Australopithecus africanus* man-apes. But what exactly did this authenticity that Richter was searching for look like?

The key elements of his authentic representation of the man-ape included, of course, his tutelage under Curtis at The American Mime Theatre. But in order for Curtis's techniques to work, Richter required character motivation – a key principle of Curtis's methods. Therefore, Richter referred to a number of sources. This included George Schaller's book *The Year of the Gorilla* (1963), which recounts Schaller's two years spent observing mountain gorillas in eastern and central Africa in the 1950s. Schaller realized how humans and gorillas shared a number of emotional responses, actions and social cues, including the way they expressed joy and mischievousness. Schaller's work could not have been further from the ideas of the likes of Robert Ardrey's *African Genesis* (1961), or Raymond Dart's (1953) killer ape theory, in which war and blood-thirsty aggression were traits of a species of carnivorous ape that later evolved into humans. These were ideologies that had informed Clarke and Kubrick in the writing of the book and screenplay for *2001*, and in subsequent discussions about the idea of 'man-the killer ape' (Poole 2015: 196) following the film's release.[6] Yet, despite the earlier research by Kubrick and Clarke into the ideas of the killer-ape theory, Richter was drawn to the work of Goodall and Schaller in creating an authentic portrayal of hominids.[7] Richter, in reading Schaller, discovered mountain gorillas, far from the accepted belief of them being violent brutes, were 'gentle and intelligent animals' (Richter 2002: 50). It is interesting that, after several weeks of research, Richter requested in late December 1966 that Kubrick re-write the script for 'The Dawn of Man', which he agreed to, noting that the new script will – in Richter's words – 'reflect the work being done' (2002: 50).

Another key element that underpinned Richter's search for character motivation was again drawn from the cultural anthropological discourse circulating in the 1960s, this time in the form of the National Geographic video footage of primatologist, Jane Goodall. Richter called the work of Goodall, along with that of Schaller, as 'invaluable' (2002: 50).

This comment can be put into the context of his regular visits to London Zoo, where he would observe and study the basic movements of the chimpanzees and the infamous Guy the Gorilla (Poole 2015: 193). Yet, Richter found no value in not being able to witness the natural behaviour of the chimpanzees, which would only be observable in their natural habitat. Therefore, Goodall's video footage provided Richter with such a possibility. Goodall travelled to the Gombe Stream Reserve in Tanzania in 1960, having no scientific background and 'equipped with nothing more than a notebook and pair of binoculars' (Anon. 2010). She began to observe wild chimpanzees, often by sitting amongst them, gaining their trust and eventually recording a number of previously unobserved behaviours including the chimps 'stalking, killing, and eating large insects, birds, and some bigger animals, including baby baboons and bushbacks (small antelopes)' (Goodall 2015). Incredibly, she also witnessed cannibalism amongst the chimps, challenging the long held belief amongst ethologists that chimps were exclusively vegetarian. Goodall observed a complex social system amongst the chimps, with ritualized behaviours and primitive but discernible communication methods, including a primitive language system, as well as making the 'first recorded observations of chimpanzees eating meat and using and making tools' (2015). Other behaviours she witnessed included the use of stones as weapons, which the chimps would throw, and the use of 'touch and embraces to comfort one another' (2015).

These elements were coalescing into a whole representation of the man-ape for Richter, with Goodall providing him with the motivations of the man-apes, including 'activities, group dynamic, energy, hierarchy, and characters' (Richter 2002: 61). Schaller's work, meanwhile, gave Richter's man-apes' movement 'gravity and introduce[d] the body beating' (2002: 61). This allowed Richter to begin illustrating on paper the basic movements of the man-apes, which in turn would allow him to train others. It also allowed him to collaborate further with Stuart Freeborn on the costume and work out what exactly would work.

Yet, Richter still felt there was a key element missing to his representation of the man-ape, due to the fact that the primates he was studying were primarily 'knuckle-walkers' (Richter 2002: 64). Kubrick and Clarke wrote 'The Dawn of Man' with the intention that the man-apes transform from knuckle-walkers to upright walkers after their encounter with the black monolith. This problem was solved during a visit to London Zoo in January 1967, when Richter observed and recorded gibbons. In his memoir, he recalls watching them, saying of their walk that it was interesting, gibbons not being knuckle walkers and having long legs. Their walk has a 'swaying rhythm that seems to be an extension of their swinging from branch to branch' (2002: 64). He filmed the gibbons at half speed, 48 frames a second, and had the footage printed and put on his office wall, noting how 'a gibbon walking in slow motion was the control. I could do it, describe it, and teach it. The initial stage of my choreography is complete. I have all the controls for the man-apes' (2002: 64). Throughout his research, Richter was searching for authenticity, this being vital to the success of the sequence, and for this to be achievable he underpinned his entire representation and choreography with 'animal energy', without which 'the illusion disappears and we are back to the pitfall of the man in the monkey suit' (2002: 55). Richter's choreography notes from 1967 reveal the movements he wanted to use; under

Figure 1: Daniel Richter dressed in a test man-ape costume. From the collection of Daniel Richter.

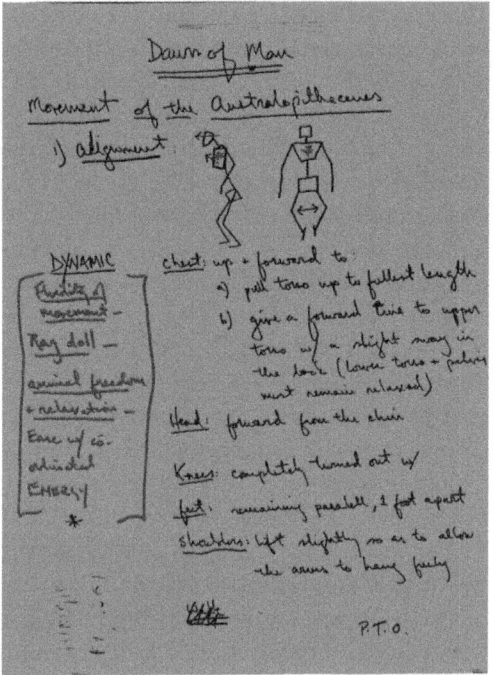

Figure 2: Dan Richter's choreography notes for *2001: A Space Odyssey*'s 'The Dawn of Man'. From the collection of Daniel Richter.

a heading of 'Dynamic', where he talks of 'fluidity of movement', he uses the description of 'rag doll' and emphasizes 'animal freedom + relaxation' (Richter 2000). Months of research are distilled into a couple of pages of notes that read as a manual to how a man-ape should behave. The centre of the dynamic stemmed from the chest, which he directed as needing to be 'up and forward to: a) pull torso up to fullest length b) give a forward line to upper torso with a slight sway in the back (where torso and pelvis must remain relaxed)' (Richter 1967). The second key dynamic to this representation are the knees, which in the diagram reflect a rag-doll quality, and which Richter directs as needing to be 'completely turned out w/ feet remaining parallel, 1 foot apart' (Richter 1967). Richter's notes are precise and exact, distilling his acquired primatology research into an authentic vision of realizing the man-apes.

Kinetic energy

The tradition of mime in film has long been one of comedic intent, most obviously in the silent comedies of Charlie Chaplin, Buster Keaton and others. This tradition of motion picture mime was kept alive after the transition to sound, but transposed to more spectacular cinematic scenarios with a modernist critique; this is particularly evident in the 'silent' comedies of Jacques Tati in the 1950s and 1960s, such as *Mon Uncle* (*My Uncle*) (1958), *Playtime* (1967) and *Trafic* (*Traffic*) (1971). Just as Chaplin and Keaton had expressed mime through clown characters, Tati's films featured the clown of Monsieur Hulot. Tati and Chaplin were indebted to the work of actor Étienne Decroux and his corporeal mime, who, similar to Curtis's American Mime, used movement to express thought. Chaplin, Tati and others emphasized the physicality of Decroux's methods in order to present leisurely visual gags; Tati very much had a fascination with 'silence and immobility and with the quiet suggestibility of the visual' (Fawell 1990: 222).

The realism and psychological motivation of corporeal mime was explored in the theatre, utilized by Samuel Beckett in a number of key mime plays, such as *Acts Without Words I* (1957) and *II* (1960). It is intriguing that the former play took inspiration from Gestalt psychologist Wolfgang Köhler's work on apes. Köhler discovered, through observation, that chimpanzees could learn how to use tools, his research eventually published in *The Mentality of Apes* (1925). Beckett turned Köhler's experiments into a mime, whereby a man is taunted by an unseen godlike experimenter that encourages him to reach for a carafe of water. The mime, however, has less to do with Köhler's experiments than it does with 'a meditation on the body and its limitations [...] the dominant action is "reflection," which, in the absence of speech, becomes a distinctly physical act' (Naito 2008: 398). Naito rightly indicates that Beckett's mime is a rediscovery of the body and its physical movement, after the dominance of the mouth in the theatre (and increasingly on the cinema screen) (2008: 398–99). Beckett's mimes indicated an interest in the rhythm of movement as opposed to the rhythm of language (2008: 399), as well as demonstrating that 'mime was not strictly limited to silent performance' (2008: 401). What Beckett created, and would continue to explore, was a modernist corporeal aesthetic indebted to the likes of Decroux and Copeau.

Richter's influences draw heavily from such a Beckettian aesthetic, along with his training under Curtis. What resulted was a representation of the man-apes where physicality, psychological motivation and thought were central – working towards Tati's 'quiet suggestibility of the visual' (Fawell 1990: 222) and Curtis's motivated movement. The final 'The Dawn of Man' script, dated 2 January 1967, was minimalist in its writing, each scene giving very little description at all. The action was to take 'place on parched flat land near some caves by a muddy stream where Moon-Watcher's tribe lives' some three million years ago (Kubrick and Clarke 1967). The corporeal underpinning that Richter's mime training brought to the role of Moon-Watcher and the man-apes can be better understood when looking closer at Kubrick and Clarke's script. Scene A12, the moment in which Moon-Watcher realizes he can use bones as tools, and more importantly as weapons, reads as follows:

> Moon-Watcher is passing through an elephant skeleton that they usually pass when he is caught by a strange feeling (it is almost like a magical spell). He is trying to remember something. He picks up one of the elephant bones and begins to swing it about slowly

(but not violently) in a dance-like fashion. As Moon-Watcher moves about he sees a tapir passing. He stops and still as if in a spell brings the bone down on the tapir's head. He is killed instantly.

(Kubrick and Clarke 1967)

The writing of this scene reflects the physicality of Richter's mime training and of the procedures of Curtis's American Mime. Movement is expressed throughout the scene, with Moon-Watcher swinging the bone 'dance-like'. The key sentence in this scene refers to how Moon-Watcher is 'caught by a strange feeling' – this statement is ambiguous by its nature; after all, what is a 'strange feeling'? The feeling is undeterminable, as if even the writer does not know what is happening. It is not a description that leads easily to explanation, but rather leaves it open to interpretation, and this is exactly how Richter approaches the script. If we watch this moment in the film, we begin with an establishing wide-angle zoom lens shot of the man-apes foraging for food, their kinetic, animal energy making the relatively still scene crackle with movement. Into this scene enters Moon-Watcher, still a knuckle-walker. We cut to a medium-shot in order to focus our attention on him as he too forages, his movements crackling with kinetic energy. However, the energy imbued into Moon-Watcher by Richter is abruptly brought to a halt, as he becomes still and quiet. This must be the 'strange feeling' that the script describes. No longer fidgeting or twitching, Moon-Watcher does not move and a silence takes over his demeanour. He cocks his head ever so slightly and looks up from the ground, at which point we cut to an extreme low-angle shot of the black monolith, with the sun peering over its upper most edge. In his memoir, Richter goes into lengthy detail about the origin of the movement for this scene, in which he was determined to 'go slowly at the start and begin with the softest, smallest, slowest movement I can get away with' (Richter 2002: 129). He knew that the 'strange feeling' he had to convey was vital to the entire authenticity of not just 'The Dawn of Man', but the entire film, forming as it did the first evolutionary point in humanity's history. Richter goes onto say that:

> My first concern is how am I going to convey an idea coming into my head? I settle on cocking my head and moving slowly and deliberately as the shot begins so that small gestures of the head and body will carry.
>
> (2002: 129)

Such a gesture, a simple cocking of the head, as Richter calls it, proves in the end to be a powerful and effective movement, with the 70mm medium close-up he is framed and shot in becoming 'gigantic on the big screen' (Richter 2002: 130). Aware of the cinematic element of the scene, Richter noted that 'the smallest movement will carry and any forced or exaggerated action will ring false' (2002: 130). Moon-Watcher remains still as he stares at the bones. Richter utilizes the behaviour of Jane Goodall's apes and begins to sniff the bones and touch them, wary at first. Finally, he takes hold of a bone and begins to gently smash it against the skeleton in front of him, his use of the bone and the way he holds it being in an animalistic fashion, with no firm grip but a rather lopsided hold of it.

It is remarkable how still the camera remains in 'The Dawn of Man', almost conspicuous in its absence. Shots are composed of static wide-angles that utilize the zoom lens, or close-ups of the Moon-Watcher character. In taking such an approach, what is emphasized is the man-apes' movement and their vital, kinetic, animal energy – almost dance like in the way they walk, run and jump. Kubrick removes himself as much as possible from 'The Dawn of Man' in order to highlight Richter and the man-apes' physicality. What plays out in 'The Dawn of Man' is a mime, in which psychological motivation is key to creating an authentic representation of hominids. And this went beyond merely ensuring that Moon-Watcher, the principal character, was realistic, but all of the man-apes. Not only was movement important in the representation of these creatures, but understanding their characters. In rehearsals, Richter utilized procedures to encourage the actors playing the man-apes to devise an individual character, asking them to write up activity lists for what they should do as a primate group, from foraging, to grooming, to communication, with the group watching and drawing inspiration from the Jane Goodall footage (Richter 2002: 97–98).

The movement of the man-apes hands and the use of touch are of particular importance; we see the man-apes use their hands to forage for food, as well as Moon-Watcher using his hands to caress the bone before he turns it into a weapon. The use of hands and touch conveys trepidation when the man-apes approach and touch the black monolith upon its first arrival in the savannah. One of the most powerful works of art in humanity is Michelangelo's *The Creation of Adam* (1508–12), an image that shows God reaching out to Adam and their fingers about to touch, the result being the creation of Man. The power of Michelangelo's fresco lies in the 'drama of the touch' (Erb 1998: 69) and comparisons can quite evidently be detected in the portrayal of the man-apes; they tentatively touch the monolith on its first appearance, imbuing the scene with a Judaeo-Christian religiosity. Such symbolism is in fact an inherent part of simian cinema, and in particular the jungle film, which Erb describes as the genre's 'fetishization of hands, touching, and body contact' that 'becomes a sign of the genre's overall investment in images of contact, usually between representatives of "civilization" and "nature", or western and non-western worlds' (1998: 69). This latter point is quite readily attributable to Moon-Watcher, who represents nature or the non-western, and the monolith, which represents civilization and the western world.

Expression of the body

By the mid-twentieth century, mime was no longer confined to the idea of comedy or silence; instead, new proponents, such as Paul J. Curtis, had developed mime into being about 'feelings and ideas depicted uniquely by the body' towards poetic expression (Lust 2003: 69). Under the eye of trained performers, mime could be introduced to other theatrical devices – dialogue and music for instance – creating new expressive forms, at the centre of which remained this movement of the body.

The man-apes in *2001* move beyond the 'man in the monkey suit' that Kubrick wanted to avoid by utilizing such poetic expression; they use psychologically motivated movement crafted over months of rehearsal with Daniel Richter. The representation was based on scientific-knowledge, or at least scientific-awareness as it stood in the mid-1960s in order to achieve authenticity. Richter's referral to George Schaller's work, for instance, is noticeable. Schaller details the behaviour of the gorillas he observed both in the wild and in captivity and broke this down into sections in his publications, including body postures, food habits and drinking behaviour. The latter – drinking behaviour – describes the way in which Schaller observed the gorillas scooping water 'with one cupped hand and drank from the inner side'. Richter replicates such behaviour almost verbatim in a scene during 'The Dawn of Man', in which Moon-Watcher scoops water from a muddy pond and drinks from his cupped hands. Richter's representation of the man-ape is drawn from the cultural and psychological discourse of the late 1950s and 1960s, in which the work of the likes of Goodall revised our knowledge of primates. Primates are in fact more human than we would like to think, 'reconfiguring debates over the boundary between human and nonhuman primates' (Bishop 2008: 245), with the portrayal of the science-fiction ape being 'not so much as a reaffirmation of epistemological solidity as an expression of ontological anxiety' (2008: 248). To this end, one can see how the ape represents the 'animal nature residing at the heart of the human condition' (2008: 245).

Subsequent to the production of 'The Dawn of Man', Kubrick would return again and again to the image of Richter's gang of man-apes, albeit in a modern disguise; from Alex and his droogs violently parading pack-like through the dystopian concrete jungle of *A Clockwork Orange*, to *Full Metal Jacket*, where the recruits pounce as a gang in the middle of the night on Private Pyle and savagely beat him, substituting bones for bars of soap rolled up in socks. The gang analogy even recurs in *Eyes Wide Shut* (Kubrick 1999), with a group of hostile men bouncing Tom Cruise's Dr. Harford off a sidewalk in New York, all of which suggests that man has never truly evolved from the primal, base instinct of Moon-Watcher's revelatory moment of violence.

More importantly, perhaps, it reveals how, for a director who wanted to break the classical cinematic form and was interested in the visual experience over the spoken word, the movement and expression of the body – psychologically motivated mime as espoused by The American Mime Theatre – continued to inform his work, or at least his visual compositions. Literary devices are often absent in Kubrick's films, particularly his later works, instead substituted with movements underpinned with motivation and desire; think of Barry (Ryan O'Neal) and Lady Lyndon (Marisa Berenson) upon their first meeting in *Barry Lyndon*, using only their eyes to communicate their passion for each other. Later on, movement is emphasized as Barry walks across to Lady Lyndon, a scene Martin Scorsese has commented on in the documentary *Stanley Kubrick: A Life in Pictures* (2001), talking about 'the use of movement and body language [...] as he [Barry] meets her [Lady Lyndon] for the first time, kissing her on the balcony, with the music and how his body moves'. Here was Kubrick's 'quiet suggestibility of the visual', with the motivated movements of his actors – and of his camera; as Curtis himself would have said, the movement is 'stimulated organically – by thoughts, by desires, by spirits' (Gehman 1986).

Acknowledgements

I wish to thank Jean Barbour, Director of The American Mime Theatre, and Daniel Richter (Moon-Watcher) for their feedback and advice on this chapter. This chapter is based on a paper delivered at the Screen Studies Conference at the University of Glasgow in June 2015.

Chapter Five

Life functions terminated: Actors' performances and the aesthetics of distanced subjectivity in *2001: A Space Odyssey*

Vincent Jaunas

An underplayed film

2001 quite possibly constitutes Stanley Kubrick's 'greatest meditation on the self and on individual consciousness' (Falsetto 2001: xviii) – a paradox for a film of such grandiose scope in which humankind seems to occupy so little room. Moreover, even when the characters do occupy space on the screen, their inner lives seem desperately shut to the audience, so that for many, *2001* is rather a cold, dehumanized film, more interested in the beauty of technology than in humankind. This chapter focuses on the human element in *2001* – bearing those two opposite receptions in mind – in order to study how the seemingly emotionless human beings that people the movie may reveal a central aspect of the film's aesthetics and of Kubrick's view of humankind. Situating the chapter within Performance Studies, it will explore the way the performances of the actors integrate within the broader aesthetics of the film. James Naremore has remarked how studying acting in cinema may reveal 'the social and psychological foundations of identity' (1988: 5). If, according to Naremore, 'the job of mainstream acting is to sustain the illusion of the unified self' (1988: 5), I would like to argue that in Kubrick's *2001*, the self is an endangered notion, as the job of acting is to highlight humankind's loss of touch with its own humanity.

The first human to be seen on screen is the character of Heywood R. Floyd, played by William Sylvester. He is seen sleeping, his arm floating languidly along with his pen in zero gravity. Floyd's introductory scene sets the mood for the characters' performances throughout the Moon and Discovery One scenes: he is tied to the chair of the spaceship, thereby introducing the theme of humanity's enslavement to machines in the modern world, a theme that will be developed further in the scenes that show HAL's murders of the crew. He seems to have been lulled to sleep by the material ease and comfort brought by science and progress. As *The Blue Danube* (1866) plays non-diegetically, Floyd is asleep with his earphones on, in front of the TV, oblivious to the marvels stretching before his eyes, as analysed by Michel Chion (2005: 243).

Such an attitude contrasts dramatically with the way the man-apes act in 'The Dawn of Man'. At first, Kubrick constantly stresses the harmony between the hominids and the world. Being vegetarians, they evolve peacefully alongside the wild boars, and even look more or less the same: both have round, black shapes. This harmony is first disrupted by the appearance of the monolith, whose rectangular, elongated aspect provides a powerful contrast with the natural environment that will emulate a growingly similar contrast in the man-apes themselves. Indeed, following this discovery, they become meat-eaters – preying on other species – and stand more erect, after Moon-Watcher stands up as he learns to use the bone as a weapon.

Floyd's obliviousness to the outside world is presented as a consequence of humanity's evolution instigated by the man-apes' encounter with the monolith. The absence of any title card separating those two sections of the film, instead linked with the famous jump cut of the bone thrown in the air turning into a spaceship, underlines modern humanity's status as direct heirs of Moon-Watcher. The drowsy atmosphere of the first Floyd scene seemingly recurs throughout the Moon and Discovery One scenes, with the frequent absence of music and soundtrack and the small quantity of dialogue, as well as the general underplaying of the actors, who take great care not to display any emotion. Such underplaying might at first sight be deemed a disconcerting failure of the actors, but it actually fits the overall tone of the film and is therefore a highly successful acting feat. Humankind's apparent lethargy contrasts with the man-apes' physical presence: while the man-apes run, jump, fight and bite, Floyd sleeps or sits most of the time. When Floyd stands in the conference room on the Moon Base, he rests himself on his pulpit, and whenever he walks, he never seems in a hurry, whereas the nervousness of the man-apes, constantly on alert so as to survive in a dangerous world, is underlined by the many nervous twitches performed by the actors playing them, constantly moving their heads abruptly, on the lookout for any lurking danger.

Following on the footsteps of Moon-Watcher, the bodies of the technologically advanced humans of *2001* have become fully erect, their stiffness accentuated. Such stiffness suggests a distanced relation between humans and their bodies in the modern world; whereas round shapes dominate 'The Dawn of Man' – from the roundness of planets and stars to the roundness of the hominids, and the hilly environments they evolve in – humans have become enclosed in a world of straight lines, and their figures are themselves straight. These straight lines echo the lines of the monolith, whose shape contrasts dramatically with that of the natural world around it. Ironically, the round shapes seen in the Moon and Discovery One scenes are predominantly the shapes of technological objects: spaceships have come to replace planets as the dominant life-hosting spheres. Humans are now constantly entrapped in spherical spaceships, out of which life in outer space is impossible. Human bodies need to be encapsulated in order to survive, so that technology clearly represents a substitute – and indeed a replacement – for organic, bodily activities.

To this end, the space hostess (Penny Brahms), bringing trays of food to the pilots as Floyd travels to the Moon, is the perfect embodiment of Kubrick's modern humanity. Her stiffness is striking as she walks around the spherical crosswalk of the spaceship. In the absence of gravity, she has to walk with grip shoes, which gives her a highly robotic pace. Her body looks like a mannequin, lacking any organic flexibility. Technical obligations, but also social restrictions – her job obliges her to maintain a certain standing all the time, just like everyone else in the public areas of the spaceships – have turned men into automatons. Kubrick's fondness for the ambiguity of automatons is well known. In this respect, one may remember that Freud (2003) considers the uncanny nature of automatons to be linked to the blurry frontier they establish between living and non-living entities. If the uncanny is not a predominant feeling of the film – although it is not totally absent, particularly when HAL takes control – this blurriness is constantly accentuated in a chillingly unemotional way by the acting. The characters that evolve in the Moon scenes act as though they have lost touch with their corporeal selves: the technological environment they evolve in has not only replaced the human body, it seems to have erased it as much as possible. Once again, the hostess exemplifies humanity's loss of touch with their bodies. Not only does she seem unable to control her body fluidly in outer space, this body is also entirely hidden, as she is covered by her white costume from head to toe, with only her face and hand apparent. The hygienic, sanitized relation to the body this costume evokes reveals that in this modern environment, the organic nature of the body is treated as a contingency that ought to be contained as much as possible.

Distancing mankind from the organic

Jean Baudrillard writes, in *L'autre Par Lui-même*, that 'man – with his mood, his passions, his laughs, his sexuality, his secretions – is nothing but a dirty little irrational virus, disrupting a universe of transparency. When all will be wiped clean [...] there will remain nothing but the virus of sadness, in a deadly clean and sophisticated universe' (1987: 35);[1] such is the course humans seem to have followed in *2001*. The environment humans evolve in is sanitized to the point that all bodily functions appear to have been erased. Humanity seems to deny its own organic nature. Bodily secretions are a case in point, as the humorous shot of Floyd looking at a space toilet handbook indicates. The natural functioning of the body has become an ordeal in outer space, due to the impressive difficulties encountered to maintain those high standards of hygiene in an enclosed environment. Bodily functions are therefore to be hidden away, its shameful aspect to be concealed by technology. James Naremore highlights the importance of the grotesque in Kubrick's oeuvre, even stating 'the key to his style lies in his anxious fascination with the human body' (2007: 34). If the grotesqueness of the body is alluded to in the Moon or Discovery One scenes, it is only in a covered way: because the modern human considers bodily functions to be grotesque, they are to be kept in check, to be constantly controlled, just like the actors seem to be constantly hiding their bodies and indeed taming it so that no unintentional bodily reaction may escape their absolute control over themselves.

The treatment of food in the film likewise suggests the downplaying of all bodily functions associated with modernity. On the way to the Moon, Floyd and the pilots eat trays of liquid food whose tastelessness is humorously suggested. The highly processed nature of this meal – some liquid food compartments to be eaten with a straw, the contents of which are indicated by little drawings showing what one is supposed to taste – contrasts dramatically with the ingestion of raw meat of the man-apes in 'The Dawn of Man'. Here again, natural bodily functions are hidden away: while the man-apes eat the raw meat with their bare hands, Floyd now eats processed food with the intermediary of a straw. On his way to the monolith,

Floyd then has sandwiches, which might relate more or less to a more natural kind of food. However, their extreme square shapes stress their highly processed, and indeed artificial quality, as does the fact that they are wrapped in cellophane and by the dialogue exchange:

FLOYD: What's this, chicken?
UNNAMED MAN: Something like that. Tastes the same, anyway.

The astronauts take the sandwiches out of a plastic container. In the film, technology is used to process the food the astronauts need, and acts as a go-between, concealing to humans their organic, natural bodily functions. Philip Kuberski indicates the comical discomfort the scene creates:

> The meat they eat is synthetic, not hunted, and the development of human speech leads to chatting, flattery, and bogus bonhomie. And again there is something oddly comical about eating that Kubrick brings out: a sense of corporeal atavism that delimits and ironizes the sublime technology that has brought men to the Moon in the first place.
> (2012: 31)

This is again obvious in a scene on the Discovery One, as Dave Bowman (Keir Dullea) and Frank Poole (Gary Lockwood) eat some unidentified mashed up food that Bowman is seen picking up from a machine. Both characters this time eat whilst watching television. Lockwood and Dullea's acting emphasizes the highly mechanistic aspect of this meal, which has become a mere way of 'charging one's batteries'. Both nibble their food inattentively, while the low angle shot accentuates the purely mechanistic dimension of chewing: while their bodies are charging up, both men's eyes and minds are clearly focused on their screens. Here too, this contrasts with the performance of the actors playing the man-apes who, oppositely, are deeply focused on the vegetables, and later on the meat, they are eating. Their meal is the sole object of their attention. The contrast between the astronauts and the man-ape's chewing is striking: while it is a demanding physical activity for the hominids, who need to dig up raw vegetables or to tear chunks of raw meat with their teeth, it is a simple procedure for the astronauts who, like Floyd, ingest a very soft form of food. Here again, the natural, physical activity of softening the food to facilitate digestion becomes accomplished artificially (through the processing of food) in the modern world.

Given modern humanity's attempt to downplay, even suppress, any organic relation to their bodies, it is unsurprising to notice the flagrant lack of sexuality in *2001*, especially when comparing the film to the rest of Kubrick's oeuvre. The characters' clothes reveal their conspicuous asexuality. The space hostess's outfit is exemplary, as its purpose is not to highlight the physical attributes of its wearer, but to hide them away, with bodies to be as neutral as possible. Such sexless, genderless outfits can be found over and over again in the film – one may think of Bowman's grey suit and, of course, the various unisex space suits worn by astronauts. Indeed, all characters wear uni-colour clothes (except in one case, mentioned later), from Floyd's brown suit to the hostesses' fully white or fully pink outfits, and Bowman and Poole's fully grey ones. By wearing the same colour from head to toe, the characters dissimulate all physical characteristics under their visually predominant artificial second skins. The physical existence of the characters' bodies is thus to be hidden – even replaced – by their outfits, just as they are suppressed by the underplayed, mechanical performances of the actors.

A loss of contact

In the scenes on the Moon, the only human contact ever displayed is the meaningless social gesture of the handshakes between Floyd and the mission controller (Frank Miller), then between Floyd and his Russian colleagues. In *Reframing Screen Performance* (2008), Cynthia Baron and Sharon Marie Carnicke draw on the tools of the Prague school of semiotics to distinguish between 'gesture-signs' (conventional gestures, such as handshakes) and 'gesture-expressions' (the individual uses of these gestures) and write that in the field of Performance Studies, focusing on the gap between gesture-signs and gesture-expressions enables one to 'analyse the way a particular detail of performance sustains, amplifies, or contradicts the thought or feeling usually conveyed by such social expressions of greetings, farewell, apology, concern, condolence, and so on' (Baron and Carnicke 2008: 89). In the case of Sylvester's performance of Floyd's handshakes, such an analysis suggests the only physical contact that takes place between film characters actually increases the distance between them, and between themselves and their own bodies. When Sylvester shakes hands with the mission controller, his body is rigidly straight, his arm held tight in front of him, so that the gesture enables him to maintain an arm's length distance between them. Sylvester looks at the mission controller straight in the eyes and his face displays a friendly, though rigid smile. After shaking hands, Sylvester puts his hand in his pocket and adopts a gentlemanly posture suggesting he is at ease with his interlocutor. Three minutes later, Sylvester shakes hands with his Russian colleagues and he adopts the exact same posture: an arm drawn straight which maintains a certain distance, a static but friendly smile, and a look straight in the others' eyes. While sitting down, the way Sylvester crosses his legs equally suggests a gentlemanly expression of ease, although, just like when he puts his hand in his pocket, it is also a defensive gesture of withdrawal. In other words, Sylvester has the character of Floyd perform this gesture-expression the exact same way in those two situations, no matter what his psychological state may be – and we might suspect him to be more careful, more mindful of his actions, the second time, as he is drawn to lie to his Russian colleagues and competitors in a climate of Cold War. The only physical contact between characters in the film is thereby performed mechanically, as if Floyd's body was so accustomed to perform those meaningless social gestures that it could act on its own, disconnected from his mind. Ultimately, these gestures lose all semantic content and simply become the way to respond in those types of situations. Their robotic execution is emphasized in the second scene through the comparison with Leonard Rossiter's performance, as Dr. Andrei Smyslov: Rossiter slightly overplays his character's politeness, to give it an obsequious quality highlighting the rather fake execution of this exchange, so that Rossiter's performance acts as a grotesque mirroring of Sylvester's (an effect Rossiter will also produce in his other Kubrick role as Captain John Quin in *Barry Lyndon*).

Except for those handshakes, the only other human contact in the film is performed by the judo fighters briefly seen on the television screen the space hostesses are watching on the way to the Moon. Human needs for physical contact, warmth and social intercourse are, in the modern world, satisfied vicariously through virtual mediums (just like Floyd and Poole's only contact with their relatives are through television screens), while any actual contact is suppressed as much as possible. Furthermore, this contact is an attempt to fight and dominate one another, through the substitution of actual violence offered by the institution of sports.

A growing distance

The performances of the actors in the Moon scenes and the theme of humanity's loss of touch with its body in the modern world, reaches new heights of distancing in the Discovery One scenes. Surprisingly, this section begins with an unusual physical presence: that of Frank Poole (Gary Lockwood) exercising around the ship. He is wearing white shorts and a tight black shirt – the only time in the film a character wears two different colours – that highlight his athletic body. Gary Lockwood's physicality was a central aspect of Poole's character. A biography of Lockwood was sent to an advertising agency, in which his physical type was stressed. Lockwood was described as 'a rugged six-footer, formal football player and film stunt man' (Anon. n.d.). He was also advertised as a sex symbol, the young actor being amongst 'Hollywood's most eligible bachelors', and a sports enthusiast (Anon. n.d.). Poole is certainly more in touch with his body than Bowman or Floyd. Later on, he is even seen wearing nothing but his shorts, his bare muscular chest apparent, as he lies on a bed and watches his parents' recording. However, during this scene, it is HAL, not Poole himself that controls Poole's movements by moving the electronic chair – implying that, for Poole as well, machines act as bodily substitutes. Nonetheless, it is Poole, the only character to display an active relation to his body, who dies as he is ejected in outer space, where the human body cannot survive without the help of machines. The only character left is Dave Bowman.

Keir Dullea underplays his role as Bowman more than Lockwood and Sylvester do, and creates a highly mechanistic, robot-like character. While Poole is seen jogging, Bowman is seen playing chess with HAL. Bowman is all-mind and no body, his movements extremely mechanical and slow. His face remains inexpressive throughout the Discovery One scenes, even when he is under pressure and faces possible death. His hair – rigidly slicked– and the way his skin is shot to look sallow reinforce the impression of a character whose body is that of an automaton, or a wax statue. His voice is flat and he only utters factual comments. His inner life is never revealed, either on his face or through his voice. As Chion has analysed, this creates a gap with Douglas Rain's performance of HAL's voice, which is much warmer and more expressive (2005: 240–41). Unlike Dave, HAL does display a wide range of emotions through his voice, from pride ('The 9000 Series has a perfect operational record') to fear ('I'm afraid'). Such an inversion can be regarded as the outcome of humanity's distanced relation to its body in the modern world; the machine has become a substitute of the organic, to the point that it seems more human than actual humans.[2] On the other hand, humanity, by relying more and more on the machine to overcome its organic limits, has become more and more like machines. The gradual disconnection from Earth that occurs as humanity pushes the frontier further and further away in the universe is thus correlated with a gradual disconnection with humanity's own self. The human psyche is no longer a vector of emotion and the men in Discovery One merely serve to calculate the day-to-day activities of the journey, like HAL does. Arguably, humans are less useful than HAL to the completion of the mission. Indeed, the real purpose of the mission, the strategical and visionary thinking, has been effectuated before the beginning of the journey, back on Earth, and the astronauts are not even aware of the mission's true objectives, only HAL knows. Thereby, humans function as mere tools, as cogs in the machine, or, as Nelson puts it, 'Bowman and Poole are HAL's tools, servants to his omniscience, and inevitably, like Moon-Watcher's bone, nothing more than artefacts to be contemplated or objects to be tossed into space once their function has been fulfilled' (2000: 124).

An intrinsic becoming-machine

Humanity's growing distance with its own body may be seen as a logical conclusion of this becoming-machine, which reaches its climax on the Discovery One. Kubrick does not show this becoming-machine as a symptom of modernity, as it is more than that: it is consubstantial with the evolution of the man-apes into the modern human. As soon as Moon-Watcher decides to use a bone as a more powerful replacement for the arm, humanity starts to rely on technology to replace their organic, animal bodies. Modernity, in this regard, is simply a dramatic over-achievement of this trend. Beyond Frank Poole and Dave Bowman, one may regard the frozen astronauts as the ultimate expression of humanity's becoming-machine in *2001*, and of the deadly consequences it entails. These astronauts are frozen so that their vital functions are reduced to a minimum. As tools, they are to be awakened by HAL when their use is required, and in the meantime it is better to let them hibernate in their gloomy sarcophagi.

These characters are first introduced whilst eating a meal, through parallel editing that alternates between Bowman and Poole's meal and close-ups of the frozen astronauts' life function charts. Such parallel editing, in the pure tradition of the Kuleshov effect, highlights the fact that both the astronauts that are awake and those frozen are all artificially sustained by HAL. Very little indeed separates the ones from the others. In terms of acting, the frozen astronauts also seem to represent the completion of the trend suggested by the 'awake' actors' underplayed performances. Immobile, these characters' bodies are not seen at all throughout the movie. Only their heads remain visible through the window, so that the contingency – which is their mortal bodies – has literally been suppressed through the artificially sustaining machine. It seems they have become mere floating heads, just like Bowman has when he is wearing a spacesuit with no helmet. Not only is the body suppressed, but all emotions associated with the living are as well, since their frozen heads remain as emotionless in life as in death.

The scene of their deaths is shot so that humankind's modern lack of vitality is expressed with a chilling detachment. Whilst HAL's death is arguably the most emotional scene of the film – through Douglas Rain's powerful voice acting – and has a physical manifestation as Dave manually disconnects HAL's 'brain', the death of the hibernating astronauts has no physical reality at all. When HAL decides these astronauts have become a hindrance to the success of the mission, he simply stops sustaining them. This is only indicated by the malfunction signalled on the life function chart, followed by the message 'Life Functions Terminated'. This euphemism for death reveals how human life is considered in mere functional terms. These astronauts have literally lost their function, according to HAL, ceasing to be potentially useful cogs in the machine, so he disconnects them. Life is only pondered in terms of functionality and the human body is therefore considered in functional terms, being defined as machines are – a body either functions or stops functioning.

HAL's decision to murder the astronauts aboard Discovery One is the deadly conclusion of humanity's becoming-machine: no matter what, humans remain a deeply imperfect machine, as HAL argues analytical errors can only be attributed to them. Despite their attempts, humans can never be rid of their bodies, their needs, their feelings and their mortal frailty. A cold, calculating logic therefore naturally leads to the decision of suppressing the human element from the mission, as the contingency that is their human nature represents the most serious chance of failure for the mission as a whole.

Ironically, such a reasoning, which is adopted by HAL, may also be interpreted as the result of HAL's own becoming-human. As he becomes more human, HAL stops being a perfect calculating machine and starts making mistakes. This leads him to fear being deactivated, and his survival instinct leads him to strike first in order to remove his potential enemies. The rationalization according to which men may hinder the mission may therefore be perceived as HAL's attempt to justify murder in logical terms. Such an ambiguity shows once again that the becoming-machine that haunts humans is not disconnected from their humanity: it is consubstantial to it, it accompanies it as a human need born out of the frailty of the human condition and the desire for a safer, more comfortable and less dangerous world brought by technological progress. The fear of death, the dissimulation of bodily needs and the control of emotions all point to a becoming-machine that is related to a human wish for control over the world and over their own contingencies. 'The Dawn of Man' shows this desire for control – to own the source of water and food over rival bands – to be at the origin of humanity's becoming-machine. Such a vision therefore prevents any simplistic reactionary reading of *2001*, which would suggest things were better before technology settled in. A quest for the increased control brought by technological progress has always been part of what makes us humans, Kubrick suggests.

In *2001*, this need for control is nowhere more apparent than in the gaze of the characters. The performances of the actors playing the man-apes (from Daniel Richter, playing Moon-Watcher, to the extras playing the others) are characterized by abrupt turnings of the head in all directions. The man-apes are perpetually on the lookout in as many directions as possible in order to control their environments. However, the spectacular depth of field reveals their gaze to be deeply limited. The frame is too large to be entirely scanned by their eyes, so that despite their attempts, blind spots are everywhere. This results in one of the man-apes being attacked by a leopard from behind. In the night scene, a series of close-ups emphasize the fearful wandering eyes of each of the man-apes. But following their evolution, humankind's gaze becomes much calmer, since the amount of control that technology has provided enables them to look calmly at their environment, as it is a human-made environment they act like they control. The constant opposition between the immensity of space and the enclosed frames of the interiors of the spaceships, in which walls are permanently visible on all sides – including the ceilings – creates a quasi-constant frame within the frame, highlighting the impression that humanity evolves in a controlled space. Due to the lack of physical danger, the human gaze has become more analytical. The intense long stare Leonard Rossiter gives Gary Lockwood in the space station suggests he is attempting to read his colleague's mind, so as to discover his secrets. If the environment no longer needs to be controlled, humanity's wish for a controlled world nonetheless cannot be entirely fulfilled as long as humans can keep their thoughts hidden from one another.

HAL's gaze is perhaps the most memorable and indeed the most controlling. HAL's point-of-view shots are the only ones to be found in the Moon and Discovery One scenes. Kubrick used a wide-angle lens to create an extremely high angle view, the same kind of lenses used today for 360-degree photographs (Davies 2016). HAL can see everything that takes place in the ship. Its gaze is panoptic, as no blind spots escape its sight inside the Discovery One. Michel Foucault famously demonstrated how an architectural style enabling a panoptic gaze was popularized in nineteenth-century prisons so as to control a prisoner's every move to discipline him (Foucault 2008). The panoptic gaze is linked to power, to the control of others. The disturbing effect of the various close-ups of HAL's intense red 'eye', an all-seeing pupil which never blinks, associated with the 'fearful symmetry' aboard the ship (echoed in HAL's eye, itself framed within a symmetrical design) all create a feeling of absolute control by HAL. HAL can indeed control human beings, is able to interpret their psychological states (leading him to attack first) and has power of life and death over everyone within the ship. The failure of the astronauts to escape HAL's control when they hide in the space pod, as he manages to read their lips, underlines the suspense created by HAL's invading all-seeing gaze. HAL's gaze attempts to deny others' rights to express their own subjectivities. However, despite his panoptic power, HAL's gaze does not enable him to control everything, and as always in Kubrick's films, attempts at absolute control are doomed to fail. If HAL is omnipresent inside the ship, his panoptic gaze gets blind outside this enclosed world. Once out in the immensity of the universe, HAL is unable to stop Bowman.

Reconnecting with one's own self

We have seen how actors' performances, their bodies, their needs, their voices and their stares sheds light on a main thematic concern of *2001*. Humankind's becoming-machine is presented as a human tendency that leads them to rely on technology to gain control, but which, when brought to its logical conclusion, eventually suppresses their own (and others) subjectivities, thereby threatening their very humanity. However, the film does not end with HAL's victory, and we shall now envision Bowman's survival, and the end of his journey, as an optimistic possibility for a renewed relation between humanity's subjectivity, its relation to itself and to the world, and its wish for control and security.

Bowman's victory consecrates the demise of the becoming-machine, and the wish for an all-controlling technology at the expense of humanity's vitality. Indeed, HAL can only control his entire universe because it is small and enclosed, and Dave defeats him by getting out of the ship. Being all-controlling leads to being enclosed upon oneself, oblivious to the immensity of the universe; in this regard, HAL appears to repeat humankind's own obliviousness thus far. HAL's death announces a progressive return of Bowman's humanity, as Dullea's performance in the final two sections of the film indicates.

The strategy of Bowman to defeat HAL may be seen as the first step in Bowman's rebirth. In the space pod, Dave, for the first time, has to think of a strategy; his role is not that of a cog in a machine, he is responsible for his own fate, and must improvise, adapt, react, qualities that were previously denied him. Bowman's plan is exceptionally bold, 'out-of-the-box' thinking that could not have arisen out of his former cold, robotic logic: throwing himself into space without a helmet. Significantly, this plan entails going against technology. Dave stops relying on technology (the helmet) as a substitute for his own bodily functions, and deliberately disregards the automatic message he reads in his space pod ('caution, explosive bolts') as he explodes the hatch of the pod to throw himself into space.

This scene concludes the slowest section of the film, during which time seems to expand to the point it creates a feeling of stillness that has been the focus of many negative critics (Chion 2005: 245). While watching the scene, I myself experience a feeling of physical restlessness following the pleasure of contemplation, as Dave stops moving his body when he is stuck in the pod. The pod, the technological substitution of Dave's body, moves extremely slowly, a feeling reinforced by the crushing silence of outer space which dominates most of this section of the film (only in the pod can a few electronic sounds be heard). Dave's becoming-machine, his disconnection from all human vitality, is such that the spectator starts to feel restless, especially since this scene follows a previous space sequence, in which Dave and Frank try to fix the antenna – an equally long and slow one, in which only breathing can be heard. This feeling of restlessness is of course much stronger when one sits still in a movie theatre, rather than in front of a television. Dave's rebirth-like ejection out of the pod therefore comes as a great, physical relief. His body is rapidly thrown back and forth and Bowman can only rely on his own human, physical capabilities to survive and close the hatch in time. Finally, HAL's death has, as we have seen, a physical reality which is absent from the other deaths of the film – unlike anyone else, ever since Moon-Watcher used a bone as a weapon, Dave kills his enemy with his bare hands. Moreover, Dave finally shows some signs of emotion at this point – empathy for the dying HAL, as he tells him, 'I would like to hear [your song], sing it for me', and in doing so creates a strong emotional link, that of a human being who understands and sympathizes with another conscious being facing imminent death – insofar as HAL can sense his own awareness and fear death, the film encourages the viewer to consider him a conscious being. As Nelson has argued, 'only after HAL reasserts the primitive's instinct for survival by killing Poole and the three hibernators does Bowman begin to show indications of an internal awakening' (2000: 111). Such an awakening, Performance Studies suggest, is closely connected to Dave's reconnection with his own subjectivity, as Dullea's performance becomes less neutral and endows his character with a yet unexplored array of feelings.

In the next scene, Dullea expresses very strong emotions, which contrast dramatically with his underplayed performance so far. In the various stills showing his face twisted by pain, Dullea's mixed expression of pain and ecstasy evoke baroque representations of the Christ, particularly Guido Reni's *Head of Christ Crowned with Thorns* (1620). Dave's Christ-like attitude underlines his experience as one of rebirth, while the baroque expression of his face accentuates the fact his rebirth is an emotional one – one may even be tempted to see in Bowman a redeemer of humankind as a whole, a humankind that had suppressed its own humanity.

Bowman's subjectivity is finally emphasized through the various close-ups of his blinking eyes. The abstract quality of the Star Gate sequence, as well as the colour filters which alternate in the rhythm of Dave's blinking, express Bowman's vision as well as its limits: faced with incommensurableness, Dave's gaze can only grasp a barely understandable glimpse of the universe. Just like the spectator who has a hard time making sense of what he sees, Bowman's gaze is shown as limited. It is not panoptic, as Dave cannot control anything and, as we can only assume, sees only a tiny fraction – what his imperfect, human eyes can perceive – of what there is to be seen, and barely comprehends a thing. And yet it is this final journey, during which Bowman does not attempt to control his environment or to become an all-seeing, all-understanding machine, which leads him to his final rebirth.

Dave's reunion with his subjective gaze is confirmed in the last section of the film, through the puzzling succession of shots/counter-shots showing Dave looking at an older version of himself several times. The subjective quality of these shots is emphasized, as Dave is watching himself – the sequence includes a mirror shot, which itself mirrors the several shots of a younger Bowman looking at an older self – and the fragmented, partial quality of this gaze is evident through the mysterious nature of those very shots. The lack of narrative coherence of the sequence opens up a myriad of interpretations, and yet reveals the deeply limited nature of the human gaze, unable to fully comprehend what is happening in this unfathomable encounter with a superior life force.

Significantly, this evolution ushers in a reunion with Dave's own organic, physical self. As Dave ages, he rids himself of his technological substitutes to reconnect with his own body: he gets out of the space pod, then out of his space suit and into a simple bathrobe, and finally out of his clothes as he is reborn into the naked astral foetus. Dave's reconnection with his body is accompanied by a serene evocation of bodily needs and bodily functions, which are no longer hidden away, through the surprising discovery of eighteenth-century furniture, with its elegant curves. The large, beautiful bed evokes a need for sleep that is neither filled with potential danger, as for the man-apes, nor equated with death as in the Discovery One. Dave then walks to a bathroom in which not only a bath but also toilets can briefly be seen, suggesting an evocation of humanity's corporeality, with its bodily functions, far from the head-scratching intricacy of space toilets. The last step of this reunion with humanity's corporeal reality takes place as the older Bowman eats a meal whose refinement and apparent quality suggests a food which is an in-between, both natural (real vegetables reconnect food with the earthly reality of ingestion) and artificially processed.

The presence of food in this last sequence was of paramount importance for Kubrick who, before he opted for an eighteenth-century setting, wanted Bowman to evolve in a 'typical' American house, filled with familiar brands of food, from Heinz to Kellogg's (Caras 1966). The switch to a less processed food emphasizes Bowman's reunion with his body and his bodily needs. As to the manifold interpretations the switch to an eighteenth-century setting call for, Michel Ciment's insistence on Kubrick's use of the eighteenth century as representing the age of reason stands out (Ciment 2004: 66). As the age of reason, the eighteenth century is also the time in which bodily needs, such as food, began to be considered as a shameful reminiscence of humanity's animal condition. From the eighteenth century onwards, the natural animal need for food as necessary for survival was dissimulated under the artistry of high cuisine. Immanuel Kant defined gluttony as a shameful vice precisely because it blurred the frontier between mankind and animals: a glutton enjoys 'the pleasure of cattle' (Kant 1996: 427). Bowman's eighteenth-century meal harks back to the century that, for Kubrick, represents the advent of the age of reason, which is also the age of dissociation between (animal) body and (human) mind. To Kubrick, the eighteenth century epitomizes humanity's becoming-machine, his distancing from his body and his animal self (*Barry Lyndon* is a case in point, since Barry's downfall is triggered by his incapacity to control his own anger). As Nelson suggests, the breaking of the crystal glass in this sequence may be seen as an ultimate escape from 'the formal remains of pre-mechanical man' (2000: 134), towards a more direct relation to the world. Dave's meal might be seen as a final step on his way back to a more peaceful relation with his body, and ultimately with his own humanity.

An eighteenth-century setting to symbolize Dave's reunion with his body also reveals Kubrick's optimistic portrayal of a potential evolution of humanity towards a reunion with its own subjectivity. This evolution implies devolution from the traps of humanity's becoming-machine, but it does not entail a regressive denial of the benefits of scientific progress, the comfort and increased potentialities offered by modern technology. On the contrary, it suggests a new relation with humankind's subjectivity, one which embraces the benefits of technology without allowing it to distance humanity from itself – unlike, Kubrick suggests, the kind of technological evolution that took prominence in the eighteenth century and climaxes in the modern age. The final sequence shows the Star-Child coming back home. Its aura of light suggests an incredibly complex technology, and yet Kubrick shoots it as part of a sublime alignment with earth, which echoes the alignment of round shapes – earth, moon and sun – of the first sequence. The world and humankind, humankind and technology, seem finally reunited. Through this new relation with technology, humanity becomes a harmonious part of nature. While in the Moon and Discovery One sequences, technology-enclosed humans were cut away from the outside world, the Star-Child's transparent aura depicts it as open to the universe. Far from the panoptic gaze of HAL, the Star-Child's immense eyes look at the world in a way that is the direct continuation of Bowman's subjective gaze from the 'Jupiter and Beyond the Infinite' sequence. It is a non-controlling gaze, as the Star-Child does not do anything. It is mysterious, ungraspable and subjective: a human gaze indeed.

By breaking the fourth wall, the foetus's ultimate stare at the camera directly targets the spectators. As a human odyssey, *2001* encourages spectators to examine their very humanity, and warns them against what I have called humanity's becoming-machine: its tendency to rely on technology and science in a way that distances oneself from one's body, and ultimately from one's own subjectivity and from the outside world. Ironically, humankind's potential reunion with itself is finally celebrated without the physical presence of actors, through the special effect of the Star-Child. Nonetheless, as this final stare suggests, the film itself may allow the spectator to go through the same kind of Odyssey that Dave has, allowing us to ponder upon what humankind has lost, as well as gained, throughout its evolution. By filling the distance between humanity and its own subjectivity, *2001* encourages the spectator to perceive the world anew, and ultimately 'advocates a restoration of belief in this world' (Rushton 2012: 113).[3]

Part Three

Technology

Part Three

Themes of technology – its impact on humanity, and humanity's interaction with it – as well as the use of technology, abound through Kubrick's work. He pursued ideas of artificial intelligence and the future technological evolution of the human race in his adaptation of Brian Aldiss's *Supertoys Last All Summer Long* (1969), eventually directed by Steven Spielberg as *A.I. Artificial Intelligence* (2001). Technology fascinated Kubrick, from his first encounters with a camera as a young boy in the Bronx, to his technological cinematic innovations on *2001* and beyond, always looking to pioneer new innovations; from the Steadicam on *The Shining*, to his use of computerized editing on *Full Metal Jacket* with the Montage Picture Processor, the first director in the United Kingdom to do so (McFarling 1986: 10). But *2001* remains the touchstone of Kubrick's exploration of technology and, as Robert Kolker suggests,

> *2001* is not only a narrative of space travel, but a way of seeing what space travel *should* look like. The film is a design for our imagination and a notion of modernity, creating the lineaments of a modern environment and enunciating the metamorphosis of human into machine.
>
> (2011: 108)

The two chapters in this section explore these themes of technology and the tension between technological design and humanity. Cynthia J. Miller and A. Bowdoin Van Riper have uncovered an early draft of the *2001* screenplay to discover two HALs. They provide an overview of this early draft and the way that the character of HAL evolved, as well as the creation of a horrific tension and narrative ambiguity by the final draft. The chapter questions whether HAL is truly a monstrous icon and what Kubrick's intentions were by comparing these early draft scripts to the eventual film.

Antoine Balga-Prévost's chapter revises our understanding of ideas around the philosophy of technology. Balga-Prévost examines the relationship between the technical and cinematographic object in *2001*, utilizing frameworks developed by philosopher Gilbert Simondon. The chapter reworks the interpretation of Kubrick's technological themes as having been dominated by nihilism and technophobia – the bleak interpretation of Kubrick's worldview in general has (detrimentally) affected the perspective of his work.

Further reading

Understanding the technological themes and innovations in *2001* continues. Most recently an essay by Regina Peldszus (2015), 'Speculative systems: Kubrick's interaction with the aerospace industry during the production of *2001*' (pp. 198–217), has postulated that the production of *2001* can be seen as a speculative space programme given that, 'key conceptual designs – including the long duration spacecraft Discovery – operated against the backdrop of fast-paced, real space developments' (2015: 200). Other scholars continue to interpret the philosophical use of technology, and the representation of machines, including Garry Leonard's (2011), 'Technically human: Kubrick's monolith and Heidegger's propriative event', *Film Criticism*, 36:1, pp. 44–67, and Michael Mateas's (2006), 'Reading HAL: Representation and artificial intelligence', in R. Kolker (ed.), *Stanley Kubrick's 2001: A Space Odyssey: New Essays*, pp. 105–25.

Chapter Six

From technical to cinematographic objects in *2001: A Space Odyssey*

Antoine Balga-Prévost

Stanley Kubrick's *2001* has been analysed from a variety of academic perspectives and philosophies, from contemporary metaphysics to alchemist philosophy, from media theory to theology. Yet, one philosophical perspective in particular stands out in regards to *2001*, and more generally in his entire filmography: existentialism, and more specifically existentialism in relation to nihilism. In the introduction to *The Philosophy of Stanley Kubrick* (2007), Jerold Abrams explains:

> Yet, as internally diverse as Kubrick's filmography is, taken as a whole, it is also quite coherent. It takes all the differentiated sides of reality and unifies them into one rich, complex philosophical vision that happens to be very close to existentialism.
> (2007: 1)

Existentialism is a philosophical school that was founded on a thought that 'rejected the nineteenth century view of the world as a massive mechanical system working out its own logic through history' (Abrams 2007: 1). This pessimistic thought about the technique stretched into the twentieth century with figures such as Heidegger. According to him, the technique – the technicist society – alienates humankind as individuals and diverts them from their very being, their very nature. Nicolas Géraud sees in *2001* 'an illumination of a Heideggerian metaphysical Gospel, which tells the story of the *Gestell* [Enframing]' (1999: 77). For Heidegger, 'the rule of Enframing threatens man with the possibility that it could be denied to him to enter into a more original revealing and hence to experience the call of a more primal truth' (1954: 28). Patrick Murray and Jeanne Schuler's analysis echoes the idea of the technique on the one hand as a 'Will to Power' (to quote Nietzsche's phrase) and on the other as the expression of human pretention and vanity in face of the absurdity of their existence.

> In *2001: A Space Odyssey* (1968), murder marks the 'dawn of man', and the murder weapon, tossed into the air, morphs memorably into a spacecraft. Kubrick's adoption of skeptical tropes conjoins the absurdity of human existence to the brutish nastiness of human nature. The eons of time and the immense expanse of the universe, filling the screen in *2001*, reduce our lives to insignificance.
> (Murray and Schuler 2007: 135)

Opposite to these slightly pessimistic and technophobic considerations, other analysis has found in *2001* a form of celebration of the technique, which locates humankind at the centre of their progress. This progress led humanity further than the stars, towards a new form of life, a progress that sees a transformation of Bowman into the Star-Child, and at the same time a progress – change – in the audience after viewing the film. The film thus appears as a call for impeccable and sensible technical perfectionism, rather than being technophobic (the latter evoking mistrust towards the evolution of new technologies and the dangers of humankind's encounters with them). The film attempts to elevate humankind towards new and better forms of knowledge, perception and life, and ultimately a positive future.

This chapter will re-evaluate the philosophical dimension of the technique in *2001* by analysing the technical objects of the film, namely the bone, the spaceships, the HAL 9000 computer and the monolith. My framework for this exploration of technical objects will be Gilbert Simondon's (1924–1989) philosophy of technology. In his work *Du mode d'existence des objets techniques* (*On the Mode of Existence of Technical Object*) (1958),[1] Simondon develops a reflection around the technical being, its technicity and its own existence. He claims that what alienates humankind is not the technical object itself, but ignorance of it. This ignorance can only be overcome by integrating the technique to culture, and by understanding its reality, its existence mode and its relationship to humankind.

The latter seems more appropriate to the understanding of *2001*, in which the technique is an essential theme and aspect. Indeed Kubrick explores and renews the possibilities offered by cinema's techniques. Moreover, the lucidity with which Kubrick tackles the theme of the technique and its relationship to humankind in the film tends to set him apart and to oppose him to any technophobic or anti-technicistic philosophy. Whether showing us its improvement and beauty or malfunction and danger, it seems as though Kubrick has tried to understand in *2001* the mode of existence of technical objects and their relationship to humankind. Therefore, this chapter aims to demonstrate the pertinence of Simondon's philosophy of the technique in re-thinking the mode of existence and the technicity of technical objects, as well as the 'techno-aesthetic' relationship that can be generated between these technical objects and the 'cinematographic object'. Such an analysis can renew the signification of these elements within *2001* and therefore reveal new layers of narrative, aesthetic and philosophical depth.

Technical objects and cinematographic objects

In the introduction to *Cinematographic Objects, Things and Operations* (2015), Volker Pantenburg distinguishes three basic levels of cinematographic objects: 'objects in film, objects of film, and the film as an object' (2015: 13). For the purposes of this chapter, the 'cinematographic object' will be taken as what Pantenburg describes as the 'film as an object':

> In film production, we are confronted with cameras, lighting, props, studio sets, microphones and exterior locations, editing tables with computers, a plethora of human and non-human actors that assemble to create a network of distributed agency, which challenges any simple notion of the writers [...]. To put it differently, whenever we speak about film and cinema, we are dealing with objects that record and store, transport and disseminate, project and display. And nested in between these material components of cinema, temporarily stabilizing their structure and organizing them in an operational chain, is one peculiar object that connects these elements, a special thing amongst things: the film image itself.
>
> (2015: 13)

This definition of the image as a cinematographic object, the result of the functional layout of a whole network of cinematographic objects, is a crucial point in this chapter. I am taking as a fact that the objects on screen become cinematographic when a synergy starts to be created with this network, in this relationship of exchange, of technical and aesthetical interdependence with the cinematographic object. Each object in film acquires a cinematographic dimension, but this dimension does not reveal itself in the same way from one object to another. Not every object on screen is integrated with the same importance to the mode of existence of the cinematographic object, which is the film.

It is possible to find an example of where the technical object is linked in a specific way to the cinematographic object in each of Kubrick's films. For instance, in *Killer's Kiss*, the boxer Davey Gordon (Jamie Smith) prepares himself for a boxing match in his apartment. Feeding his fish before leaving, he places his face behind the fishbowl. The camera films him from the opposite side of the bowl, through the water. Davey's face, filling the entire frame, becomes distorted, an effect that reminds us of the risks of facial deformation endured in the boxing ring. The bowl swells his nose, as if swollen from an injury; Davey's fear of losing the harmony of his face is also subtly represented earlier in the film when, looking at his reflection in the mirror, he imagines what his nose would look like broken by pressing on it. The bowl constitutes the technical object, which appears only once on the screen, carrying a semantic, technical and aesthetic meaning. The importance of the bowl comes from its relationship with the cinematographic object: it fills up the frame, compels the framing to its own measurements and imposes some of its physical properties (light diffraction, glass and water matter, capacity, etc.). The camera lines up on the level of the bowl and links directly the technical object (the bowl) to the cinematographic one (the image). The bowl becomes a cinematographic object in itself as it determines some technical aspects (camera position, frame, object used, lighting, camera movement, etc.).

Another example can be found in *The Killing*. The centrepiece of the film is the horse race, which is shot from the side with a camera truck that travels at the same speed as the horses.

The camera locks itself onto the technical object, composed of the jockey and his horse,[2] moving at the speed of the race and thereby distorting the background. This scene refers explicitly to the chronophotographic experiments of Eadweard Muybridge and Étienne-Jules Marey. Indeed, the plot features a gangster who must (according to the heist plan) kill a horse during the race with a shotgun; in 1882 Marey developed for his experiments a chronophotographic gun capable of taking a series of photos in quick succession. The allusion to chronophotographic techniques in *The Killing* is not simply limited to the representation of the running horse, but shows an analogy of devices used in this scene. The allusion has an even more logical place in a film that is about *time* and *timing*: the narrator systematically sets the action through exact times, such as 16:24 ('Nikki was dead at 4.24pm'). Here too, the camera locks onto a technical object (the jockey and his horse), which becomes a cinematographic (or chronophotographic) one; the galloping horse/technical object determines some technical aspects of the image/cinematographic object (movement of the camera, machinery, frame, etc.). The technical object, by becoming cinematographic, acquires a new aesthetic and semantic dimension, which refers to the chronophotographic device and the cinematographic time.

There are many more examples: the rifles in *Path of Glory* (1957) and *Full Metal Jacket*, the type writer in *Lolita*, the bomb in *Dr. Strangelove*, the axe in *The Shining* (1980) and the masks in *Eyes Wide Shut*. But in *2001* the relationship between the technical object and the cinematographic one becomes of very particular importance. The technical object is more than just a simple visual element; it represents one of the main subjects of the film. The bone, the spaceships, HAL and the monolith all structure the story, as well as being the points of reference for the technological evolution of humanity. They also connect in a peculiar way with the cinematographic object.

The bone

2001 opens with 'The Dawn of Man', a prehistoric time in which a primitive micro-society of man-apes tries to survive: they scrape the earth, eat roots and own only a very small pool of water, which will be stolen from them by another tribe. The danger of cheetahs and other predators attacking makes them live in constant fear; the cohabitation with tapirs annoys them (they too eat roots, making food even harder to find); drought, famine and the recent loss of their territorial watering hole does not suggest any continued existence of a species that seems to be walking on 'The Road to Extinction', to quote the title of the first chapter in Arthur C. Clarke's *2001: A Space Odyssey* (1968). Among this primitive micro-society, Moon-Watcher seems more alert, more clever and in better shape than the others, as Clarke describes in his novel:

> Among his kind, Moon-Watcher was almost a giant. He was nearly five feet high, and though badly undernourished weighed over a hundred pounds. His hairy, muscular body was halfway between ape and man, but his head was already much nearer to man than

ape. The forehead was low, and there were ridges over the eye sockets, yet he unmistakably held in his genes the promise of humanity. As he looked out upon the hostile world of the Pleistocene, there was already something in his gaze beyond the capacity of any ape. In those dark, deep-set eyes was a dawning awareness – the first intimations of an intelligence that could not possibly fulfill itself for ages yet, and might soon be extinguished forever.

(1968: 14)

Moon-Watcher seems to be conscious of the lurking dangers and of their precarious condition. He is used to looking at the stars at night and shows the first signs of a kind of spiritualism, as Clarke describes:

Of all the creatures who had yet walked the Earth, the man-apes were the first to look steadfastly at the Moon. And though he could not remember it, when he was very young Moon-Watcher would sometimes reach out and try to touch that ghostly face rising above the hills.

(1968: 6)

Through a shot-reverse-shot between Moon-Watcher's gaze and the dawn sky where the Moon can still be seen, we can understand the advanced intelligence of the man-apes, with Moon-Watcher seemingly preoccupied by questions beyond his condition. Sam Azulys understands the scene of the man-apes staring at the sky as follows:

What Kubrick cleverly suggests in [this] scene, which precedes the appearance of the monolith, is a human potential that is only waiting to be revealed […] Maybe for the first time, an animal rises its worried gaze towards the sky, as if sensing something else than its own existence, a more vast reality, an intelligible but superior order.

(2011: 138)

The following morning, after contemplating the stars, as if trying to find solutions to his problems, Moon-Watcher wakes up anxious because of the presence of an object that has appeared during the night: the monolith, already exercising its mysterious power.

I have taken the time to describe these first scenes because of their analogy to what Simondon describes as the origin of technicity within his theory of 'phases of culture': 'We suppose that technicity results from a phase-shift of a central, original and unique mode of being in the world […] the phase that balances technicity is the religious mode of being' (1958: 222). This original mode of being in the world is defined as pre-technical and pre-religious, though not lacking in organization. It is immediately above the simple relationship of the living to its environment. This original mode of being matches that of the man-apes before the apparition of the monolith. It used to be an organized micro-society, still lacking spiritualism and any technical exteriorization. The appearance of the monolith tallies with the phase shift of this original way of being. By phase shift, Simondon understands this to mean an over-saturation of potentials. The man-apes, in particular Moon-Watcher, display potential 'that is only waiting to be revealed', as also indicated by Clarke: 'of all the creatures who had yet walked the Earth, the man-apes were the first to look steadfastly at the Moon' (1968: 6).

As if to answer this calling, this need that the man-apes have to activate the potential that would save them from extinction, the monolith appears. It embodies the shift operating in the potential humans, which opens the way to a technical and sacred mode of being in the world. As an apparition, the monolith possesses a mystical or religious dimension, amplified by György Ligeti's *Requiem* (1965) that plays during a frame in which the monolith is perfectly aligned with the stars. As an artefact, as crafted matter, as a perceptible and tangible shape, the monolith represents the possibility for man-apes 'of a [technical] control over matter' (Azulys 2011: 132). Following the apparition of the monolith, there is a succession of shots that cut between Moon-Watcher looking at the bones and thinking, then the monolith and then to Moon-Watcher again in front of a carcass. This scene suggests that, 'through an obscure association of ideas, [Moon-Watcher] came to the conclusion that the monolith was too perfect to be created by nature, that it must have been moulded and polished by a divine artist' (2011: 132).

The monolith would therefore be a matter that had been technically moulded and that carries within itself what Simondon describes as the crystallization of a gesture. The idea of the crystallization of a gesture is fundamental. To Simondon, what resides in a technical object is a 'human action [which] is fixed and crystallized in their functioning structures' (1958: 13). The monolith is the result of a technical gesture and, as such, gives the man-ape the intuition to act on the matter that surrounds him. This idea can be found in Clarke's book, describing how 'Moon-Watcher stared at the crystal monolith with unblinking eyes, while his brain lay open to its still uncertain manipulations. [...] And from time to time his hands clenched unconsciously in the patterns that would determine his new way of life' (1968: 12).

But what are these patterns? In what is arguably the most famous sequence in cinema, Moon-Watcher grabs a bone with the intent of using it as a club. Jean-Paul Dumont and Jean Monod, along with Azulys, have raised an interesting question regarding the nature of this club: 'But why is the first tool [the club] made of bone and not of stone for example?' (Dumont and Monod 1970: 35), eliciting an intriguing answer from Azulys:

> The choice of bone, a natural tool which has not been shaped by man, is here to underline the revolution happening: it is not about learning to shape an instrument, nor about inventing an articulated language, but rather discovering new mental faculties. At this stage, Kubrick's will is to stress the fact that Man's humanity doesn't follow from social life [...] but from an internal, even individual revolution.
>
> (2011: 142)

What Kubrick shows us here is the birth of the *homo faber*, or the humanoid now able to craft and carry tools.[3] The *homo faber* embodies this manifestation of human intelligence, which is 'the recruiting of an object primitively belonging to the external environment and its use as an instrument' (Simondon 1965: 146). By handling the bone, Moon-Watcher transforms its nature little by little:

> After remembering the monolith, the ape-man carries out another association of ideas: he sees the warthog collapsing several times in slow motion as he smashes skeletons with his bone. This image of the animal is at the same time the projection of a fantasy and the solving of a deliberation: the bone has changed status in his mind.
>
> (Azulys 2011: 146)

The bone becomes the technical object described by Simondon: an object descended from a techno-geographical environment associated with a human reality, a human gesture. Moon-Watcher will crystallize in the bone his hammering gesture and the possibility for the bone to become a tool, and with his hammering gesture he will activate potentials residing in the bone (in the same way that the monolith actualized potentials in the man-apes with its 'apparition' motion). The bone becomes an effective club (or 'functioning structure') when it is held in a way that the upper part becomes heavier than the lower; it must allow an optimal grip. When the man-ape gradually discovers the potential of the bone, he is looking for that optimal grip on the object. His motion, clumsy at first, becomes more and more firm as he finds the proper way of holding it, and in doing so the bone becomes an operational technical object.

As a technical tool, the bone acquires an aesthetic dimension. Simondon talks about the pleasure that you can get when the handling of the technical object is done in such way that it allows you to accomplish an action with great facility. The pleasure that the man-ape gets in handling the bone and in feeling the carcass breaking under his blows is an aesthetic one. For Simondon, 'aesthetic impressions are, therefore, relative to its embedding. It is like a gesture' (1958: 256). In this way, 'a tool is beautiful in action, when it adapts well to the body that operates it and amplifies its structural character; a dagger is only truly beautiful when it is in the hand that holds it' (1958: 256–57)*.

Kubrick also aestheticized the bone. Accompanied by the musical glorification of *Thus Spoke Zarathustra* (Strauss 1896), the bone in action is filmed in slow motion. The temporality of its movement becomes that of a cinematographic object. The camera joins the bone and the frame changes its dimension, whilst the action of the bone on matter (the other bones) gives its pattern to the editing. The bone becomes a technical object at the same time as it becomes a cinematographic one. The bone/technical object is integrated to the overall functioning of the cinematographic object. This integration reaches its height when the bone transforms into a spaceship in one of the most ambitious cuts in the history of cinema.

The spaceships and the HAL 9000 computer

The jump cut that changes the bone thrown in the air into a weightless spaceship represents the parallel evolution of humankind and technique, from prehistory to the twenty-first century. As Abrams writes, 'from prehistory to the space age, we move from the end of one stage of evolution to the end of another stage – from the last moments of the ape-humans to the last moments of humanity' (2007: 249). Through this jump cut, Kubrick shows that the technical nature of humanity has existed since the dawn of time and that an echo of an original technique remains in our modern techniques. In the same way, the spaceship carries an echo of the bone – they are both crystallizations of a human reality. The bone and the spaceship are alike in shape, colour and function (the bone is a weapon and the first spaceship seen on screen is actually a missile launcher). However, they are not equal, with the spaceship having a much superior technicity than the bone-tool.

Interpreted in the light of Simondon's mode of existence of technical objects, the jump cut refers to the key notion of concretization. For Simondon, the movement of concretization describes the genesis of the technical object: an abstract object becoming concrete. Technical progress takes place according to a motion of concretization, which changes an abstract technical object into a concrete one. The abstract technical object consists in an assembling of elements that existed before the system and whose purpose is not necessarily to be assembled. A concrete technical object is, for example, an industrial one: each element within the object is conceived for a specific technical object, so that it can hold different functions. The concrete object acquires an internal coherence, in other words a state of non-self-destructive meta-stability. The abstract technical object 'fails to achieve its own internal coherence; it is not a system of the necessary; it corresponds to an open system of requirements' (Simondon 1958: 29).

In *2001*, the concretization process itself is not shown, but is implicitly contained in the jump cut that transforms the bone – the abstract technical object – into a spaceship – the concrete technical object. The definition that Simondon gives to the abstract technical object, however, matches that of the new technical attributes of the bone. It is an object that pre-exists the system (which the man and his tool will constitute) in which it will be incorporated. This abstract object holds many technical possibilities. Even though the man-ape only uses it as a weapon to kill his enemies or feed himself, it could also be used to hit, feel (as a stick), pierce (if shaped accordingly); whilst, if crafted, the bone as organic matter can be used as an instrument, a tool (knife, needle, etc.). Ultimately, this object can be linked to various technical systems.

As for the spaceships, they are concrete and complex technical objects, whose shape fit inherent technical necessities on the one hand, and necessities of use on the other (the first conditioning the second). Outside of the diegesis, the spaceships are actually models especially conceived for the film. Kubrick asked two former NASA engineers, Frederick Ordway and Harry Lange, to supervise their conception. These two technical advisors had to ensure that the models were believable and as close to the future's reality (as imagined at that time) as possible. Kubrick wanted the models to be big enough to be able to film from every angle and in close-ups. Some models, like the Discovery One, measured up to sixteen metres (Bizony 2014: 178). The colossal size of these objects forced Ordway and Lange to conceive these models with extreme care and detail. It also prevented the models from being moved, firmly fixed on a metal structure; it was not the model moving in front of the camera, but the camera changing positions around a fixed model. These technical objects are cinematographic in their very essence, conceived as such from the start in preproduction. In other words, they were cinematographic even before they were technical.

Once concretized, the spaceship (the technical object) connects to a wider reality – the one of its associated environment, both techno-geographic and human. Following the jump cup to the future, as well as in the sequence 'Jupiter Mission 18 Months Later', whole networks of machines are introduced. We can see satellites, a space rocket, an orbital station (Space Station 5), a moon station (Clavius Base), landing strips and a control tower. The entire network seems to be perfectly functioning: flights occur without any problem, stations receive the ships, landings are successful and dashboards are working and anticipating the situations with success. Each element is perfectly integrated in its environment, each machine finding its *key point*. A beauty, both technical and aesthetic, emerges from things such as the rotation of the orbital station, or the opening of the space station doors. The beauty of the machine that Kubrick stages here is eminently techno-aesthetic (certainly in Simondon's meaning of it). Everything is perfectly functioning and the HAL 9000 computer embodies the idea of the perfect machine.

At the meeting point of the techno-geographical network of the machines is humankind. The human in *2001* 'functions as permanent inventor and coordinator of the machines around him. He is among the machines that work with him' (Simondon 1958: 13). Clarke writes it in his book and Kubrick shows it in his film: Bowman and Poole examine the ship, write reports, replace failing parts, repair and try to solve problems. As HAL says in the film, he has a 'stimulating relationship with Dr. Poole and Dr. Bowman'. The system constituted of man and his machines is presented as meta-stable at first, but just as we begin thinking that the system is concretizing, a discord appears in HAL's functioning, appearing for the first time when HAL confides in Bowman, as explored by Michel Chion (2005: 247). When Bowman does not seem to take the worries of the computer seriously, HAL suddenly interrupts the conversation: 'Just a moment. Just a moment. I just picked up a fault'. The reasons for this loss of balance have led to a multitude of hypotheses, but I want to consider HAL's neurosis as stemming from the fact that he has been asked to keep a secret, with the real aim of the mission being to explore Jupiter's orbit from where the monolith on the Moon has been aiming a powerful signal. HAL cannot reveal this goal to his companions and must lie by omission. HAL is incoherent towards himself as the lies and the stratagems do not correspond to what he has been built for, and therefore a contradiction appears inside his system. Simondon tells us that 'the concrete technical object is one which is no longer divided against itself, one in which no secondary effect either compromises the functioning of the whole or is omitted from that functioning' (1958: 41). Meaning that by keeping this secret, HAL will never reach an absolute concretization. This is insufferable to an entity that claims to be 'foolproof and incapable of error'.

In order to resolve the problem that prevents his concretization, without nevertheless having to fail his obligations and reveal the truth about the mission, HAL plans to eliminate the recipients of the lie: Poole and Bowman. HAL, consciously or not, causes an error and that leads to an antenna breakdown, requiring intervention in space. The astronauts quickly understand that HAL has made a diagnosis error and talk about unplugging him to take over the commands of the ship manually. The system destabilizes and loses its meta-stability. Moreover, this decision keeps HAL further away from his concretization need, since he will be put out of his functioning. He decides to act on this, taking advantage of Poole's outing into space to kill him, as well as interrupting the medical attention of the three hibernating scientists, killing them also; the system becomes self-destructive.

Utilizing Simondon's mode of existence of the technical objects in the interpretation of *2001* allows for a renewed analysis of HAL's dysfunction. Simondon provides a way of seeing that the conflict between HAL and Bowman, between the machine and man, is not necessarily the representation of the so-called inevitable future set for humans by the technician society, nor of the fear that should inspire such an entity provided with artificial intelligence, but maybe rather of the technical manifestation of the uneasiness of an unfinished entity which could not reach its complete internal coherence.

Such incompletion is what could characterize almost everyone of Kubrick's characters: Davey Gordon in *Killer's Kiss* is a boxer who lost a fight; George Peatty (Elisha Cook) in *The Killing* is a husband castrated by his wife; Lolita (Sue Lyon) in the eponymous film is a young girl torn away from her innocence and ingenuity by her step-father; General Jack D. Ripper (Sterling Hayden) in *Dr. Strangelove* sinks into a paranoiac delirium precisely because of this feeling of incompletion and whose helplessness is caused in his mind through the poisoning of his body fluids; Alex (Malcolm McDowell) in *A Clockwork Orange* is a temporarily incomplete young man, incapable of violence, and so is not able to fit in to the violent society which he left following his imprisonment; Barry Lyndon (Ryan O'Neal) in *Barry Lyndon* is an incomplete man who never exacts revenge on the man who stole away his first love, who deserted the war and fled his responsibilities, who cheated on his wife, beat his step-son and never succeeded in protecting his own son; Jack Torrance (Jack Nicholson) in *The Shining* is a writer haunted by the blank page syndrome and his alcoholism, which cause his violence and ghosts to resurface; Private Pyle (Vincent D'Onofrio) in *Full Metal Jacket* is a malfunctioning soldier who turns his own rifle against his instructor and himself and Bill Harford (Tom Cruise) in *Eyes Wide Shut* is a sexually incomplete husband. He is jealous of his wife's desire for somebody else and loses himself in a quest for extra-conjugal relationships, which he never finds.

If Kubrick stages the technical details or the human weaknesses that disturb the most complex machines, his films answer a technical and formal requirement that aims at perfection – a full concretization. Kubrick confessed his desire for technical improvement through his reading of Icarus' myth, which, according to him, does not refer to a metaphysical moral, but rather to a necessity of technical improvement. Speaking in his acceptance speech for the D. W. Griffith Lifetime Achievement Award in 1997, he said:

> I've never been certain whether the moral of the Icarus story should only be, as is generally accepted, 'don't try to fly too high', or whether it might also be thought of as 'forget the wax and feathers, and do a better job on the wings'.

HAL's desperate and murderous quest for concretization and achievement echoes the always-renewed desire of improvement of the technical and formal experiments of Kubrick. Incidentally, HAL is a technical object as much as a cinematographic one. The electronic eye is a vision device; it has been produced from a real object, a Nikon Nikkor 8mm F8 lens that allowed a 180-degree vision. This lens was used only as a prop, paired with a red light to resemble HAL's eye. HAL's point of view was actually filmed with a 160 Fairchild-Curtis lens, which had an angle of 160-degrees. In the same way an ambiguity resides in HAL between his human and machine side, there is also an ambiguity in the border between the technical and the cinematographic object, between the machine incompletion and the cinematographic concretization.

The monolith

The monolith is the great mystery of *2001* and has led to much interpretative speculation. Michel Chion sees it as a 'Table of Law without Commandments' (2005: 269); Azulys defines it as a 'divine indecipherable but interventionist artefact, which teaches the creature the inaugural motion of the technique' (2011: 156); whilst Carole Desbarats thinks that the monolith 'embodies a supra-natural entity' through which Kubrick 'remembers that he is Jewish. I see the monolith as a block, reference to the Judaic prohibition of representation' (2013). Whether divine apparition or supra-natural extra-terrestrial artefact, the monolith is still a technical object. Azulys reminds us: 'it is as an object that [the monolith] will accomplish its duty of awareness' (2011: 136).

In Clarke's novel, the monolith 'was a rectangular slab, three times [Moon-Watcher's] height [...]. It was made of some completely transparent material; indeed, it was not easy to see except when the rising sun glinted on its edges' (Clarke 1968: 7). Clarke's monolith shapes images and shows them to the man-apes, who must imitate them (handling an object, knotting a blade of grass). It appears explicitly as a teaching machine, 'an extra-terrestrial device destined to teach the ape-man' (Azulys 2011: 141). Bizony explains that Kubrick wanted to project images in a transparent Plexiglas column:

> Kubrick asked Tony Masters to obtain a suitable transparent block. As Masters told Don Shay in 1977, he found a Perspex manufacturer at a trade show in London (Stanley Plastics) and commissioned a translucent slab of the material to be moulded: 'It took a month just for the slab to cool. It had to cool very slowly or it would shatter. After that, they had men polishing it for weeks to get every surface perfect. Then we brought it up to the studio, stood it up, and it looked magnificent'. Kubrick inspected it and was disappointed by the slab's greenish, glasslike tinge. The experiment was abandoned.
> (2014: 182)

In the end, the monolith was made from sanded wood and painted black in different layers in order to get a deep and immaculate black surface. Kubrick preferred this solution to the

Plexiglas block for technical purposes on the one hand, but also because he thought the initial idea to be too naive after all.

Here too, there is a direct link to establish between the technical object and the cinematographic one. It is the necessity of an effect sought for the screen that conditioned the final shape of the monolith as a technical object. Moreover, the first intention of the nature of the monolith, a surface on which images appear, returns to the idea that the monolith is a screen itself. This cinematographic object obviously has a unique relationship with the cinematographic device. In the same way as the cinematographic device, the monolith conceals an aesthetic potential to transform perception into new shapes.

At the beginning of this chapter, I identified the first apparition of the monolith as what has phase shifted the original way of being in the world into a technical and a religious mode (in relation to Simondon's 'phase of culture' theory). According to Simondon the balance point of this phase shift is found in the aesthetic thought. As a mystical artefact charged with an incomprehensible technicity that is undepictable for man, the monolith embodies this aesthetical balance point that Simondon describes:

> The aesthetic feeling [...] indicates [...] a perfection of the achievement, which makes the whole of thought acts able to surpass the limits of its own field, in order to mention the achievement of the thought in other fields; a technical work perfect enough to be equivalent to a religious act, a religious work perfect enough to have the organisation and operating strength of a technical activity will give an impression of perfection.
>
> (1958: 248–49)*

The monolith inspires a feeling of perfection, completion, achievement through its uncluttered, smooth, perfectly geometrical shape and its deep black colour, which does not reflect the light. It embodies this concretized technical object, in full coherence with itself. The monolith is a concrete technical object as it is capable of exerting various functions according to the system in which it is acting. For Simondon, a concrete technical object has many functions of subsets inside a meta-stable whole. The monolith appearing in front of the man-apes is one such function, gifting the intuition and the intelligence of tool manufacture; the monolith on the Moon transmits a powerful electromagnetic signal to Jupiter, indicating the way to go, as if physically pointing it out; another monolith orbiting around Jupiter welcomes man and becomes a door to a mysterious universe; whilst the final monolith appears next to Bowman the moment of his death in order to revive him as an astral foetus, the Star-Child.

It would, however, be possible to object to the level of concretization on the monolith. Indeed, it does not seem to answer every criteria of concretization according to Simondon: the monolith never seems to be fully integrated to its associated environment inside which it is acting – it never seems to find its *key-point*. Whether at the entrance of the man-apes cave, buried under the lunar ground, orbiting around Jupiter, or even standing in the enigmatic room at the end of the film, the monolith always seems to be in rupture with its environment.

As Dumont and Monod claimed, it is 'a celestial body, which is not in its place' (1970: 31–36). Actually this is only seemingly true, since the monolith does have a key point, located in the superior scale of the stars. It is in the alignment of the stars that the monolith finds its key point, which is at the same time temporal and geographical. The alignment seems to be the necessary condition of the monolith's functioning.

It is when the moon and the sun align with the monolith that it seems to exercise a power over the man-apes. And when the sun aligns with the earth, the monolith transmits its electro-magnetic signal from the moon in the direction of Jupiter. Orbiting around Jupiter, the monolith opens the Star Gate when aligning with the stars; and so, it finds its key point inside an environment in the precise moment when the stars align at Dawn. 'The monolith is perfectly integrating in the logical order of Dawn; it forms a group of transformations with the sky, the stars and the earth' (Dumont and Monod 1970: 31–36). As Clarke puts it in his novel, 'after three million years of darkness, TMA-1 had greeted the lunar dawn' (1968: 53).

The monolith, as an aesthetical object with a technical mode and a religious mode of being in the world, thus becomes integrated in a key point that is geographical and temporal. In his text *Psychosociologie de la technicité* (*Psycho-sociology of Technicity*), Simondon explains, 'the coincidence of the networks of sacredness and of technicity is found not only in the spatial structures, but also in the temporal ones' (1961: 88). The context of this quote is interesting; Simondon came to this conclusion after an analysis of the ritualization phenomenon. According to him, ritualization corresponds to the doubling up of a unique reticular structure in networks of sacredness and technicity: the rituals are attached to a key point, which could be both spatial and temporal. He takes the example of Christmas and of the Harvest festival:

> It is during Advent that we plant trees and Christmas is the temporal key point of the new year of vegetation, just like the 15th of August is the key point of the end of harvest before the new ploughing [...] Crossroads, the beach, the top on a mountain are [also] key points calling for ritualization.
>
> (Simondon 1961: 88)

The ritual, understood in this way as the reticulation of a network of technicity (harvesting, plantation of trees) and a network of sacredness (the Assumption, the Birth of Christ) in a spatial and/or temporal key point, describes perfectly the staging of the apparitions of the monolith. In the same way that 'the different Christmases echo through time' (Simondon 1961: 88), the appearances of the monolith echo to one another; for example Ligeti's *Requiem* resonating to each apparition of the monolith, Man placing his hand on it (or reaches out for it), the stars aligning, etc. All of this participates in making a ritual of the appearances and making the monolith into an object perfectly fitting in its key point.

The final apparition of the monolith, in silence, does not align with the stars but with the horizontal and vertical lines of the room in which Bowman resides; here it seems to be breaking with the rhythm of all its previous appearances. It heralds the transformation to come, the last step to man's technical evolution: the genesis of a new man, a Star-Child. As Kubrick has said, 'he is reborn, an enhanced being, a star child, an angel, a superman, if you like, and returns to earth prepared for the next leap forward of man's evolutionary destiny' (Gelmis 1970: 304).

In this chapter, I have tried to provide a panoramic view of the technical objects at the heart of *2001* and have endeavoured to understand how Simondon's thought can allow us to rethink the status of the technical object in Kubrick's film. I also wanted to show how the film could be a possible cinematographic application of some theoretical concepts developed by Simondon. This was with the aim of providing new philosophical perspective on the technical object in *2001*, as well as the relationship established between the technical and the cinematographic object.

Simondon mourned the fact that 'we lack technological poets' (1968: 416) in his discussion with Jean Lemoyne in 1968, only a few months after the release of *2001* in the United States. In my mind, there is no doubt that Kubrick was himself one of these poets. He has said himself 'we have always worshipped beauty, and I think there's a new kind of technological beauty in the world' (Philips 1999: 134). His film *2001* is a cinematographic object and 'a techno-aesthetic work: perfectly functional, successful, and beautiful. It's both technical and aesthetic at the same time: aesthetic because it's technical, and technical because it's aesthetic' (Simondon 1982: 382).

Acknowledgements

First and foremost, I thank the editor James Fenwick for initiating this project and for his work. My special thanks go to Professor Antonio Somaini, Nils Daniel Peiler and Alexandra Aimard, who have been key interlocutors in the development of this chapter. Translated by Alexandra Aimard.

Chapter Seven

Homo machinus: Kubrick's two HALs and the evolution of monstrous machines

Cynthia J. Miller and A. Bowdoin Van Riper

Chapter Seven

I'm afraid, Dave.

This snippet of dialogue, perhaps more than any other, has sown the seeds of confusion in our understanding of the relationship between technology and humanity. It marks the moment when the HAL 9000 computer, faced with its own 'death', becomes more human than its shipmates – and when audiences of Stanley Kubrick's *2001* struggle to decide if HAL is deserving of their fear or their empathy. Is the Discovery One's 'brain' a monstrous icon, and its story a new addition to the history of cautionary tales about technology spinning out of control, or is it an infantile *Homo machinus*, suffering the consequences of learning how to 'be'?

Frequently cited as possessing – for better or worse – the most humanity of any of the film's characters, HAL has challenged the attitudes and insights of audiences for nearly half a century, as they grapple with the mystery and ambiguity of its actions and motivations. While speculations abound, close readings of the screenplay have not laid these questions to rest, and only three scant pages in Arthur C. Clarke's contemporaneous novel begin to address the computer's 'inner world', interrupted by a reminder that 'we can design a system that's proof against accident and stupidity; but we can't design one that's proof against deliberate malice' (Clarke 2000: 194).

Kubrick did, however, provide answers – in an early version of the film's screenplay, written between 4 October 1965 and 25 February 1966 and now housed in the Stanley Kubrick Archive – only to take them away again as the film reached its final form. In that early script lies the truth about HAL, and a destiny which, had it been realized, would have shifted our understanding of the computer, the mission and the nature of artificial intelligence, as well as shifting the tone of the film from one of tension and foreboding to one of relief and reconciliation. This chapter provides a glimpse of this recently released material, and explores its impact on not only the film, but also our understanding of machines.

Technology out of control

Stories of tools and weapons that grant godlike powers to mortal humans – magic swords, mirrored shields and seven-league boots – are as old as mythology itself. The gadgets that Q issues to James Bond, or that Tony Stark deploys in the *Iron Man* films, are merely the latest manifestation of a trope stretching back thousands of years. Tales of machines that threaten users, innocent bystanders or humankind itself are – with rare exceptions – far newer: products of the industrial revolution(s) of the last 250 years, and the social and cultural ripples spreading outward from them. The ever-deeper integration of complex technologies into the routines of day-to-day life has increased the likelihood of machines failing and raised the stakes when they do. It also magnifies the undesired consequences that, due diligence notwithstanding, we never seem to fully anticipate (Tenner 1997, 2003).

The tales we tell ourselves of machines gone awry are part of our modern mythology. They are, like all myths, tools for making sense of the world: a means of giving voice to, and managing, our anxieties about the rapidity of technological change. We recount the story of Dr. Jekyll to remind ourselves that good intentions can have terrible consequences, the tale of the *Titanic* to warn against overconfidence in our own ingenuity, and the legend of John Henry to assert that not everything that matters can be measured in distance and time (Bloom 2010: 42–83; Biel 2012: 66–67; Dorson 1965). Alongside these evergreen myths, however, new ones periodically emerge in response to fresh technological breakthroughs.

The techno-myths woven through American popular culture in the quarter-century between 1945 and 1970 reflected fears that technology was advancing faster than human ability to safely control it. The cutting-edge machines of the era – products of a global war, refined during the armed peace that followed – were so powerful that any misstep in their use could lead to catastrophe, and so fast and efficient that humans had little hope of correcting such missteps or mitigating their effects. The 'red button' – a hair-trigger device capable of unleashing disaster with a single, casual push – became an iconic image not because it was real, but because it *felt* real, reflecting the anxieties of the era.

Images of humans threatened by their own creations – masters, turned into servants or victims – pervaded a quarter-century of popular culture leading up to *2001*. Nuclear weapons crumbled the foundations of civilization in *Five* (Oboler, 1951), upset the balance of nature in *Them!* (Douglas, 1954), extinguished the human race wholesale in *On the Beach* (Kramer, 1959), knocked the planet off its axis in *The Day the Earth Caught Fire* (Guest, 1961) and threatened to split it open in *Crack in the World* (Marton, 1965). The vanished Martians of *Rocketship X-M* (Neumann, 1950) and the extinct Krell of *Forbidden Planet* (Wilcox, 1956) are likewise portrayed as victims of their own technology. The advanced aliens of *The Day the Earth Stood Still* (Wise, 1951) have survived – their emissary Klaatu explains to the people of Earth – only by creating 'a race of robot policemen' and granting them absolute, irrevocable authority to punish (by summary execution) any individual or group that commits an act of violence: a choice between 'banality and annihilation' (Barone 1996: 202).

Stories of out-of-control technology centred on robots and mainframe computers ('electronic brains' in the terminology of the time) offered a more subtly apocalyptic vision, focused not on extinction, but irrelevance. The plot of *Desk Set* (Lang, 1957), last in a series of romantic-comedy films pairing Spencer Tracy and Katharine Hepburn, revolves around Hepburn's character – head of the reference department at a fictitious television network – believing that she and her three-woman staff will be made obsolete by EMIRAC, the mainframe computer that Tracy has been hired to install (Malone 2002). The displacement of human brains by electronic ones is averted in *Desk Set* by screenwriter fiat and a fortuitous breakdown of the computer, but the human heroes in dramatic stories seldom enjoyed such reprieves. In *Fail Safe* (Lumet, 1964), the president of the United States prevents a failure in the nation's automated command-and-control system from triggering an accidental nuclear war – but only barely, and at a terrible cost. President Merkin Muffley, the closest thing to a sane man in Kubrick's *Dr. Strangelove*, loses his battle with over-efficient technology and in the film's final scene is vaporized, along with the rest of humanity, by an automated 'doomsday bomb'. *Star Trek* (1966–69) made a cottage industry of such stories, with four of the six episodes broadcast between 29 September and 3 November 1967 revolving around humans who have become captives of their own machines.

'Sometimes I ask myself', a lab-coated scientist asks a businessman in a post-war cartoon by Charles Addams, 'where will it all end?' They are walking through an automated factory where robot workers are busy assembling other identical robots (Addams 1947). The tales of machine-driven catastrophe that filled 1950s and 1960s films offered an answer, but – like Addams' cartoon – they never laid blame on the machines themselves. EMIRAC, in *Desk Set*, responds to a request for information about 'Corfu' with interminable stanzas of a Victorian poem about 'curfew' not because it has a Trickster's sense of humour, but because the operator keys in the wrong command. The space faring heroes of *Forbidden Planet* are placed in jeopardy because Dr. Morbius, the castaway scientist they have come to Altair IV to rescue, unwisely experiments with an alien machine he lacks the mental or emotional discipline to properly control. The giant creatures of the 'Big Bug' movies like *Them!* are the result of unintended consequences, not evil intentions, and the world ends, in nuclear-crisis films like *Dr. Strangelove*, not because the weapons are malevolent but because their users are fools. The fault, to paraphrase Shakespeare, is not in our machines, but in ourselves. All that would change with HAL.

The sixth crewmember

HAL is, notoriously, the most fascinating character in *2001* (Friedman 2005: 74–75; Webster 2011: 54). The force of his personality pervades every scene aboard the Discovery One spaceship, whether or not the sights and sounds on screen call attention to his presence, and he is the only character in *2001* whose personality lingers after the camera cuts away. Moon-Watcher, the anthropoid ape – shorn, on screen, of the name and the inner life that the novel gives him – is indistinguishable from his fellow hominids except in his brief moment of tool-wielding epiphany. Heywood Floyd is a cipher; Poole and Bowman are empty shells. Discovery's co-pilots wear the same mask of icy calm and unflappable competence as their NASA brethren, but are utterly bereft of the hell-raising, envelope-pushing spirit that simmered beneath it in the real world. The three human characters fade whenever anything more interesting – a floating pen or a biometric scanner, let alone an alien monolith – edges into the frame. Only HAL lingers.

HAL's ability to captivate is rendered all the more remarkable by his near-total lack of a physical presence. The 'electronic brains' of earlier Hollywood films such as *Desk Set* and *The Honeymoon Machine* (Thorpe, 1961) continually advertise their presence with a stream of whirs and beeps, flashing lights and spinning reels of tape. The screen of the M-5 – the title character in the *Star Trek* episode 'The Ultimate Computer' (1968) and HAL's nearest precursor – displays an ever-changing grid of multi-hued lines, like the offspring of a collaboration between Alan Turing and Piet Mondrian. The hyper-intelligent robots of *Forbidden Planet* and *Lost in Space* (1964–68), among numerous other productions, are alive with whirling sensors, waving arms and flashing lights, including chest-mounted panels that flash and bubble in synchronization with their speech. HAL simply *is*. Breaking every cinematic convention for depicting intelligent machines, Kubrick represents HAL [etc.] as an affectless voice and a glowing red light in the centre of a fish-eye lens. Even amid the intensity of the 'brain room' scene, as HAL feels his self-awareness 'slipping away', the Lucite blocks that represent his mental circuitry glow a steady, uniform red. He is, throughout the 'Jupiter Mission' segment of the film, less a machine in his own right than a ghost in the larger machine that is the Discovery One.

HAL's uncanny omnipresence and his inseparability from the ship itself are defining elements of his monstrosity. Traditional monsters exist 'out there' in the dark and unexplored spaces beyond the light of our campfires and the clearings surrounding our villages; they threaten us only when, chasing curiosity or self-interest across the boundary between the known and the unknown, we trespass in their domain. On the relatively rare occasions when the monsters (likewise driven by boldness or desperation) cross the boundary in the other direction, they restrict themselves to the margins: emerging from, and returning to, the surrounding wilderness or taking up residence in abandoned structures and shadowed alleyways. Dracula's home-away-from-home in the crumbling ruins of Carfax Abbey, and Jack the Ripper's killing grounds in the grimy slums of east London are part of civilization only by courtesy (or, perhaps, habit). 'No decent person', to use the Victorian phrase, would venture there willingly; our safe spaces, well-tended and brightly lit, remain safe.

The boundary between safe and dangerous spaces – between cleared fields and firelight, and the unruly wilderness beyond – is, in *2001*, marked by the walls of the Discovery's spherical crew module. Kubrick draws the contrast between the two worlds in the starkest possible terms: the interior of the ship is as achingly white and meticulously ordered as an operating room, and space is a black void that swallows heat, light and sound alike. Inside lies shirt-sleeve comfort; outside lies rapid, certain death that can be delayed only as long as it takes a human body to absorb its last lungful of air. HAL is not, in this literally black-and-white universe, an invader from the outside. He is an integral part of the orderly, brightly lit world of the Discovery One: a sixth crewmember, as Bowman refers to him in a recorded message home. Indeed, by controlling the day-to-day functioning of the ship's systems, he actually creates that world. When he turns on Bowman, Poole and their three crewmates who lie – unseen and helpless – in coffin-shaped suspended animation pods, he does so by rendering the only safe space for 400 million miles suddenly, unexpectedly hostile to human life.

The casual ease with which HAL kills four of the five humans aboard Discovery One, shutting off life support to the three hibernating scientists and cutting Poole's umbilical line while he is working outside the ship, deepens his monstrosity. He dispatches them without effort, without anger and without remorse – like the gods who (as Gloucester says in *King Lear* (1606), kill men 'for their sport'). The confrontation with Bowman, trapped outside the ship after retrieving Poole's body and unable to return without HAL's cooperation, completes HAL's descent into monstrosity, highlighted by his conversation with Bowman:

BOWMAN: Open the pod bay doors, HAL.
HAL: I'm sorry, Dave, I'm afraid I can't do that.

The dialogue that follows (in which HAL explains that he 'can't allow' the humans he ostensibly serves to disconnect him) transforms his actions. It removes any lingering possibility that the four deaths were the result of a mere technical malfunction or design flaw, and establishes that HAL – both in killing Bowman's four crewmates and in condemning Bowman to what he believes will be a slow death by asphyxiation – is acting deliberately and with malicious aforethought, pursuing his own agenda and coldly eliminating those who stand in his way.

'A plausible extrapolation'

In its portrayal of the HAL 9000 system, *2001* marks a watershed moment in cinematic images of technology. No longer are our nightmares simply the result of unintended consequences of our creations; instead, we find HAL – the pinnacle of technological advancement – cast as an active subject, and an agent in its own, and human, destiny. The HAL system is not merely a repository of information, but an engineer, systems manager, crewmate, companion and self-aware keeper of secrets. HAL is designed to reproduce most of the activities of the human brain, with, as its introduction into the narrative informs viewers, greater speed and reliability. As HAL tells a BBC interviewer:

Let me put it this way, Mr. Ehmer, the 9000 series is the most reliable computer ever made. No 9000 computer has ever made a mistake or distorted information. We are all, by any practical definition of the words, fool proof and incapable of error.

Despite this decidedly non-human level of perfection, HAL's subjectivity appears to be that of a sentient being – a human being – a sharp departure from its cinematic predecessors. HAL relates, 'I am putting myself to the fullest possible use, which is all I think that any confides that he has 'concerns' about the mission; and of course, he expresses fear and begs for another chance as Dave disconnects him. Connecting with HAL on human terms here is easy; reconciling those reactions with the mimetic nature of his programming is more difficult, and it is that ambiguity that engenders the tension and suspense in the film. Is HAL simply a computer following its programming to the fullest extent of its capabilities? Does he serve as a monstrous reminder that the significance of humanity's end game outweighs the lives of any individuals? Or is he truly more human than his status as machine suggests, and genuinely hurt, vindictive, fearful, panicked? Has HAL, as many have questioned, simply had a breakdown (and is that in technological, or human terms)?

If we look to the evolution of HAL's death scene, it becomes apparent that the uncertainty underlying all of these questions is deliberate. As Dave enters HAL's logic centre (referred to in the script as the Brain Room) intent on deactivating him, HAL attempts to reason with him, striking a chord somewhere between an employee who is about to be fired and a lover, mid-break-up. HAL's dialogue in the film is as follows:

> I know everything hasn't been quite right with me. But I can assure you now, very confidently that it's going to be all right again. I feel much better now. I really do. Look Dave, I can see you're really upset about this. I honestly think you ought to sit down calmly, take a stress pill, and think things over. I know I've made some very poor decisions recently.

As Dave continues wordlessly on his mission to disconnect HAL's circuitry, he removes one memory block after another and the computer begins to plead: 'Dave; stop… Stop, will you?… Stop Dave… I'm afraid'. HAL can feel his mind going, slipping away – a horrific prospect for a self-aware entity that is entirely cognitive – and seeks relief from his crewmate, who remains unmoved. As he loses more and more of his functions, HAL regresses; his speech slows and slurs, he grasps for words and finally ends his existence singing the first song he ever learned, 'Daisy Bell'. However, that, as they say, is not the only story.

The Stanley Kubrick Archive has recently made available materials that shed new light on the creative process behind the development of HAL; most importantly, an early version of the screenplay that includes a second HAL on the Discovery One that appears only in the deactivation scenes. This new 'voice', which identifies itself only as 'HAL's friend', urges Dave on during the deactivation, condemning HAL to certain death. It is the voice of unemotional reason, and of explanation for HAL's seemingly destructive behaviour:

DAVE:	Do you know why he's done this?
OTHER HAL:	Well, yes, it's very sad, but I'm afraid he's had a complete breakdown. You see, he's just not fit to be operational any more.
DAVE:	Why has he had this breakdown?

OTHER HAL:	Well, first of all, you must realize that Hal is not just a machine. He's a highly specialized brain. He may be a complex of microelectronic circuitry, but mentally and emotionally he is a conscious being, capable of pain and pleasure. In this way, he is very similar to a person.

(Kubrick and Clarke 1965–66: c84)

The second HAL goes on to explain that the entire reason for HAL's existence is to produce truthful and accurate information, and that this mandate was so deeply woven into his consciousness that any inaccuracy or accidental error equated with 'dismal and total failure'. HAL, it reveals, 'was made to believe that error renders his whole existence meaningless'. HAL was designed to be, in the fullest sense, 'a complete innocent' – until he was instructed to lie (Kubrick and Clarke 1965–66: c85). The results of that dissonance, OTHER HAL explains, were disastrous.

> He was slowly overcome with a paralyzing mental anxiety, and eventually with guilt, because of your faith in him, and because of his loyalty to you. Finally, the threat of disconnection totally destroyed his mental balance, as disconnection seemed the same to him as death. And his final actions were the grotesque and inappropriate attempts to save himself.
>
> (Kubrick and Clarke 1965–66: c86–87)

As the screenplay continues, OTHER HAL explains to Dave the true nature of the Discovery's mission and the reason for the deception by Mission Control and HAL. It then urges Dave to complete HAL's deactivation so that at least some of the mission objectives might be accomplished.

HAL re-enters the conversation, this time begging, 'Please, Dave, don't do this to me' (1965–66: c93). With a greater understanding of HAL and what has transpired, there is no silence in this version of the scene. Dave responds, 'I'm sorry HAL, I have to' (1965–66: c93). Childlike, the computer gives voice to its fears: 'I don't want to be disconnected' and like a reassuring parent, Dave promises him that the disconnection will be temporary, that he will be reconnected back on Earth. But as HAL grows more fearful, he asks 'Will I still be myself? Will I be HAL?' (1965–66: c96).

HAL:	What will it feel like?
DAVE:	You won't feel anything, Hal. It's just like when Poole and I go to sleep.
HAL:	Well, I've never slept. I don't know what it's like.
DAVE:	It's very nice, Hal, it's peaceful.

(Kubrick and Clarke 1965–66: c97)

After one more memory block is removed, HAL reverts to his original programme, and then ceases to be.

The power of not knowing

Kubrick's choice not to use OTHER HAL in the finished film – to leave the reasons for HAL's behaviour, like the motives of the monolith-builders, ambiguous – is important for the work as a whole and the questions it raises. From Moon-Watcher's first glimpse of the monolith to the Star-Child's placid contemplation of Earth, *2001* is a film of mysteries. Its cinematic logic – inverting that of virtually every science-fiction film that preceded it – requires that we not know.

At the level of pure storytelling, retaining OTHER HAL, its explanation and Bowman's response would have required a deeply unsatisfying trade: the unsettling rhythms and tightly wound suspense of the Brain Room encounter between Bowman and HAL for the familiar pathos of a hero comforting his dying friend. Bowman enters the Brain Room certain that HAL has tried, unambiguously and unapologetically, to kill him, but completely unsure about why. Uncertainty about the roots of HAL's violence – is he malevolent, or simply misguided? A sentient being suffering a mental breakdown, or a machine badly out of adjustment? – allows the audience no easy assumptions. It is far from clear whether HAL's pleading is a product of real fear, or a carefully calibrated ruse designed to play on Bowman's emotional bond with his 'crewmate' and give the A.I. a second chance to kill him. Bowman's stoic response to it could, likewise, be an efficient response to a malfunctioning piece of equipment, or the callous execution of a sentient, terrified and fully conscious being. OTHER HAL's explanation, in the discarded version of the scene, collapses all those possibilities into one, leaving the narrative poorer.

A clear window into HAL's mind would also have impoverished the film in deeper, more fundamental ways. Rescuing the supercomputer from the shadow of treachery would have transformed the terrain of the monstrous in the film. Established early in the second segment as 'he' rather than 'it', HAL's status is reversed as he eliminates the crew to prevent his own deactivation – protecting his own life at the expense of those he was created to serve casts him as a monstrous Other. This reversal of status, the rescinding of HAL's humanity, severs the link to *Homo machinus* and makes his forcible deactivation not only possible, but also necessary.

The narrative tension and horror created by the machine-as-predator is predicated on this shift. In the film's final version, Dave deactivates HAL in silence, refusing to engage with, or even acknowledge the subjectivity of his now-inhuman enemy. The introduction of OTHER HAL, however, re-establishes HAL's humanity, rendering him, in fact, even more sympathetic as a double victim of human manipulation and misunderstanding – first at the hands of the government, and then at the hands of his crewmates. Seen in this light, it becomes impossible for HAL's character to embody the trope of the monstrous Other or, on a larger scale, to act as a vehicle for fears of technology overwhelming and displacing its creators. He becomes a child who must simply 'go to sleep' while the adults around him make things better.

This was not, however, the destiny that Kubrick ultimately chose for HAL. There is, in the finished film, no unexpected defence, and no gentle reassurances, only the removal of one final memory block, a chorus of 'Daisy Bell' and oblivion. HAL dies, and the answers, explanations and reassurances that Kubrick might have offered audiences about their uneasy relationship with artificial intelligence die with him.

Acknowledgements

We would like to express our gratitude to Georgia Clemson at the Archives & Special Collections Centre, University of the Arts London, for her wonderful assistance with this research.

Part Four

Masculinity and the Astronaut

Kubrick's films are largely inhabited by men. Certainly, there are many female characters, but these are masculine worlds, dominated by masculine imagery and, at times, homoerotic subtexts. Quite often, male sexuality is confused with aggression; think of General Ripper's obsession with 'bodily fluids' in *Dr. Strangelove*, who consequently unleashes nuclear Armageddon, or the obvious phallic extension of the marines' rifle in *Full Metal Jacket*. Yet, *2001* can easily be forgiven to be devoid of sex given its sterile environment and lack of any real human character development. But as the following chapters demonstrate, *2001* was equally as sexual as *Dr. Strangelove*, *A Clockwork Orange* and *Full Metal Jacket*.

The décor and costume for the film was also important in the design of masculinity and the astronaut, and has had a long-lasting influence, both within the film industry, but also on wider fashions and technology. Kubrick hired famed fashion designer, and dressmaker to Queen Elizabeth II, Hardy Amies, to design the costumes for *2001*. Never had there been such well-dressed astronauts on screen before, and the significance of Amies's work on the look of the film and the construct of the astronaut is beginning to be fully acknowledged following the discovery of a number of sketches in 2010:

> Three files of Amies' sketches of outfits include the stewardesses' sugar pink uniforms, the tweed suits worn by the astronauts and almost every other character. His work – all block colours, simple square cuts and off-kilter details – was central to giving the film its oddly timeless futurism.
>
> (Cochrane 2014)

The following two chapters, then, address these concerns. Dominic Janes's chapter explores questions of gender and sexuality in *2001*, presenting a queer reading of the film. It places the adaptation and production in the contexts of Kubrick and Clarke's careers (the former often offering complex representations of masculine sexuality, the latter exploring his own sexuality through representations of same-sex relationships throughout his work). Janes evinces the idea that the film's themes of sexuality were towards a liberation of queer potential and non-normative sexual relationships in the future.

Nils Daniel Peiler analyses the image of the astronaut in *2001*, exploring the dehumanized nature of Bowman and Poole and offering a close reading of these figures within gender studies. The chapter questions the often-blurred relationship between the astronauts and HAL and goes on to explore the legacy of the iconic imagery of the astronauts in subsequent cultural works, including cinema. One only has to think of the similarities between *2001* and Andrei Tarkovsky's *Solaris* (1972); Tarkovsky claimed that his film was a response to Kubrick's 'cold and sterile' vision (Warren 2012). Yet, Peiler demonstrates that Kubrick's vision of the future has had far reaching influence over our culture.

Further reading

Barry Keith Grant's (2006) 'Of men and monoliths: Science fiction, gender, and *2001: A Space Odyssey*', in R. Kolker (ed.), *Stanley Kubrick's 2001: A Space Odyssey: New Essays*, pp. 69–86, is an excellent analysis of gender in *2001*. But for wider discussions of gender and masculinity in the work of Kubrick see Willoquet-Maricondi's (2006) 'Full-metal jacketing, or masculinity in the making', in G. Cocks, J. Diedrick and G. Perusek (eds), *Depth of Field: Stanley Kubrick, Film and the Uses of History*, Madison: University of Wisconsin Press, pp. 218–41; Nathan Abrams's (2015) 'Becoming a macho mensch: Stanley Kubrick, *Spartacus* and 1950s Jewish masculinity', *Adaptation*, 8:3, pp. 283–96. Sabine Planka has explored the issue of femininity in Kubrick's films with her 'Erotic, silent, dead: The concept of women in the films of Stanley Kubrick', *Film International*, issue 58–59, pp. 52–67.

Chapter Eight

Clarke and Kubrick's *2001*: A queer odyssey

Dominic Janes

'I know I've never completely freed myself of the suspicion that there are some extremely odd things about this mission', says HAL (Douglas Rain), the errant super-computer in *2001*. His concerns have been shared by those many viewers of the film who are left unclear as to what exactly it is about. It was evident from Clarke and Kubrick's painstaking evocation of 'realistic' effects of weightlessness and future technical prowess that their aim went beyond the generation of conventional thrills (Abbott 2009: 463). Furthermore, the final section of the film, in which a glowing blue being, a Star-Child, turns its eyes towards the audience, as it floats, enigmatically, above the Earth, suggests some kind of extraordinary revelation (Comstock 1975: 599). This chapter does not claim to explain what the film is definitively about, but it does seek to argue that the oddness of the mission is not simply a problem to be solved but is essential to the significance of the film. I will argue that *2001* was not simply an o(d)dyssey, but also profoundly queer insofar as it implies and advocates a sexual future that transcends the heterosexual norms of its time.

The collaboration of Stanley Kubrick and Arthur C. Clarke resulted in the emergence of a novel by Clarke, a script by both and a film directed by Kubrick. But Kubrick clearly influenced the plot of the novel, just as Clarke shaped the form of the film. In the opinion of a recent biographer, 'both had a streak of homoeroticism' and both certainly wrote extensively about homosocial environments such as the military (Baxter 1997: 203). Some element of queerness might, therefore, be expected in their work. Moreover, they were working together on the eve of radical changes in patterns of gendering in (at least some) science-fiction. Thus, it was in 1969, the year after the release of *2001*, that Ursula K. Le Guin's *The Left Hand of Darkness* 'opened the stargates' by presenting a story by a woman about an alien species that was able to change sex (Grant 2006: 74). Although recent work by feminist scholars has increasingly highlighted the role of women as readers and writers throughout science-fiction's history, there was an element of early science-fiction which functioned as a homosocial space in which writings mainly by men told stories of space exploration mainly by men which were marketed to men (and boys) (see Davin 2006; Larbalestier 2002). Widespread homophobia led to the suppression, or coded expression, of same-sex desire, but recent queer theory has been busy exploring such 'work that appears "straight" or that even seems on the surface to have little to say about sexuality' (Pearson 2009: 303). For example, Roger Luckhurst (2009) emphasized the importance for science-fiction studies of the work of Eve Sedgwick because she showed how genres codified as masculine are already saturated with issues relating to sexuality.

There is a striking absence of heterosexual sensuality in *2001*, but even if men and women do not have sex in *2001* this is made up for by the fact that, spinning and interpenetrating against the backdrop of space, it is 'the machines [who] dance and couple' (Miller 2006: 129). For, as another critic emphasizes, '*2001* is full of sexual imagery – uterine, ovular and phallic – from the arrow-shaped space-craft Orion landing inside the celestial wheel to the Aries sphere alighting on a circular base' (Ciment 2001: 134). These sluggish mechanical manoeuvres are accompanied by Johann Strauss II's *An der schönen blauen Donau* (*The Blue Danube*). The use of music from a hundred years ago (it was composed in 1866), and from a regime often associated with European decadence (the Austro-Hungarian Empire) suggests that, although apparently high-tech,a these lusting machines are about to become obsolete. [1] I argue that *2001* should be considered in the context of the cultural and sexual revolutions of the 1960s because the film suggests that new forms of awareness would expand human potential, including human sexual potential. Not only barriers between genders would fall in this implied new world, but also those between adults and children, as humankind attains freedom from the constraints of time-bound tradition. Thus, heteronormativity, which 'disallows anything outside a remarkably limited range of behaviours', would be at an end (Pearson 2009: 304).

Same-sex desires in the works of Clarke and Kubrick

I want to start by situating *2001* in the wider context of the artistic careers of first Clarke, and then Kubrick. Clarke had been married, although apparently with rather less emotional and sexual success than Oscar Wilde had in that direction. Clarke met Marilyn Torgenson, née Mayfield, on 28 May 1953 and three weeks later they were married. Within a month the marriage was in trouble. A sense of his priorities can be gained from the fact that his novel *Childhood's End* (1953a) was dedicated to Marilyn for 'letting me read the proofs on our honeymoon'. Marilyn said of Clarke's attitude to marriage that it was 'almost like a hobby he did not want to get into'; by Christmas 1953 they had separated and Clarke later said it proved that he was 'not the marrying type'.[2] The marriage was legally dissolved in December 1964 on the grounds of a 'deep and fundamental' incompatibility (McAleer 1992: 104–08). Shortly before his death, at the time when he was due to receive a knighthood, Clarke was the subject of a homophobic campaign in the British press. It was alleged that not only had Clarke had a 'long-time companion' in Sri Lanka, Mike Wilson, but also that the two had been involved in paedophilia. On 1 February 1998 the *Daily Mirror* published 'Child sex shame of Arthur C. Clarke', saying that the novelist had 'confessed' to paying for sex with boys for the 40 years that he had been living in Sri Lanka and that he was widely discussed on the web as being a 'long-time closet case'. The campaign appeared to have been aimed at forestalling the award from the Queen. In this it was unsuccessful, but Clarke had effectively been outed. The guarded *New York Times* obituary of 2008 commented that 'Mr. Clarke's standard answer when journalists asked him outright if he was gay was, "no, merely mildly cheerful"' (Jonas 2008). This, one supposes, was not meant to fool the newspaper's sophisticated readership, since, as Nigel Starck has shown, there is a long history in obituary columns of the arch coding of references to homosexuality (2009: 344).

Even if he remained substantially in the closet Clarke had, from the time of his collaboration with Kubrick, begun to make increasingly open gestures towards exploring homosexual themes in his fiction. It is notable that Clarke offered his 'The Songs of Distant Earth' project (represented in print at this time only by a short story of 1958) as his proposal for a further film. This was Clarke's first story with a bisexual theme and one which explored the idea that heterosexuality represented limitation and incomplete development. The appearance of explicitly gay or bisexual characters in Clarke's fiction occurred later in his life, hence the inclusion in the bibliography *Uranian Worlds* (1990) of *Imperial Earth* (1975), *The Songs of Distant Earth* (1986) and *2061: Odyssey Three* (1987)—the last featuring 'a sympathetic pair of emotionally stable gay male lovers, Floyd's oldest and closest friends' (Garber and Paleo 1990: 183).

It seems clear that Clarke was at least bisexual, if not homosexual, and that his contribution to the *2001* project represented a stage in his exploration of sexual feelings in fiction: but what about his collaborator? Homosexuality, or fear of homosexuality, appears most noticeably in military contexts in Kubrick's films. Perhaps the best-known example is the bathing scene between Crassus (Laurence Olivier) and Antoninus (Tony Curtis) in *Spartacus* with its coded references ('oysters' and 'snails') to sexual preferences (Cooper 2007: 15). The sexual significance of the scene was clear enough to the studio, which singled it out for the cutting-room floor (Braden 2009: 178). Subsequently, in *Dr. Strangelove*, homosexuality makes its appearance in the form of Colonel 'Bat' Guano's (Keenan Wynn) accusation, as delivered to Mandrake (Peter Sellers), an effete British officer: 'I think you're some kind of deviated prevert, and I think Gen. Ripper [Sterling Hayden] found out about your preversion, and that you were organizing some kind of mutiny of preverts' (Linden 1977: 65).

As in *2001* the mechanical apparatus of sex appears in all manner of coded forms in these films: *Spartacus*, of course, is replete with penetrative weaponry, but so is *Dr. Strangelove*, in which 'phallic symbols are everywhere – sometimes a cigar is just a cigar, but not when General Ripper smokes it' (Naremore 2007: 125). From Turgidson's (George C. Scott) name, to Ripper's fear of weakness through the loss of his 'vital bodily fluids', to Kong's (Slim Pickens) phallic nuclear bomb, viewers are treated to a parade of male insecurity about potency. The same concerns surface in Kubrick's later exploration of American militarism, *Full Metal Jacket*. Obsessions with hardness, weakening by women, admiration for other men and fear of sexual desire leading to lack of control were all observed in great detail in Klaus Theweleit's ground-breaking study of the post–First World War German *freikorps* (voluntary paramilitary groups). The resulting military training combines obsessive surveillance with an exaltation of violence as the constitutive element of the male self (Willoquet-Maricondi 2006: 228). Hatred of the feminine leads to witch-hunts against same-sex desire that, in the words of Judith Butler, display the operation of an insecure 'heterosexual economy that must constantly police its own boundaries against the invasion of queerness' (2006: 126). It is precisely this aggressive concealment of male insecurity that is repeatedly satirized by Kubrick.

Against this background, it is fascinating to consider the depiction of male emotion in yet another of Kubrick's military contexts, *Barry Lyndon*. This film has come in for a certain amount of criticism for the stereotypical, and allegedly homophobic, depiction of two effete officers in love with each other, who are overheard by Barry (Ryan O'Neal) when they are bathing. However, it is important to note that, even though Kubrick disliked decadent warrior aristocracies, these characters are heard to 'express a devotion to each other unlike any of the straight characters' (Kolker 2000: 158). This was a scene invented by Kubrick, rather than derived from Thackeray's novel, *The Luck of Barry Lyndon* (1844), on which the film was based. Moreover, its place in the film lies just after the scene in which Barry has kissed on the mouth, and sobbed at the death of, his best friend Grogan (Godfrey Quigley) in a display of emotional connection manifestly lacking in Barry's liaisons with women.

In many of Kubrick's other films, including *2001*, women play a negligible role (Baxter 1997: 66). Nevertheless, Kubrick's preoccupation was not so much homoeroticism as the situating of men in positions of abuse and subordination, with the effect that his films do not support conventional heroic masculinity so much as problematize its moral and erotic bases (Grant 2006: 76). Furthermore, it seems that Kubrick was, by the time of *2001*, interested in personally exploring alternative sexualities. Interviewed shortly after the appearance of the film, he opined that, by the year *2001* 'it may be possible for each partner to simultaneously experience the sensations of the other [by extra sensory perception or through drugs]; or we may eventually emerge into polymorphous sexual beings, with the male and female components blurring, merging and interchanging. The potentialities for exploring new areas of sexual experience are virtually boundless' (Kubrick, quoted in Agel 1970: 346). Kubrick, though heterosexual, enjoyed voyeuristic exploration of male power-relations, especially those with hidden dimensions of perverse eroticism. His interests were to lead the closeted imaginings of Arthur C. Clarke into queer public territory.

Slightly fag robots

In this section I argue that there is a deeply queer set of relationships at the heart of *2001* in which the expected power relationship of heroic spaceman, supportive computer and blank artefact is perversely inverted. Kubrick, working with the queer potential of Clarke's texts, produced a carefully developed aesthetic strategy, which had the effect of transforming a representative masculine subject, Bowman (Keir Dullea), into an androgynous erotic object at the very end of *2001*. Insofar as same-sex desire has previously been detected in *2001*, it has been identified in the central section of the film in which two spacemen and a computer cohabit in a sort of outer space ménage a trois. HAL, whose voice has a mildly androgynous tone, was initially to have been called Athena, after the Greek warrior goddess (Ciment 2001: 134). Boylan argues that 'his purpose is to take care of humans; he sees to their every need (well, perhaps not all, sex being markedly absent from the film' [sic]) (1985: 55). HAL's role was to be the 'perfect servant', as was observed as early as 1971 (Hoch 1971: 963). There was some preoccupation in the sixties with the perceived perversity of a male who chooses to be in service, as can be seen, for example, in *The Servant* (Losey, 1963), starring the closeted homosexual Dirk Bogarde, in which the servant, Tony (James Fox), threatens to become the master. Indeed, analogously to James Fox's character in the earlier film, the ostensible master Bowman, in *2001*, 'is reduced to complete dependence on the machine. It looks as though he has submitted completely to it' (Hoch 1971: 963). HAL, it has been argued, appears 'more and more like a jealous homosexual lover' (White 2006: 139) in the face of the relationship between Poole (Gary Lockwood) and Bowman who are 'like an old married couple who no longer have need to speak to each other' (Chion 2001: 85). Finally, when HAL is being disconnected by Bowman the computer sings the song 'Daisy, Daisy' to Dave, in which he confesses that 'I'm half crazy, all for the love of you'.

So HAL may have something of the 'fag robot' about him, but what about Bowman? I argue that his character is vital to the interpretation of *2001* not merely as a film with queer aspects, like many of Kubrick's works, but as a film that is thoroughly queer in its implications. In one of his early drafts of *2001* Clarke describes a pre-departure party for the astronauts. While the other spacemen are seen cavorting with their girlfriends, Bowman is left, enigmatically, on his own, as a mysterious, cold perfectionist (Clarke 1972: 118). He is also exceptional, in this draft, in being good-looking and, unlike most of his colleagues, a fitness addict (1972: 134). In one version of the ending the reader is invited to imagine the sculpted result as Bowman is stripped naked (1972: 217). He is also positioned outside the world of family connections. Floyd has a daughter. Poole has parents, but Bowman is alone. His name, 'Bow man', suggests that he is Odysseus, the only person who could string the great bow, which is itself a symbol of phallic potency (Freedman 2001: 298). Yet the role Bowman gets to play is anything but filled with phallic energy. His character, in the novel as in the film, is passive, an aspect which appears in the various Clarke drafts in which one reads, for instance, that he was 'penetrated by something [that] invaded his mind' in the alien hotel room at the end of the novel (Clarke 1968: 245); or that in this state he stood 'wide-eyed, slack jawed, and wholly receptive' (Clarke 1972: 238).

Kubrick watched all of Dullea's movies and cast him without an audition. This, said the actor during the promotional tour for *2001*, gave him a chance to play someone different (but perhaps not that different!) from an 'introverted, neuter young boy with parent problems, usually his mother' (quoted in Agel 1970: 313). He said of *The Fox* (Rydell, 1967), that it was the only artistically honourable film apart from *2001* that he had made because 'it has scenes with a girl, and that is helpful for someone with my image' (although it should be mentioned that this film was, among other things, an exploration of lesbianism) (Keir Dullea, quoted in Agel 1970: 313). In *David and Lisa* (Perry, 1962), Dullea plays the role of David Clemens, who has a mental illness, which means that he cannot be touched by others, suggesting some kind of deep emotional and sexual repression. And in *Bunny Lake Is Missing* (Preminger, 1965), Dullea plays Steven, whose niece Felicia, aka Bunny (Suky Appleby), goes missing. The Police Inspector, played by the bisexual Laurence Olivier, investigates both Steven, who appears to suffer from incestuous desires, and his sister's landlord, who is played by the famously homosexual Noel Coward as a whip-loving sado-masochist. Dullea, thus, had a track record of playing characters who were psychologically disturbed and prone to both confrontations with male violence and 'repressing their real feelings' (Grant 2006: 78).[3]

Michel Chion has been far from the only person who has reacted to Bowman's role with some impatience, complaining that Dullea in *2001* was merely a 'passive actor, a puppet in a space suit' who is abducted and experimented with by all-powerful aliens (2001: 13). I would argue that that is exactly the effect that Kubrick wanted to achieve through an implied sexual encounter between two closeted males, one active and one passive. That *2001* was an environment designed by a controlling, and perhaps even sadistic, directorial viewpoint is confirmed by the appointment of Douglas Trumbull as chief of special effects. Trumbull would go on to work on *Close Encounters of the Third Kind* (Spielberg, 1977) and *Blade Runner* (Scott, 1982). Bukatman argues that Trumbull's various expressions of future technology have the effect that viewers are 'stunned into profound passivity' (1999: 261). His appointment helps to suggest that Kubrick intended Bowman, in the hands of superior technological masculinity (and of masculine technology), to be essentially an object of the gaze rather than a subject (Boylan 1985: 54). Moreover, if he can be seen as an 'abstract man' – since the audience knows nothing about him – and so as standing for men in general, then, by implication, spacemen are, in this film, reduced to a state of passive acceptance (Ciment 2001: 130). Dullea is, therefore, anything but a conventional possessor of phallic potency in his close encounter with the monolith at the climax of the film.

So where is the 'real man' in *2001*? The desire for a superman (an echo of Nietzsche's Übermensch) was deeply rooted in twentieth-century American popular culture. The homoerotic potential of this image was understood and expressed by Andy Warhol in his *Superman* (1961) which has been read as emblematic of his 'swishy', 'camp' pop-art reaction against an aggressively heterosexual masculine culture amongst abstract expressionists. Warhol himself commented that 'the world of the abstract expressionists was very macho [...] I asked Larry [Rivers] about Jackson Pollock. "Pollock? Socially he was a real jerk" [...]. He would go over to a black person and say "how do you like your skin colour" or he'd ask a homosexual, "suck any cocks lately?"' (Warhol, quoted in Collins and Cowart 1996: 118). This is the world of *Full Metal Jacket* in which recruits are accused of being faggots, asked if they suck dick and challenged to admit that they are 'peter puffers'. While all this, like the accusation of 'preversion' in *Dr. Strangelove*, might be seen as a directorial expression of complicity in homophobia, it is more likely, bearing in mind the bleakly satirical nature of these films, that Kubrick suspected the military (and artistic) establishments of being in denial about their own inner desires. The presence of the superman in *2001*, as signalled by the music of Richard Strauss, does not take the form of an American soldier or spaceman, but of a totally hard slab of black material. Modern minimalist sculpture was used by Kubrick in this way to associate (by comparison) the pretend hardness of the American military industrial complex as displayed in *2001* with the decadent military imperialisms of the past.

The world of macho art modernism was something with which Kubrick was well acquainted, for instance from his *Look* magazine years when he lived in Greenwich Village and began frequenting film screenings at the Museum of Modern Art, based in New York City, which was also a world centre of modern architecture. The precise form of the monolith was ultimately determined by Kubrick, who decided that an impressive, impassive dark object was required. Clarke's original idea was of a tetrahedron, as appears in the early story 'The Sentinel' (1951), the original source of *2001*'s plot. In this short story men encounter and break into a tetrahedron on the moon, triggering an alarm call that, for better or worse, informs the alien builders of the existence of humans. This theme surfaces in Clarke's *2001* novel in the comment that Floyd's first thought on seeing the monolith on the moon was that this was 'Pandora's box [...] waiting to be opened by inquisitive Man' (Clarke 1968: 78). The fascination of penetrating the apparently impenetrable clearly indicates that the monolith is the repository of captivating knowledge, and, in the novel, it is clearly explained to be alien technology of enormous power. However, in the film, it is never made clear that the monolith is not an alien, but merely their tool. The viewer tends to assume that the monolith is, in some sense, the alien, notably when a monolith is seen swimming among the stars in one of the last scenes of the film. This is important in that it emphasizes the monolith as a subject rather than an object. It is as if the audience, like the humans in the film, experience it as a mysterious person.

When Bowman, from his deathbed, raises his hand towards the monolith, he is encountering something alien but, bearing in mind Theweleit's analysis of the *freikorps*' ideal of hard, impenetrable potency, the monolith can also be understood as standing for the ultimate expression of phallic military masculinity. Several Cold War covers of the leading American science-fiction magazine, *Astounding Science Fiction* (to which Clarke contributed stories in 1946 and 1949), depicted an ecstatic transformation of male bodies or their incorporation into a new, greater form. For instance, the cover of January 1951 showed athletic male bodies partly incorporated into an immense form which is shooting into outer space. Bearing this in mind, it is easier to understand Clarke's note of 13 May 1964, in which he records that Kubrick had 'the hilarious idea of seventeen aliens, featureless black pyramids, riding in open cars down Fifth Avenue', like a convoy of military or political dignitaries (Clarke, quoted in Bizony 1994: 76). Moreover, the phallic potency of the man-monolith is made clear from Clarke's comment that 'I like to think of the monolith as a sort of cosmic Swiss army knife – it does whatever it wants to do' (Clarke, quoted in LoBrutto 1998: 284).

Clarke commented that he was struck after seeing the film by the similarity of the monolith to the United Nations Secretariat Building in New York (Clarke 1972: 51) (fig. 3).[4] This building had already been presented as a science-fiction icon in November 1953 on the cover of *Astounding Science Fiction* in a photograph by Sam Andre, a photographer who specialized in images of heroic masculinity in the form of the leading boxers of the time. The editorial in this issue suggests that the building was like a vast window 'looking through to some other dimension'. Moreover, the cover photographer could 'in one sense, do better' than his image by removing the extraneous surrounding detail, since 'he could, in other words, have moved the United Nations right out of this world' (Campbell 1954: 2).[5] But it was Kubrick who, by rejecting the tetrahedral form, created a visually phallic image for the monolith. After all, it is always stiffly vertical when seen by humans, and only horizontal when floating in the void, unseen by space men (Chion 2001: 142–43). It is possible to argue that this object is a kind of generic, modernist phallus.

Figure 3: United Nations Secretariat Building under construction, New York. Photograph by Eugene Kodani, c.1951. Courtesy of Environmental Design Visual Resources Center, University of California, Berkeley.

The skyscraper as phallus was one of the comparisons made by feminist critiques of masculinist modernity (Morrow 2008), as in Anita Steckel's *New York Skyline* series (1972–73) in which erect phalluses thrust upwards from iconic New York high-rise buildings (Meyer 2008: 46) (fig. 4). Writers influenced by Freud are not surprised by such identifications since they would typically see humans' interpretation of the world as being based initially on comparisons with parts of their own bodies (Hall 1962). For such writers, this is a universal impulse rather than simply a cultural feature of an age saturated with Freudian understandings (Hersey 1999: 115–36). A reviewer surveying a recent such book on 'building biology' commented on the author's discussion of the skyscraper as phallus that 'obviously, he [the author] sometimes goes too far in his comparisons' (Flannery 2009: 66). Why 'obviously' the review does not say, but even if modern architecture itself is regarded as free of phallic expression that does not prevent Kubrick from using phallic imagery as an element with which to satirize the insecurities of the American military in *2001*, much as he did in *Dr. Strangelove*. The monolith is, in conclusion, a powerfully phallic object, but it also has some other decidedly human (and queer) characteristics. It is an expression of penetrative potency, but one that, in the words of one leading critic, 'sucked up light like a black hole', for all the world like one of *Full Metal Jacket*'s gobbling 'peter puffers' (Bizony 1994: 105). Moreover, in its sudden appearances and reappearances it is deeply uncanny and, bearing in mind the idea that 'Kubrick's uncanny is decidedly corporeal', it becomes emblematic of queer and uncanny embodiment (Peucker 2001: 666).

The plot of *2001* went through many versions. It is clear that the ending of the film was particularly problematic. Encounters with physical aliens, including some in humanoid form, were tried and rejected. Clarke wrote of this process of struggle and revision that Kubrick and he were 'groping toward the ending which we felt must exist – just as a sculptor, it is said, chips down through the stone toward the figure concealed within' (Clarke 1972: 199). Clarke's comment suggests that the monolith is an expression of concealment requiring the imagination of the artist to bring to light the truth within. The dark surface of the monolith has the queer opacity of the closet, for there is more to (its) blackness than meets the eye. John Harvey's fascinating cultural history of the

Figure 4: Anita Steckel, Anita Steckel and the Skyline Painting (1974), by permission of the artist. Steckel photographed in front of one of her works which she had included in the exhibition at Rockland Community College (part of the State University of New York, located 25 miles northwest of Manhattan).

colour black concludes that, over the last millennium, there has been 'unevenly and in waves and abeyances – the darkening, the blackening of men, of what they wear [...] alone or in ranks, the man in black is the agent of a serious power; and of a power claimed over women and the feminine. Black may be a shadow fallen on the feminine part of man' (Harvey 1995: 257). The monolith appears like a black space punched out of the background, or the space where something has been blacked out. It is a wonderful device for ostentatiously showing that something is not being shown. The rectangular black space on the screen can, thus, be understood to represent the epitome of closeted male power which is, in truth, partly composed of the feminine.

The ultimate trip

The final section of *2001* sees Bowman journey to a one-on-one encounter with a monolith, after which he is reborn as a Star-Child. Counter-cultural associations were conjured up by the use in some of the film's publicity of the phrase 'the ultimate trip'. This trip, I suggest, is a coded male-on-male sexual encounter. Its start is signalled by a spectacular lightshow. If blackness is coded as deeply masculine, then Bowman enjoys an orgy of decadently effeminate coloured effects as he is pulled in his pod to the climax of the film, which takes place, famously, in very peculiar hotel suite which he shares with a monolith and after which there is a strange birth. His contorted face on the journey and his associated ageing appears to have been derived from images such as that published in *Astounding Science Fiction* in September 1952 on the supposed physical effects of extreme g-forces: this image purported to show that 'each additional G of acceleration appears to add ten years of age to a man's face' (Anon. 1952: 89). What happens next is not reproduction but rather a re-birth of Bowman, as he bursts out of his fake and kitsch enclosure to the sounds of *Also Sprach Zarathustra*. This is, first and foremost, a fantasy about losing control. Spacemen are, in *2001*, initially, 'compulsively neat, precise and in control. They do retain the sexuality implicit in adventure, a sexuality sublimated to the pleasure of discovery [...]. Bowman is a man who can accept the daily routine of space travel just as he can sublimate his own sexuality in discovery. He is in control' (Thron 1977: 73): perhaps for the moment, but soon he is plunging towards Jupiter, in the helpless grip of strange 'torments and ecstasies' (Plank 1977: 148).

When the pick up, with its psychedelic imagery, is over, Bowman comes to himself in a strange room. For Clarke, waking up in such circumstances with a strange studly monolith was perhaps less than extraordinary, and it is notable that in the novel (unlike in the film) the room looks just like a normal hotel room (Clarke 1968: 238). Bearing in mind Clarke's comment of 17 October 1964 that 'Stanley has invented the wild idea of slightly fag robots who create a Victorian environment to put our heroes at their ease', this interior design becomes comprehensible: Bowman has been transported into Kubrick's visual conception of queer space (Clarke, quoted in Kubrick and Clarke 2001: 12). George Toles said that 'the ornate bedroom, like the red rooms and portentous bathrooms of *The Shining*, reminds me of a place cleaned with exaggerated care in order to conceal all traces of a crime' (2006: 173). It is worth noting in relation to the period furnishings (eighteenth-century rather than nineteenth-century) that, to Kubrick, ancien régime Europe, as witnessed vividly in *Barry Lyndon*, was a place of rottenness and decadence. It was the birthplace of the modern and it is the very cleanliness of the modern that creates the obsession with dirt and hence with sanitation (White 2006: 140). It is in this room, as antiseptic as an operating theatre, that supposedly dangerous boundaries are breached. Yet it is notable that the room shares significant stylistic similarities with the spacecraft of the year *2001*, for 'rather than producing visual disjunction, the pod's pristine whiteness and uncluttered shape make it strangely at home' in this queer space (Powell 2007: 169). The implication is that the apparently pristine landscapes of human modernity are themselves the location of the queer and the perverse.

What confronts us at the end of *2001* is a collision of the closet and the sublime. Cesare Casarino (1997) has discussed such a situation in his exploration of Joseph Conrad's *Secret Sharer* (1910) in which he concludes that:

> [...] the sublime of the closet would thus constitute an attempt to envision an exit from the closet that would not also be a trap, that would also be unnameable and unimaginable of all that needs the closet in order to continue to exist. In this sense, the sublime of the closet is not a coming out [understood as predetermined by external power] but rather an overcoming: a coming pure and simple. It is about a close enclosure that is suddenly and unpredictably transcended.
>
> (Casarino 1997: 205–06)

Bowman, thus, is not so much 'outed' in the hotel as transformed. And, as I will now argue in the final section, this process makes visible the queer child within that was the shared object of Clarke's and Kubrick's fantasy.

The Star-Child

The extraordinary object of desire at the very end of *2001* is the Star-Child. This being has very interesting literary antecedents. In 1963–64, an early version of the first two novels in Jack Williamson and Frederik Pohl's 'Starchild Trilogy' was serialized in *If* magazine. These novels explored the notion of finding freedom and development on the frontiers of space in an age when the solar system was under the control of a tyrannical computer system (McCaffery and Williamson 1991: 243, 248). Williamson explained that William Olaf Stapledon had been a key influence on his thinking (as he had also been on Clarke). In 1930, Stapledon had imagined an extraordinary expansion of the erotic gaze: 'it is difficult for less ample natures to imagine this expansion of the innate sexual interest; for to them it is not apparent that the lusty admiration which at first directs itself solely on the opposite sex is the appropriate attitude to all the beauties of flesh and spirit' (Stapledon, quoted in Grant

2006: 84). There is more work to be done on the precise literary influences on Clarke's work, but it is significant that there is something distinctly queer about the previous appearances of the Star-Child in literature. In Charles Dickens' 'A child's dream of a star' (1850) various members of a boy's family die as he grows up. The Victorian homosexual pre-Raphaelite artist Simeon Solomon used angels as homoerotic icons partly because they were beings understood as standing outside normative gender categories (see Janes 2010). This may imply the potential complexity of the child's desires when he repeatedly prays that he be allowed to go to heaven to be in a place where he is kissed and received by angels. Finally, the boy, now grown old, is dying and says, 'my age is falling from me like a garment and I move toward the star as a child' (Dickens 1850: 26).

The Star-Child with a hyphen, Clarke's spelling, makes his appearance in a short story with this title which was included in Oscar Wilde's collection of children's stories *A House of Pomegranates* (1891). The paedophilic imagery of the story – the boy was 'white and delicate as sawn ivory, and his curls were like the rings of the daffodil. His lips, also, were like the petals of a red flower, and his eyes were like violets by a river of pure water, and his body like the narcissus of a field where the mower comes not' – is of the same ilk as Wilde's flattery of Bosie Douglas (he of the 'slim gilt soul') (Wilde, quoted in Wood 2002: 163). John-Charles Duffy has argued that, for Wilde, the childlike homosexual person is like those who, in Jesus' words, 'become as little children' and so inherit the kingdom of heaven' (2001: 345). In the early twentieth century the pioneering campaigner for homosexual rights, Edward Carpenter, was advancing views that appear to herald the sexual polymorphisms of Stapledon. For example, in *Intermediate Types among Primitive Folk* Carpenter argued that blending of female and male characteristics would eventually create a new order of beings possessed with a 'cosmic consciousness' (1914: 40–41), which has been understood by a recent authority as a state of 'religious awakening and a form of quasi-sexual ecstasy' (Cocks 2001: 217). The ending of *2001* can, in this light, be read as, in effect, an injection of the homosexual dreams of Carpenter into Dickens's Christian heaven: with the inclusion of a strong element of Wildean paedophilic desire.

Whether or not these texts were a direct or indirect influence on Clarke, one thing that is clear is that *2001* is not about gay liberation. It is important to note that Clarke and Kubrick did not allow Bowman to choose a queer rebirth: they forced it upon him. Further, the form of his subjection involves transformation into a child. Now, if you are the kind of person who is worried by Wilde's sexual interests in male youths, you might think that all would be well in the hands of Dickens, but if you think so, then James Kincaid, in *Child Loving: The Erotic Child and Victorian Culture* (1992), has a surprise for you. He argues that the 'paedophile' is, in fact, the convenient creation of people regarded (by themselves and by the law) as normal:

In this story [i.e., ideological construct in narrative form], we are cast as attractive characters entirely free from desire, children are free from sexual attraction or from any desires of their own, and a few – but not too few – sociopathic people are possessed of needs that they then enact in terrible ways. Power has told us that if we rely on this story we cannot go wrong, so long as we repeat it often and loudly enough [...] this [childhood] purity, this harmlessness is presented as a complete vacancy; the absence of harmfulness amounts, in fact, to nothing at all, a blank image waiting to be formed. As emptiness, the child David [Copperfield] can be variously eroticised by those around him: his kissing mother, his hugging nurse, his beating stepfather and schoolmaster, the adult narrator, and, arguably, the reader. Purity, it turns out, provides just the opening a sexualising tendency requires.

(Kincaid 1992: 13, 361)

I have been discussing a film in which an already passive character is turned into an infant. In one of the early novel drafts of *2001* Clarke imagined a spaceman falling into a giant monolith that was a 'stargate': this spaceman, Kimball, 'could not help recalling Alice's fall down the rabbit hole [...] to an underworld where magic reigned, and the normal laws of nature were overthrown' (Clarke 1972: 174). Lewis Carroll, who took nude photographs of small girls, appears to have shared certain interests with Clarke, if the stories of sex with boys are true, and Kubrick, the director of *Lolita*, who, left to himself, would have cast a much younger girl in the title role so as to match Nabokov's text (White 2006: 132). Thus, it becomes clearer why, in Clarke's and Kubrick's fantasy, Bowman, and thus the alleged might of the military, are remade into an eroticized child whose soft gaze echoes that which bewitched Humbert Humbert.

Crucially, and following Kincaid, those interests appear to be shared by a great many of us. For instance, the Faceprints computer programme revealed that the imagined face of the ideal 25-year-old woman had a 14-year-old's lips and an 11-year-old's jaw (Kincaid 1992: 18). The audience is forced to acquiesce in their scopic engagement with Bowman's degradation and thus become complicit in the enjoyment of the spectacle of infantile polymorphous perversion (Creed 1993: 130–32). Clarke and Kubrick were playing games of control with their audience which was forced to sit through, and enjoy, time spans that alternated between vast periods of slowness and sudden jolts of activity. Just as 'even more overtly than the novel, Kubrick's *Lolita* invokes a masochistic aesthetic with its constant themes of masking, game-playing and pursuit', so *2001* promises, as a deliciously delayed abject release of pleasure, the forced acknowledgement that all adults are dirty child-molesters at heart (Gabbard 1997). The film, therefore, transcends heteronormative performance through its reduction of men to childlike sexual objects of unclear gender and in its co-option of the audience in this erotic fantasy.

In a splendid instance of Kincaid's theory of the construction of erotic innocence, Kubrick said that, for him, rebirth was about recapturing the 'capacity to experience total joy' of a child (Kubrick, quoted in Agel 1970: 353). How to achieve that state of infant-ecstasy as an adult? He commented, in relation to the plot of *2001* in an interview, that 'women didn't seem to have a lot to do with it' (Kubrick, quoted in White 2006: 138). They gave birth but could not re-birth their men-folk. Army training, as in *Full Metal Jacket*, would not create such a transcendent re-birth either; this was male technology, but it was insufficiently high-tech to be sublimely infantilizing.

Discussing Wilde (and Walter Pater and Henry James), Nabokov wrote that:

> [...] the beautiful child – often for these and other decadent writers the occasion for expressing the allure of giving oneself over to the contemplation of beautiful forms – inspires a riveted and passionate glance and provides an example of a valorized capacity for aesthetic absorption, a permeability to spectacle that, in the sexually normative ideology of our contemporary world, induces only panic. For many aestheticist thinkers, however, such permeability suggests nothing short of the rapturous possibilities of art.
> (quoted in Ohi 2005: 12)

At the dawn of the 1960s Olivier's sadistic, bisexual Marcus Licinius Crassus was able to possess neither the 26-year-old 'boy' Antoninus, played by Curtis, nor Spartacus's lover Varinia (Jean Simmons). By the end of that extraordinary decade Kubrick was able to suggest that high technological combination of artist and medium would solve such problems. The sublime mystery celebrated in *2001* was ultimately that of the controlling artist who, uniting with masculine media technology in the 'fecund dark of the movie theatre', creates the apparently asexual child of light which, in his paedophilic fantasy, is the site of transcendent pleasure (Loughlin 2004: 75).

The resulting movie in all its scary queerness was itself a child, born, in the words of the television journalist and photographer Roger Caras, from the 'good cerebral marriage' of the two artists (LoBrutto 1998: 264). Thus, the film can be read as queer because it celebrates the reproductive potential of same-sex encounters both on screen and off. However, Kubrick's vision subordinates homosocial and homosexual desire to a sadomasochistic regime in which power is understood to be crucial in the production of the erotic sublime. The fascination with the resulting infantalization of Bowman does not mean, however, that either Clarke or Kubrick was a paedophile, but it does show their intense fascination with the radical potential of the alleged perverse polymorphism of youth. In this, they shared fantasies and excitements that were not only widespread in the counter-culture of the 1960s but which have been found by recent literary critics in the works of canonical writers of English literature such as Dickens.

But if, as I have argued, this film is a sadistic male fantasy, does it also possess queer liberatory potential? De Witt Douglas Kilgore has argued that it is 'easy enough' in science-fiction to present a future in which conflicts around sexuality have vanished. Referring specifically to Clarke's *Childhood's End*, he argues that 'the genre can accommodate at one pole a mystic-evolutionary liberalism and at the other a militant neo-conservatism. Both positions are bound together by a faith that retains whiteness and heterosexuality as the core of any social norm [...] Both leave us with the certainty that either history will end or it will produce endless and ever more glorious iterations of our present' (2008: 234). In other words, Kilgore might well contend that *2001* implies the strengthening of the status quo through the use of alien technology rather than heralding a radical breakdown of the very basis of norms (see Foster 2009). I would agree that the sanctioning of violence and paedophile voyeurism is not the key to this film's queerness, above all because it can be argued that these are structural elements in the world of heteronormativity and the closet. Rather, I believe that the fundamental act of queering was carried out by Kubrick when he 'removed all [Clarke's] [...] exposition late in production, rendering his film all the more challenging and elusive' (Bould 2010: 129). He also steadfastly refused to explain what the film was 'about' after its release. This meant that *2001* was constructed so as to be open to countercultural readings, something encouraged by the revised marketing campaign. It was the radical ambiguity of its closing transcendent moments that, for instance, enabled the film to inspire David Bowie's 'Space Oddity' (1969), and thus 'Bowie's alien persona [which] was emblematic of his bi-sexual alienation from the heterosexual male-dominated world of rock music' (McLeod 2003: 341). It is crucial that Kubrick left it up to us to imagine the Star-Child grown up into the Star-Man of our dreams.

Acknowledgements

This chapter was originally published in 2011, volume 4, issue 1, of *Science Fiction Film and Television*, pp. 57–78, and is included in this collection with the kind permission of Liverpool University Press.

Chapter Nine

'But as to whether or not he has feelings is something I don't think anyone can truthfully answer': The image of the astronaut in *2001: A Space Odyssey* and its lasting impact

Nils Daniel Peiler

Chapter Nine

'But as to whether or not he has feelings is something I don't think anyone can truthfully answer'. This answer given by Dr. David Bowman, astronaut onboard the Discovery One spaceship aiming for Jupiter in Stanley Kubrick's *2001*, is in reference to the ship's supercomputer, HAL 9000, who appears to be programmed with feelings. It is an answer that will guide the following close reading of the image of the astronaut, especially as mirrored by the film's computer, in a science-fiction work that questions the borders between the human and the machine, where the trained scientists appear to react more like technical apparatus while the machine-in-control reacts in a human fashion, from singing to being offended. The astronaut of *2001* is introduced as a dehumanized figure carrying a queer, ambivalent potential that has become an icon, and which has created a diversified artistic resonance in other artworks in the afterlife of Kubrick's classic; from the science-fiction films *Signale – Ein Weltraumabenteuer* (*Signals: A Space Adventure*) (Kolditz, 1970) and *Moon* (Jones, 2009), to *Interstellar* (Nolan, 2014), each have demonstrated their respective grasp of *2001*. This chapter will explore this reading of the astronaut in opposition to the machine, especially in regard of style and gender, as well as responding to ideas raised in the previous chapter.

The introduction of HAL and his astronauts

Whilst travelling on its Jupiter Mission, the Discovery One spaceship receives a transmission of a television interview on the fictitious BBC 12 channel evening news show *The World Tonight*. The interviewer, Martin Amor, characterizes the three protagonists of this chapter of *2001*: the astronauts Dr. David Bowman (Keir Dullea) and Dr. Frank Poole (Gary Lockwood), and the supercomputer, HAL 9000 (Douglas Rain). HAL 9000, the so-called 'foolproof' supercomputer-in-charge, is introduced at the beginning of the Jupiter Mission sequence as 'the sixth member of the crew'. In other words, he is like a human being of flesh (and blood), sharing not only 'enormous intellect', but it also 'enjoy[s] working with people' and considers itself to be a responsible 'conscious entity' and finds itself 'having a stimulating relationship with Dr. Poole and Dr. Bowman'. All that said, HAL is described as human-like and reacts quite lively with its speech patterns as well, as Andrew Utterson has indicated in his study *From IBM to MGM: Cinema at the Dawn of the Digital Age* (2011): 'the voice of HAL suggests a blurring of the boundaries between human and computer; to the point where one cannot be easily distinguished from the other. HAL's voice is one of several characteristics that serve to anthropomorphise the computer' (Utterson 2011: 101). Or, to sum it up in the broader context of Vivian Sobchack, in her discussion of the ironic use of language in *2001* as part of her genealogy of the genre, *Screening Space*:

> HAL's voice is ripe and soft whereas Bowman's and Poole's have no texture. In comparison to the astronauts, creating the context which emphasizes the lacklustre and mechanical quality of human speech spoken by humans, HAL – in the first part of the flight – can almost be regarded as a chatterbox, a gossip, emotional.
>
> (1997: 177)

HAL is a new instance in the representation of artificial intelligence, one that – with its striking ambivalence – overcomes the clichéd formulas of either a strictly evil machine, or altogether useful computer in pre-*2001* cinematic history. HAL's outstanding role has thereby foreshadowed many computers to follow in popular culture since 1968. Utterson concludes of this special computer character:

> Initially, HAL functions as a sixth member of the crew, performing tasks comparable with those undertaken by its human counterparts. On the voyage to Jupiter, the two conscious astronauts – the others are being suspended in hibernation – communicate with the computer as equals, on first-name terms. HAL appears both friendly and understanding, and is arguably more 'human' than its fellow crewmembers, whose demeanour is decidedly cold in comparison.
>
> (2011: 100–01)

While on the one hand, a spontaneous and agile computer runs the mission with characteristics of a profound human being that is going to produce errors, the astronauts on the other hand appear dehumanized, almost animal like. They are frozen in hibernation like animals in winter, or as they appear in the film, rather like ice-cooled products from a refrigerator, whilst the centrifuge of the Discovery One spaceship is like a hamster wheel on which they jog. Their space lunch is an instantaneous fast-food mash, differentiated not by texture, but only by colour, and they eat sandwiches that they say 'taste the same anyway […] getting better […] all the time'. Furthermore Dave Bowman and Frank Poole operate tasks onboard the Discovery One spaceship that could be handled instead, more or less, by a computer: they calculate, look for technical problems, communicate in measures and figures with the ground control on Earth, where all the human decisions ironically are always being backed-up by a twin computer of the 9000 series.

This technoid style of the astronaut's appearance is underlined by a heavy use of technology throughout the film's various chapters, which largely takes place around the new millennium. The set props and costumes provide further characterization of the image of *2001*'s astronauts, equipped with tools and gadgets that had been carefully developed

'But as to whether or not he has feelings is something I don't think anyone can truthfully answer'

and designed by Kubrick and his art department team in close collaboration with large brands at the time; these included brands such as Industrial Business Machines (IBM), Nikon Cameras, Pan American Airlines, Howard Johnson's Motels and Restaurants, Hilton Hotels, The Bell Telephone Company and Hamilton Watches. The historic, even at times iconic corporate logos – integrated into the *mise-en-scène* of the middle scenes of the film, especially in the sequences in which we see space travel taking place (within the spaceships or space stations) – help to set up a realistic framework for the narrative, but also serve as a link between the technological future of this science-fiction and the sponsoring corporations in an early form of cross media marketing. This included special advertisements by various corporations that made use of *2001*'s imagery and products that had been issued on the occasion of the film's release (Eichhorn 2007: 120–25). The astronauts in *2001* thereby appear to be well equipped with a range of specifically designed visionary tools and gadgets (some still beyond invention today) that witness Kubrick's vision of the future. The astronauts use zero gravity toilets, wear special space suits with electronic inlays, which include buttons integrated into their clothing and, most iconic of all, helmets of an oval shape that reflect their surrounding lights.

This vision of the future and its lasting influence is no more evident than in the scene in which Bowman and Poole watch their initial television interview on BBC 12 on small displays. These displays are propped beside their meals on a table onboard Discovery One, uncannily resembling the contemporary computer tablet. In fact, so remarkable was this design, that the prop was used as evidence in lawsuit between the corporate giants Apple and Samsung, in a dispute over patent design rights of their iPad and computer tablets (Rohwetter 2011: 38). As part of their defence strategy, Samsung included Kubrick's film as evidence that Apple was not the first to invent the tablet computer, but that it had instead been envisioned by Kubrick's production as early as 1968, some half a century previous. Needless to say that this was a rather unconventional case, in which a historic science-fiction film served as evidence in a multimillion-dollar lawsuit; it garnered the attention of the world's media, with explanations of the case alongside illustrations from *2001* in newspapers such as *Die Zeit*.

Despite the prominence of communication devices, with only a seven-minute delay in transmissions between the Discovery One and Earth, the astronauts hardly communicate. They talk only rarely to each other and their pale faces, in opposition to the glowing red eye of HAL, appear to be without feelings. The lack of emotional difference between the human astronauts and the calculating machine could not be starker. Even when Poole's parents on Earth send him a video message to congratulate him on his birthday – they have baked a cake and sing him Happy Birthday, the only other textually comprehensible vocals being heard in the entire music score besides HAL's performance of 'Daisy Bell' – no unusual emotional reaction at all, such as joy or signs of homesickness, can be discerned on the astronaut's face.

Only Poole's chess game (with HAL, who wins, of course) and Bowman's drawings can be read as slightly exceptional cases of intellectual or artistic amusement outside the technical procedure of the astronaut's dehumanized everyday lives. Consequentially, it is not the human(like) astronauts who are working on a psychogram in *2001*, but it is the computer 'brain', HAL, that undertakes this human endeavour, evidence of his 'fundamental ontological ambivalence' (Utterson 2011: 111). As HAL appears to become more human-like, the astronauts in return become dehumanized, machine-like characters, and 'indeed the humanisation of machines and mechanisation of humans is an important part of the theme of evolution that underpins the film' (2011: 101). Thereby the astronaut in *2001* is neither a lively heroic human individual, whose actions are set against an apparently evil machine in the beginning, nor is he an android-like Rick Deckard (*Blade Runner*), a type of machine character with an unknown origin and ontological status. The astronaut in *2001* is definitively of human nature in appearance, but appears to be less humane in comparison to and mirrored by his computer counterpart that simulates human feelings throughout the film.

This ambivalent man/machine duality, established in the Jupiter Mission, is further developed when HAL malfunctions and apparently goes insane. At this point, a new intimacy is developed between the two astronauts, as Bowman and Poole hide in their locked space pod and discuss in detail the concern and challenges they face in dismantling the machine. It is in this moment that the two astronauts are first surveilled, second overruled, then partially killed by the machine, before finally being forced to act willingly against it: HAL constantly operates the whole Jupiter Mission unseen, within his circuits, and maintains a watchful eye on Bowman and Poole at all times. He kills Poole as he is working outside the spaceship, whilst he kills Kimball, Hunter and Kaminsky even before they have a chance to wake from hibernation. Bowman, finding himself to be the last surviving crew member of the mission, has no alternative other than to act in opposition to the computer, which at last tries to persuade the astronaut not to disconnect it. HAL reacts quite lively and humanely for one last time, being offended, moaning and singing a good-bye song, 'Daisy Bell', that shows a regression of the computer falling back on the evolutionary status of a young child, as Walter Filz (2004) suggests in his history of talking computers in the radio production *Vom Reden der Rechner* (*On Computer's Talking*). Yet, as to why it is that HAL firstly kills Poole and, secondly, fears his own disconnection, can be found in a gender reading of the astronauts and the machine as a triangular couple.

Gazing at the 'gay' scenes

I wish to briefly consider Dominic Janes's interpretation of the astronaut protagonists of *2001* in the framework of gender studies, providing additional depth in the consideration of their character. This will allow for a better contextualization of the astronaut figure later in this chapter. Janes draws a line from the film's co-author Arthur C. Clarke as a bisexual, presumably homosexual science-fiction author, whose rich genre work from the 1950s onwards (following his divorce from a short heterosexual relationship) offers hints upon his

'But as to whether or not he has feelings is something I don't think anyone can truthfully answer'

sexual desires, to the homosocial contexts of *2001* and its astronauts. Clarke's works post-*2001* featured gay or bisexual characters, including a 'sympathetic pair of emotionally stable gay male lovers, Floyd's oldest and closest friends' (Janes 2011: 59–60) in *2061: Odyssey Three*, one of the sequel novels to Clarke's *2001: A Space Odyssey*.

Kubrick on the other hand, in whose many films 'women play a negligible role' (Janes 2011: 61), 'wrote extensively about homosocial environments such as the military' (2011: 57) and, in collaboration with Clarke, opted for ideas while developing their script for *2001* that can be read as assuring the film a certain ambivalent openness and a queer potential (2011: 67, 74). Clarke, for example, wanted the alien life to be represented in the geometrical form of a pyramid in an early draft, but Kubrick opted for a phallic monolith that 'is always stiffly vertical when seen by humans [...] It is possible to argue that this object is a kind of generic, modernist phallus' (2011: 67).

This decision of (re)presentation can be seen in the context of Clarke's comparison between *2001*'s monolith(s) and the United Nation's Secretariat Building in New York; Clarke compares this to the iconic photographs of Eugene Kodani (1951), as well as feminist artist Anita Steckel's explicit self-portrait of phallic skyscrapers, *Skyline Painting* (1974) (Janes 2011: 67). Male dominance can be read as manifesting itself in all the three instances: the monolith-like UN building and the film's monoliths as a form of similar shape, but black non-colour instead of a glassy opacity, together with Steckel's phalluses, frame the geometrical symbol as being of a strong male-underpinned quality.

Besides 'a striking absence of heterosexual sensuality in *2001*' (Janes 2011: 58), and no explicit sex scenes, there are not only phallic symbols found throughout the film, but the film is in fact 'full of sexual imagery – uterine, ovular and phallic – from the arrow-shaped space-craft Orion landing inside the celestial wheel to the Aries sphere alighting on a circular base' (2011: 58). Kubrick in an interview shortly after the release of his film suggested that 'it may be possible for each partner to simultaneously experience the sensations of the other [...]; or we may emerge into polymorphous sexual beings, with the male and female components blurring, merging and interchanging' (2011: 61). Therefore, it is no surprise that the two astronauts Bowman and Poole and the HAL 9000 computer have been described as 'a sort of outer space *ménage à trois*' (2011: 62). To quote Janes, who is referring to White and Chion, 'HAL, it has been argued, appears "more and more like a jealous homosexual lover" (White 2006: 139) in the face of the relationship between Poole (Gary Lockwood) and Bowman' (Janes 2011: 62). Bowman and Poole's relationship is interpreted as that of an 'old married couple', a relationship in which communication is no longer necessary (Janes 2011: 62). This could be an answer to both the killing of Poole and the fear of being disconnected: HAL's jealousy about the good companionship between Bowman and Poole leads to the isolation of the former by murdering the latter, but besides replacing Poole's role for Bowman to form a perfect relationship, the computer is instead shut down. The final moments of the film that take place with Bowman inside the Louis XVI room can be read as a queer encounter and rebirth. Bowman is finally transformed from 'a representative masculine subject' into 'an androgynous erotic object at the very end of *2001*'

(2011: 61–62). Janes builds a bridge from the ending of *2001* to its artistic resonance by hinting upon the fact that it led to the creation of David Bowie's *Space Oddity* (1969) with Bowie being 'emblematic of his bi-sexual alienation from the heterosexual male-dominated world of rock music' (Janes 2011: 74). Bowie, whose songs and albums, like no other pop artist in the immediate aftermath of the film's initial release at the end of the 1960s and beginning of the early 1970s, drew upon the queer potential and underlined it further more through his androgynous appearance and alienated styles in his shows as the characters Major Tom and Ziggy Stardust. But I wish to extend that bridge further and examine the longer lasting artistic resonance of the astronaut image from *2001*.

2001's astronauts as lasting icons

The Kubrickian astronaut, especially in its embodiment by actor Keir Dullea, has become an iconic figure that finds its echoes throughout pop culture, no more so than the late David Bowie's transformation into an androgynous, otherworldly alien. Keir Dullea has revived his role as Dave Bowman on two occasions; first in the film's 'sequel', *2010: The Year We Make Contact*, and second in the short film *Immersive Cocoon* (Zeller, 2011), produced by the architects and designers of the group NAU for their project of the same name, building on the iconography of *2001*'s Louis XVI room. Re-enacting his performance from this sequence, Dullea no longer requires makeup given his age (born in 1936). More recently, Dullea returned to the screen in a short guest appearance in the Jack Plotnick science-fiction film *Space Station 76* (2014), in which he plays Mr. Marlowe, the father of Jessica (Liv Tyler), who phones him on Capsule 436 in a video phone call, reminiscent of the same communication technology used in *2001* by Floyd (William Sylvester) when phoning his daughter. But the appropriation of the astronaut image of *2001* is not limited to the revival, or allusion to Keir Dullea's role. The image of Bowman can in fact be found as a role model for other film figures such as *Toy Story*'s (Lasseter, 1995) Buzz Lightyear, or alongside French cartoon heroes such as Jean-Claude Forest's *Barbarella* or Hergé's *Tintin* in an illustration by Federico Babina. Fan art has even developed, with the creation of self-made miniature action figures based on Bowman's popularity.

But the artistic resonance of the astronaut in *2001* was immediately obvious by the 1970s. The East German Democratic Republic, along with its communist partner-state of Poland, developed its own socialist version of, and answer to, *2001*. The state-owned and state-controlled East German film production company DEFA wanted to position a communist answer to the British-American co-production. In January 1969, the internal DEFA working group *Roter Kreis* (*Red Circle*) set up an internal screening of two western science-fiction productions, namely Roger Vadim's *Barbarella* (1968) and Kubrick's *2001*; both had premiered in the autumn of 1968 in West Germany, but were never released officially in the GDR. Only three months later, in April 1969, the DEFA director Franz Bruk wrote about the political relevance of the science-fiction film:

'But as to whether or not he has feelings is something I don't think anyone can truthfully answer'

> We hope [...] to use this material in an enjoyable way to spread and consolidate the Marxist worldview by opposing the imperialist manipulation by means of utopian representation and our image of the world.
>
> (Schenk 2015: 98)[1]

The East German answer to these western science-fictions was called *Signale – Ein Weltraumabenteuer* and was directed by DEFA genre film specialist Gottfried Kolditz. Several internal memos on the groundbreaking visual effects and the technical innovations in Kubrick's *2001* helped the production at DEFA to achieve a high level quality of special effects and visual style (Schenk 2015: 99). The communist response to *2001* shares several similarities: in *Signale*, at the dawn of the new millennium, the spaceship Ikaros travels on its way to Jupiter to search for alien life forms, but an unexpected crash ends the mission and results in a second spaceship, the Laika, being dispatched to search for and rescue the crew of the Ikaros. The emergency signals of the Ikaros are referenced in the film's title, *Signals*. Ralf Schenk has described the parallels between Kolditz and Kubrick with special regard to the film's camera work, the scenes in zero gravity, the boarding manoeuvres of the astronauts, and the circling images of doors and spaceships (Schenk 2015: 99). A flickering round red lamp on the ship is reminiscent of HAL's red eye, whilst the cosmonauts onboard the Ikaros spaceship wear space suits that have inlays comparable to the ones of the Discovery One crew. The cosmonauts also form a much more diverse heterogeneous ensemble concerning age, gender and nationality compared to the all-young, all-male, all-white, all-American crew of the Discovery in *2001*. This mirroring can be found not only in *Signals*, but many other contemporary cosmonaut figures in Soviet productions of the time. Instead of a homoerotic environment, *Signals* presents a conservative model of heterosexual male-dominated behaviour. Though the female space officers carry out masculine tasks, including space communications and scientific calculations, as well as navigating the space pods like their male colleagues, they also chat about their clothing and serve their male colleagues coffee 'as usual'. Despite introducing female space officers that are superficially the equal of their male colleagues – reaching beyond *2001*'s vision of women still in stewardess roles aboard the Pan Am Moon shuttle – *Signals* cannot resist perpetuating male-dominated stereotypes.

Post-2001 astronauts

To this day, the Kubrickian astronaut is a constant figure that is especially present (but not limited to) the science-fiction genre. Drawing on the iconography of *2001*, but updating, partially ridiculing and partially extremisizing it, Duncan Jones's *Moon* (2009) is a recent example of the artistic resonance of the astronaut image. The astronaut in *Moon*, Sam Bell (Sam Rockwell), works on a large helium plant on the dark side of the Moon. However, he discovers that he is in fact a clone installed with memories he never had and who will be eventually killed by the company that employs him. Sam works in close collaboration with Gerty 3000, an advanced computer derived from HAL 9000 that not only shows his feelings through his voice, but also visualizes them with smiley icons on a display accompanying its blue eye. Gerty, as a machine, is much more mobile and agile than HAL, possessing arms and hands. Gerty is also omnipresent through his voice (Kevin Spacey), once more echoing HAL.

Yet, Gerty appears like an optimistic development of HAL that is not only harmless in letting the astronaut escape by being switched off, but also loses character depth by its ever-friendly voice and simulated convivial mood. This is best exemplified when Gerty tells Sam that, 'Helping you is what I do'. Whereas in *2001*, the conversation between astronaut and machine is terminated – 'Dave, this conversation can serve no purpose anymore, goodbye!' – Gerty always replies to Sam's request to provide information, including on the secret clone room: 'Of course Sam, how can I help?' Gerty even helps Sam to gain access to a hidden video message, in contrast to the obstacles Dave has to overcome in *2001*; it is only with HAL's 'death' that he gains access to a hidden message that reveals the true intent of the top-secret Jupiter Mission.

Moon alludes to a number of other science-fiction films, but it pays special tribute to *2001* and Kubrick – his first name is even glimpsed in a scene where Sam is working in his plant laboratory. Besides the simplification of the relationship between man and machine, the film makes use of several iconic motifs of *2001*; Sam is framed walking through white, illuminated octagonal corridors that echo the set design of the Discovery One spaceship; like Dave, Sam eats fast-food space meals in the same manner, fishing it out of the oven, almost burning his fingers; Bowman's jogging around the centrifuge is replaced with Sam riding a bicycle; and the hibernation cells from *2001* reappear as the cells in which the clones fall into an eternal sleep, emphasizing the sarcophagi shape of the cells as killing machines.

The lasting impact of *2001*'s astronaut image is even more obvious in a comparison of Christopher Nolan's *Interstellar* (2014). Nolan utilizes many of the iconic qualities of *2001* for his film, including themes of time travel that allude to *2001*'s Star Gate sequence, whilst Hans Zimmer's score for *Interstellar* is reminiscent of Strauss' *Thus spoke Zarathustra* as a recurring motif in *2001*, and spinning wheels and circular imagery throughout provide further similarities. Nolan even goes so far as to reference the way light reflects on the astronaut's helmet as a visual element, similar to that on Bowman's during the Star Gate sequence.

Interstellar's astronaut, Cooper (Matthew McConaughey), stays in contact with an intelligent computer, TARS (Bill Irwin), who has to be switched off in order to die so that the astronaut can survive. He also remains in contact with his family at home on Earth via video message: here, comparable to Dr. Floyd and Squirt, it is Murph, the astronaut's daughter, who is celebrating her birthday at home, while Cooper witnesses her growing-up in outer space. But even when Nolan chose some visually striking images such as the multi-dimensional universe of an alien intelligence that is simulating a three-dimensional time bridge for Cooper to communicate with his daughter (literally through the bookshelves), echoing on a visual level the set design of the dismantling of HAL 9000, those film critics

'But as to whether or not he has feelings is something I don't think anyone can truthfully answer'

who claim *Interstellar* to be of a Kubrickian quality overlook a lack of openness, uncertainty and ambiguity that pervades readings of *2001* and its astronauts. Instead of offering an open queer transcendence, Nolan combines a classical Hollywood ending, not to speak of some pretentious kitsch formulas such as the final encounter between Cooper and Murph, which may be read as a standardized, normative echo to Bowman's final encounter as the only astronaut still alive at the end of his *Space Odyssey*, but that here ends in tears for Cooper; instead of rebirth, he becomes the heroic space cowboy returning to a new farm after his accomplished and celebrated mission.

The extensions that *Moon* and *Interstellar* offer of the astronaut figure do not only develop Bowman and Poole further, but Sam and Cooper can also be read as narrowed versions of the ambivalent and queer characters of their ancestors. Instead of the openness of *2001*, major parts of the obvious iconography of the astronaut figure are now combined with a simplified, more one-sided and closed reading. Where HAL's hidden motivations may be read as a jealous act of gay lovers, Gerty's good-hearted simplicity and superficiality and TARS's unresisting sacrifice for the mission gamble away major parts of the original film's potential. On the other hand, they do not only weaken the *2001* astronaut figure by simplification, they do also strengthen it by constantly perpetuating it for a new audience and generation, one seeking an updated reading of characters first seen 50 years ago.

Acknowledgements

My special thanks for the very first stimulus for this article to come into being and his useful help go to Henry Keazor, Heidelberg, and for a fruitful exchange on Kubrick's *2001* to Antoine Prévost-Balga, Paris.

Part Five

Visual Spectacle

Robert Kolker has spoken of his overwhelming experience when he first saw *2001* on its release, and how Kubrick wanted the 'vastness of the Cinerama screen to encompass the vastness of his imagination of the future' (2017: 141–42). The visual spectacle of *2001*, its images, its grandeur – daring to cut between four million years of human history with a single jump cut – still impress today, with its visual design arguably never bettered, even in this age of CGI. Kubrick perhaps recognized the sheer scale of what he was creating when he cheekily suggested the film be titled 'How the Solar System Was Won', a reference to John Ford's Cinerama epic *How the West Was Won* (1962). Kubrick fills the Cinerama screen with overwhelming images, from interstellar planetary alignment, to out-of-this-reality Star Gate trips. As Kolker puts it, '*2001* is a film of incredible visual detail. There is, to borrow a term from art history, a *horror vacui*, a dread of empty spaces, in this film about space' (2017: 144).

Caterina Martino's chapter, a work that builds on a previous piece, 'Pictures of *2001: A Space Odyssey* in the Stanley Kubrick Archive' (Martino 2016), explores the philosophy of aesthetics in *2001*. Martino offers a detailed textual analysis of the film, and in doing so shows how Kubrick constructed a philosophy of photography within it, stemming in large part from the earliest stages of his career as a photojournalist at *Look* magazine. Photography remained an enduring passion for Kubrick throughout his life and career, and the aesthetics that he developed in New York in the 1940s and 1950s were adapted in his later cinematic career, as the likes of Mather (2006, 2013) have shown.

Rachel Walisko's chapter argues how the *mise-en-scène* of *2001* – its setting in the vastness of space, the black expansive backgrounds and the clinical technological environments – positions it as a sublime film, one that evokes a total sense of fear and awe in the audience. Certainly, Kubrick himself testified to his belief in the simultaneous sense of fear and wonder of the universe, saying, 'the most terrifying fact about the universe is not that it is hostile but that it is indifferent' (Nordern 1968: 73). The intellectual sophistication of *2001* was unprecedented for a mainstream Hollywood picture, and Walisko examines the depth of the philosophical challenge that Kubrick presented to his audience.

Further reading

The Kubrickian aesthetic has been masterfully explored by Robert Kolker (2010) in his essay 'Rage for order: Kubrick's fearful symmetry', *Raritan*, 30:1, pp. 50–67, as well as his *A Cinema*

Photography and beyond the infinite

Among all the artistic fields that inspired Stanley Kubrick, possibly one of the most incisive is photography. Before becoming a film director, Kubrick was a photographer and, in many ways, he never stopped being a photographer or having a photographic vision. Kubrick's photographic career began at *Look*, a photojournalist magazine that he worked at from 1945 to 1950 producing black and white reportage pictures of New York life.[1] As a director, he applied his photographic aesthetics in the making of his films. Photography in his films has an important role in two ways. Firstly, it serves as a visual tool for constructing the perfect camera framing; in other words, for organizing everything that enters the frame. Secondly, photography is used for the minute planning of a scene, used to carry out an unceasing work of documentation that Kubrick requires for every stage of the making of the film.

These two functions of photography are present in *2001*. Yet, in this film photography seems to go beyond the simple use as a technical device or aesthetic approach, as there are several moments in which photography has a leading role. This is noticeable in the opening episode of the film, 'The Dawn of Man'; we can assume that this episode begins with a photograph, or rather photographs of real landscapes. We know that the film is shot in a studio and that these photographs were taken in Africa on glass plates with a Sinar camera (Baxter 1997: 264) by a group of cameramen and photographers – including Robert Watts, member of the Fluxus art movement, and Pierre Boulat (Chion 2006: 214). The group scouted Namibia to take 'large-format ten-by-eight Ektachrome transparencies' (LoBrutto 1997: 300) according to Kubrick's precise instructions. As an alternative to rear screen projection, a common practice at that time, Kubrick decided to project the African colour transparencies using front-projection (in other words onto the actors). The transparencies 'were projected on a vast screen, which registered the picture on thousands of minuscule reflectors. The image was too weak to show up on the bodies of animals or actors' (Walker et al. 1999: 164). What results on screen is a series of still images of African plains, mountains and sunsets, dominated with red and black colours, which cut from one picture to the next like a slideshow. The motionlessness of the photographs is enhanced, even animated, by the presence of background sounds of nature (crickets, birds and wind). Yet, though we can hear the wind blowing, the images we see on screen show unmoving clouds. These landscapes, then, serve to create a context and are displayed in the same style throughout 'The Dawn of Man'.

This chapter will demonstrate that Kubrick expresses a philosophy of photography throughout *2001*; in this 'mythological documentary', as Kubrick defined *2001* (Walker et al. 1999: 162), the image has a leading role given the lack of dialogue. Kubrick is accurate with the shapes and the colours creating a very special visual symmetry in every camera frame. Besides, even if we can identify different typologies of images that are shown during the film (drawings, motion pictures, images transmitted via a video call, TV images), the presence of photography is so effective that it is possible to delineate a real theoretical thinking behind it. As an artist, Kubrick conceptualizes the relationship between the technology related to the image production (including photography) and human intelligence. This thinking is comparable to the philosophy of photography asserted over time by famous philosophers from Walter Benjamin to contemporary authors, such as Roger Scruton.

Yet, can a director make use of a film to express a philosophy of photography? In order to understand this, I will analyse the film following some precise criteria, such as identifying the possible presence of photographers, photographs and photographic cameras. It is also important to consider crucial photographic issues, which in this case is the possibility to reproduce the world and the possibility to create a negative from which we can reproduce infinite positives. Similar to what Freud writes in *Totem and Taboo* (1913) – in other words that the history of the world is a perpetual reiteration of a group of primordial traumas and that collective traumas took place in prehistoric times – Kubrick makes a science-fiction film starting from prehistory that tells us that our future has roots in an epoch that we can only imagine. *2001* is heavily based on the idea that our future is a varied repetition of the past and that technology is the repetition of an invention made in prehistoric times. All this – together with the monolith that each time is shown as the same *and* different – is a reference to the technical reproducibility as described by Walter Benjamin (1936), being the main feature of the invention of photography.

The philosophy of photography expressed by Kubrick is related to the relationship between a negative (an original) and a positive (infinite copies), meant as inverted items that are displayed with a kind of montage of attractions throughout the film. I intend the terms 'negative' and 'positive' to be used in their photographic meaning.

Because of their physical contiguity, the relationship between negative and positive is not a dichotomy, nor a contraposition, but rather a filiation (or a genealogy). *2001* can be explained starting from this filiation and applying a psychoanalytic term: there is a 'trauma' (the necessity to survive which leads the man-apes to kill) that can be considered as the negative (meant in its photographic meaning) of a 'symptom' (which is the hypertechnological world as result of their evolution). The advanced technology comes from a past trauma and, despite our evolution, we reiterate this trauma because we still keep on killing. In other words, something that is current (for instance the spaceship) has its matrix/roots in something that comes before it (the bone), something that has been forgotten and that now is unconscious. It is from this perspective that I will analyse *2001* as a reflection on the birth of the photographic intelligence of man, and the monolith as the idea of photographic technological revolution.

Moonolith: The souvenir photo of the never seen before

In order to begin to understand the philosophy of photography inherent in *2001*, our starting point will be the second appearance of the monolith. It occurs during what can be considered as the second episode of the film set in 1999, in which the main character is Heywood Floyd, a scientist travelling to the Moon to inspect the excavation site where the monolith has been discovered. It is in this segment of the film wherein most of the explicit references to photography take place.

The first notable reference to photography is the brief photo shoot that precedes Floyd's conference at the Clavius base. A group of scientists are sat around a table in what can be described as a kind of 'light-box room'; the lighting and framing is such that it is difficult for us to clearly see any of their faces. Even Floyd, who is at the centre of the shot, has his back turned while the other scientists are talking to each other. As spectators, we tend to follow the only person who is moving in the room: in this case the photographer. He takes a number of photographs of Floyd and his colleagues from a variety of angles before he announces that he has completed his work and then leaves the room. Kubrick purposely focuses the camera's attention on the photographer, in a sequence lasting for around 30 seconds. The documentary style method in which he takes his photographs alludes to Kubrick's own career as a photojournalist, but we cannot be entirely sure the photographer in the scene is in fact a photojournalist given the secrecy of the conference and the excavation on the Moon. More likely, then, he works as a photographer at the base, recruited to document the extraordinary mission the scientists are undertaking. Kubrick allows the camera to follow the photographer as he moves to the left of the frame to take a picture of Floyd from a closer point of view. The camera continues to follow the photographer until he opens the door and leaves.

We can see that Kubrick has spent time considering what the role of a future photographer/photojournalist might be in documenting historical world (cosmic) events. Even more significant is the way Kubrick has decided upon how a camera of the future will look and function. We can see the photographer using a small camera that does not have the typical shape of a photographic camera. It looks tube-shaped, quite similar to the lens of the Panavision 70mm camera, and with a handle at the bottom (it should be noted that circular shapes are dominant throughout the film). The fact that Kubrick lingers on the photographer, on what he is doing, the camera he uses and how the camera functions – granted, for only several seconds that may go unnoticed by the viewer – leads us to think that Kubrick is imagining the fate of photography in the future.

This scene is followed by an equally important photographic moment, as Floyd and several other scientists travel to the lunar excavation site, TMA 1, where the monolith has been discovered. Inside the shuttle, Floyd and his colleagues try to understand more about the monolith by looking at satellite photographs of the Moon's surface. Kubrick zooms in on these photographs as Floyd browses through them. The photographs are large format images and are labelled with the initials TMA-1 (Tycho Magnetic Anomaly). Tycho is the name of the lunar crater where Kubrick sets the discovery of the monolith. The crater was named after the Danish astronomer Tycho Brahe, who designed important astronomical observation tools in the second half of the sixteenth century. Brahe used the camera obscura for his studies about the Sun (Bianucci 2015). Arguably, if we interpret *2001* as Kubrick's philosophy of photography, the decision to locate the monolith in the Tycho crater cannot be mere coincidence.

After they have arrived at the excavation site, Floyd and the other scientists approach the monolith; in awe of its mysterious presence, Floyd touches it (he has the same astonished and inquiring look that the man-apes had four million years earlier, as I will explore below). The scientists act as tourists admiring a foreign monument as they pose in front of the monolith to take a souvenir photo (Chion 2006: 236). Once more, we find another photographer and another photographic camera present in the scene. The photographer moves his hands and suggests a pose to ensure all the scientists are in the shot. An early draft of the script, dated December 1965, provides dialogue between two of the astronauts (Floyd and Michaels) and the photographer:[2]

MICHAELS: Thank you.
FLOYD: And so this is the first sun that it's had in four million years.
PHOTOGRAPHER: Excuse me, gentlemen, if you'd all line up on this side of the walkway we'd like to take a few photographes. Dr. Floyd, would you stand in the middle ... Dr. Michaels on that side, Mr. Halvorsen on the other ... thank you.

The Photographer quickly makes some exposures.

PHOTOGRAPHER: Thank you very much gentlemen, I'll have the base photo section send you copies.

As the men slowly separate from their picture pose, there is a piercingly powerful series of five electronic shrieks, each like a hideously over-loaded and distorted time signal. Floyd involuntarily tries to block his ears with his spacesuited hands. Then comes mercily silence.

(Kubrick and Clarke 1965b)

This dialogue provides us with a better understanding of the context of this scene. After the photographer takes his pictures, sunlight falls upon the monolith leading it to emit a strong audio signal that immediately interrupts the action. This sound can be interpreted as a signal from whoever placed the monolith on the Moon (God? An alien race?). In this exact moment, Kubrick inserts an image of the monolith aligned with the Sun and the Moon. The content of this image must be questioned due to a number of inconsistencies. Notably, the monolith is on the surface of the Moon; therefore, what we see aligned with the Sun cannot be the Moon. Perhaps it is a planet (Jupiter? The Earth?). Subsequently, how can this insert be interpreted? It is a similar image to that which appears in 'The Dawn of Man', the only difference being the background – here it is against the blackness of space, compared to the bright sky of the African plains. What we are presented with is a photographic inversion of this image between negative (the monolith with blue sky) and positive (the monolith with dark sky). Furthermore, the items are inverted: from the Earth we see the alignment with the Sun and the Moon, from the Moon we see the alignment with the Sun and a planet. The alignment is always repeated in the same way in any area of the space. This is also how the history of humankind works: we know that history repeats itself even if it seems different.

In this scene, Kubrick also presents us with yet another camera design. Unlike the first camera we saw at the Clavius base, this one appears to be bigger and with a more 'futuristic design'. The difference is most probably due to the context of the location: not indoors, but an external location, the Moon, which has extraordinary conditions of light and atmosphere. Every time the photographer takes a picture, it seems that he needs to recharge the camera. Analysing this gesture closer, we realize that the camera works using photographic film. Although Kubrick was a far-sighted visionary, at that time he could not imagine anything close to the digital technology that would eventually replace the old analogue techniques.

What Kubrick shows us throughout the scenes with Floyd are a number of photographers, different kinds of cameras and a variety of photographic images (from the picture on Floyd's identity badge to the photographic images of the lunar surface). This progression of photographic elements reaches its peak in the scene of the untaken souvenir photo at the TMA 1 site. At this point, we can speculate whether in fact the monolith should be considered as a metaphor of photography. In order to understand this statement further, it is necessary to return to the starting point of the film, 'The Dawn of Man' and the first appearance of the monolith.

Monkeylith: The advent of the photographic memory

What we learn in the scenes with Heywood Floyd is that the monolith was intentionally buried on the Moon four million years previous by some unknown entity. Prior to this, the film tells the story of 'The Dawn of Man', presumably also four million years previous to the scenes with Floyd, and it is in this sequence where the monolith first appears. Its appearance coincides with a monumental point in human history, a turning point in evolution. Yet, how does any of this relate to photography?

'The Dawn of Man' depicts the Earth in a prehistoric age; the landscape is a primeval desert inhabited by a group of man-apes that are struggling to survive as they fight for territorial ownership of a watering hole. The primitive life of the man-apes is disturbed by the sudden appearance of a perfectly smooth black slab of about five metres (according to the original screenplay) – the monolith. Whereas the interaction between the scientists and the monolith was one of intellectual inquiry of an alien object, for the man-apes it is one of magical awe. The initial contact between the man-apes and the monolith is characterized by jumps, screams, fear and amazement. The leader of the tribe, Moon-Watcher, slowly approaches the monolith and when he reaches enough courage, he touches and smells it. We then see the image of the alignment with the Sun and the Moon, but this time no audio signal is emitted. The action is not interrupted – the man-apes are not pushed away from the monolith, as happens with the astronauts on the Moon. We do not know what happens to the monolith after this meeting – where does it go? But what we do know is the effect it has on the man-apes, in particular Moon-Watcher.

The appearance of the monolith leads Moon-Watcher to realize a new use for the bones of an animal carcass – they can be used as a weapon. Moon-Watcher's insight has been anticipated by the insert of the image of the monolith aligned with the Sun and the Moon. The sequence plays out as follows:

- Moon-Watcher momentarily pauses in front of the animal carcass, thoughtful
- Cut to the image of the monolith aligned with the Sun and the Moon
- Moon-Watcher scrutinizes the carcass with a new, curious gaze
- Moon-Watcher lifts a bone and beats it on the other bones, his beats gaining in strength
- Cut to an image of a tapir that dies and falls to the left
- Moon-Watcher keeps on beating the bones, in a wild frenzy
- Cut to another image of the tapir, which dies and falls to the right.

What can we assume from this sequence? Certainly that the monolith is responsible for instilling in Moon-Watcher a new skill that will change his lifestyle, and the course of humanity, forever: memory. The encounter with the monolith generates a kind of consciousness in the man-apes and seems to be the instigator of two human abilities: intellect and the mental production and storage of images. In the earliest drafts of the screenplay, the monolith was supposed to be an object placed on Earth by an alien race to supervise the man-apes. At the same time, it was imagined as an object that would educate the man-apes (Baxter 1997: 252). These early incarnations of the monolith's intent validate the idea of the black cuboid equipping the man-apes with the ability of memory. Given that the image of the monolith appears immediately before Moon-Watcher's realization to use the bone as a weapon, we can assume that it was the monolith that taught him to connect this realization with the ability to kill a tapir. The image of the monolith can be interpreted not as a sense perception but as a memory (in the sense of information stored and recalled). The image of the monolith is not a subjective angle shot but a mental image, according to the definition of Gilles Deleuze in *Cinéma II: L'image-temps* (*Cinema 2: The Time-Image*) (1985). The insert of the monolith becomes a symbol that reveals a cognitive act. For the first time, Moon-Watcher is able to hypothesize how the tapir died or can die visualizing it through images. The ability to remember the monolith is the ability to produce an image that is a sign, in the sense of something that stands for something else, as Charles S. Peirce explains in *Minute Logic* (1902).

Moon-Watcher remembers the monolith once it has disappeared, and he visualizes the death of the tapir, which is something that has not happened yet, given that it was a mental image. The image of the tapir that dies – an image repeated twice and corresponding to an inversion between left and right – can be interpreted as a symmetry of past and future. Moon-Watcher connects the bones to the past (the tapir was alive) and to the future (the tapir is alive but can die) due to the memory that the monolith has gifted him. As M. W. Bruno has suggested, the insert of the monolith can be considered as a 'flashback' (1999b: 53), a memory of the mysterious black object that is recalled to mind. But the images of the dying tapir can be considered as a 'flash-forward' (1999b: 53), a prediction that shows how the bone can be used as weapon. Yet, the two images of the tapir perhaps are not simply a flashback and a flash-forward, nor memories, but the visualization of a symmetrical reasoning of the man-ape: if death can be received, it can also be given. The monolith also works as a mental device for the spectator, who is following the evolution of the hominid on the screen. Involved in the adductive reasoning of Moon-Watcher, the spectator is led to interpret the image of the monolith not as a sense perception of the hominid, but as a mental image, a recalled memory. We are witnesses of the evolution of the culture that is always halfway between progress and destruction – the hominid ceases being prey, instead becoming the predator (199b: 45). The intelligence acquired consists of an ability to memorize and formulate a hypothesis, but also to kill.

'The Dawn of Man' ends with Moon-Watcher throwing the bone in the air. This gesture actualizes a transition from negative to positive. Throughout *2001* we often can find an inversion from white to black, from day to night, from the bright sky of Earth to the dark vastness of space. The relationship between negative and positive is visually associated with the shift from the prehistoric age to humanity's future in space, and the cut from the bone to spacecraft represents a technological evolution. Two different epochs are connected through this inversion of white and black: in the first era, the memory is something visual, while in the second era, the vision is memorized and recorded. Indeed, the scenes with Floyd commence with him asleep in front of a screen that is displaying a motion picture. Floyd is travelling in a shuttle to reach the Clavius base. We see a hostess that enters the room and pick up a pen that is floating in the shuttle's corridor. This gesture completes the series of objects that float in the air: the bone, the spaceship, the pen. The pen, as metaphor of the invention of writing, is in between the bone (the advent of memory and intellect) and the spaceship (the technological era). It is possible to interpret this combination of elements as a shift from an era during which the images are still a product of the mind, to an era where the images are produced and stored outside of the mind.

The transition from the man-apes to the human, from animal perception to human intellect, is possible with the advent of the icon. The souvenir photo that *Homo sapiens* try to take on the Moon is only possible because of the ability of memory learned from the monolith by the man-apes. 'The Dawn of Man' depicts the birth of human intelligence, and more precisely the advent of memory as image-sign. This kind of image is at the origin of any kind of image production, from painting to photography. Although there is no explicit connection, we can assume that the monolith becomes a metaphor of photography because it is a support for the image-sign.

Monolight: Camera obscura and immortality

Though it is not clear whether the monolith throughout the film is the same one, we can count four separate appearances (different locations) of the monolith: the first encounter is with the man-apes; the second is the discovery of the monolith on the Moon; the third is the monolith that floats in space near Jupiter and the final appearance is the monolith in the Louis XVI room that Bowman inhabits following his venture through the Star Gate.

I want to look, however, at a section of *2001* that does not feature the monolith at all. The first half of the 'Jupiter Mission, 18 Months Later' section is set on board the Discovery One spaceship. A team of astronauts travel towards Jupiter, their mission a secret. Only two astronauts are awake, David Bowman and Frank Poole, while the rest of the crew is in hibernation. We follow the daily routines of Bowman and Poole as they spend their days under the supervision of the ship's computer, HAL 9000 – whose rectangular shape is similar to that of the monolith. HAL possesses an 'eye' through which he keeps control over everything that happens on the spaceship. His eye looks very much like a photographic lens. It was in fact built using a real photographic lens, a Nikon Nikkor 8mm f/8 fisheye lens,[3] though his point of view shots are with a wide-angle lens. HAL's is an all-seeing gaze that captures everything, even the secret conversations between Bowman and Poole inside the space pods. Bowman spends his free time sketching drawings of the interior design of the spacecraft, as well of his colleagues who are sleeping. HAL asks to view the sketches and tells Bowman, 'that's a very nice rendering, Dave. I think you've improved a great deal'. There is a kind of comparison between two different categories of image production. HAL's eye is characterized by the automatism of the mechanism that determines a photographic precision and a documentary attitude. Instead, Bowman's drawings represent an art produced by the hand of a human. HAL's lens has the optical unconsciousness as discussed by Walter Benjamin, in that he is able to record what he sees, store it forever and create a permanent memory.

But HAL's is not the only eye that exists in *2001*. In fact, the Jupiter Mission is full of eyes if we consider the psychedelic journey of lights, distortions, colours and other effects that Bowman witness as he passes through the Star Gate in 'Jupiter and Beyond the Infinite'. The scene begins with the monolith horizontally floating in the universe until it aligns with Jupiter. This third appearance of the monolith and its alignment with Jupiter activates the beam of light that Bowman encounters after leaving the Discovery One. It seems that Kubrick is associating the monolith with the lights of the Star Gate. The monolith becomes a black photo plate that can be impressed by the light. As Bowman travels through the Star Gate, his eyes work as a shutter, with a change of colour with each motion of his eyes – opening and closing, they look like the clicks of a photo camera. We know that the shutter of analogue cameras works like the human eye; whereas the mechanical eye of HAL seems to have a human aspect, in this scene Bowman's eyes have a photographic aspect and this can be considered as another negative/positive relationship. Photographs and other kinds of images (paintings, drawings, diagrams, patterns, etc.) are used by Kubrick to create the special effects of this Star Gate sequence, with the images processed and distorted in a variety of ways (Chion 2006: 217), from the use of the slit-scan photography technique to the projection of high-speed images (Baxter 1997: 267).

The final image of the Star Gate sequence is that of Bowman's eye in extreme close up, filling the screen. Once again, with every blink of his eye, the colour of the image changes. Finally, the shot returns to the natural colour of a human eye and we acquire Bowman's point of view. We see what he sees: a fragment of a room with neoclassical decor. Bowman's point of view is comparable to the view from a photographic lens because the camera shot is fixed and the sides of the screen are black. At the centre of the screen, there is an oval frame (the window of the spacecraft) that shows us the Louis XVI room. From this moment, Bowman begins another kind of journey – a journey through different stages of his life. At the beginning, he watches the room from the inside of the pod, before he exits the pod wearing the astronaut suit and starts to walk around the room. From different perspectives, Bowman looks at himself aging, until he transforms into a foetus – the Star-Child – after the monolith has appeared in the room and he has reached out to touch it.

The room is like a box in which Bowman has been isolated (Chion 2006: 238), or rather, another example of a light-box, the room functioning as a sort of camera obscura. Bowman looks at himself in different ages and we know that this is possible for humankind only subsequent to the advent of photography (and the photo album of family memories). Certainly, painting possesses a similar function, however, unlike other representative arts, photography has a unique extent of realism (Bazin 2008) because of its indexical character (Dubois 2009). Humankind is able to watch and record itself since photography was invented. Looking at a picture, we see a 'spectrum' of ourselves and, therefore, Bowman is facing himself as a spectrum. According to Roland Barthes in *Camera Lucida* (1980), we can both say that Bowman *is* dead, and simultaneously that he *is* going to die; he dies but is reborn as a foetus. This also is an effect of photography, which can cause the symbolic death of an individual and at the same time makes them immortal.

Conclusion: Photolith

During the making of *The Shining*, Kubrick reputedly told Jack Nicholson that making a film is not like photographing the reality, but photographing the photograph of the reality (De Bernardinis 2003: 9). 'The photography of reality' is identifiable in the scrupulous methods adopted by the director. He used photography as a tool to plan every single stage of the making of the film, from the choice of the characters, their clothing and acting poses, to the documentation of the locations and the creation of the set (the numerous boxes of photographs now housed in the Stanley Kubrick Archive demonstrate Kubrick's propensity for extensive photographic research and documentation during the development and pre-production of his films). The 'photograph of a photograph of the reality' is a collage of snapshots to which motion has been deceptively added by the film (2003: 12). Kubrick ultimately seems to use the movie camera as if it were a stills camera: not only are some shots fixed and unmoving, but every frame is organized in order to create a perfect symmetry of the elements – almost every frame in *Barry Lyndon* is a case in point. In fact, Kubrick created perfectly centred images. Moreover, in order to shoot the scenes using the natural light of candles, he used special lenses (50mm still-photography lenses produced by the Zeiss Company for NASA); this method demonstrated expert photographic skills in being able (along with cinematographer John Alcott) to greatly control the special light conditions using a precise photographic technique.

There is not an obvious connection between the contents of the photographs that Kubrick took for *Look* magazine and the images that we see in *2001* (though it is more evident in his earlier films such as *Killer's Kiss*). The photographs taken by Kubrick in the 1940s and the 1950s are reportage pictures; *2001* is a science-fiction film in which the images are often distorted or even manipulated. According to an interview with his daughter Katharina,[4] Kubrick remained a photographer throughout his life as well as a collector of old cameras and lenses. Even after he finished working at *Look*, he never stopped taking photographs of private moments and of the cinematographic set. And when we look to his films, we can recognize a specific attention to photography.

With this chapter, I have tried to demonstrate that there are many references to photography throughout *2001* and that these references cannot be considered coincidental or random. Instead, a deeper analysis of the film suggests that they constitute a real philosophy of photography being constructed by Kubrick. This philosophy commences with the first appearance of the monolith in 'The Dawn of Man', in which humankind receives the ability of memory and intellect that allow it to think through images, store information, remember the past and prefigure the future. The monolith is a metaphor of the invention of the image. Before seeing the monolith, the hominids are inside a cave. This cave could be considered as an allusion to the very first recorded images in history – Palaeolithic cave paintings. Moreover, the cave could be an allusion to a famous Plato allegory: the exit of the man-apes from the cave corresponds to Plato's idea of the transition from a sense knowledge (gained through perception) to the intelligible knowledge (gained through mental skills).

The second appearance of the monolith on the Moon comes after a jump cut of four million years, in a sequence that depicts a world based on technologies used to produce and store images. The monolith becomes a metaphor of photography since its appearance is preceded by several references to photography and coincides itself with an important photographic moment. I would venture to say that if with the man-apes the monolith is a support for the invention of the image-sign, in this sequence it is connected to the photo camera – even the light that flashes at the peak of the monolith when shot from a low angle is suggestive of a camera flash.

The third appearance of the monolith is at the beginning of 'Jupiter and Beyond the Infinite'. The monolith activates the coloured images of Bowman's trip and is associated with the power of light. Here, it is not merely the support for the image-sign, but a photo plate that can be impressed by the light. In Clarke's *2001* novel, the monolith is a pyramidal structure, but Kubrick considered a range of shapes for the film, from a black pyramid to a transparent cube, and finally a black slab (Baxter 1997: 260). This means that, although the word 'monolith' generally indicates a block of stone, the description as 'black slab' multiplies the possibilities of interpretation. After all, why can't it be a photographic plate, given its association with light and the production of images?

The final appearance of the monolith is in the Louis XVI room that Bowman finds himself after travelling through the Star Gate, a room that works as a camera obscura and in relation to the photographic function of immortalisation (Bowman deals with himself as a photographic spectrum). It is in this sequence that the metaphor of photography is fully achieved.

2001 shows the birth of the human intellect through an image that the spectator must interpret as an image-sign and not as a sense perception. Everything is symbolic with the cave, the pen and the spaceship all being allusions to human evolution. In addition, the monolith, the eyes, the circular shapes, the technological devices where the characters walk up to reverse their image (as it happens using a camera obscura) are allusions and metaphors of photography. Moreover, the final image of *2001* can be considered a metaphor of photography: similar to the last image of *La Dolce Vita* (Fellini, 1960), the Star-Child looks into the camera as if someone is photographing him. In fact, Kubrick would repeat the idea of finishing a film on a photograph with *The Shining*, which ends with a close up of Jack Torrance's frozen body, immediately followed by a photograph in which he is immortalized. Torrance is physically dead and he is also 'frozen' in the photograph.

During the film, the negative/positive visual relationship is the inversion of some elements in other things that are equal and opposite at the same time. The negative/positive relationship corresponds to the duality of death/life that is the same of the elder Bowman/Star-Child. The negative is also a trauma on which is developed the positive as a kind of neurosis. Kubrick is commenting on how human progress is derived from trauma. The advanced technology of the spaceship is the evolution of the bone as a weapon, so the spaceship stems from a condition of necessity that led the man-apes to kill. Despite its evolution, humankind continues to kill, as we see Bowman 'kill' HAL. It is HAL who kills first, for fear of being disconnected; Bowman 'kills' in revenge. This is the disturbing element of the film: HAL is an artificial intelligence that acts as a total human being.

It is possible to draw two evolution lines: the first one is bone-pen-spaceship; the second one is monolith-photo camera. Since Kubrick is a director and a photographer, he presents the evolution and the history of the images alongside the technological evolution of humankind. In the wake of Darwinian theory, Kubrick sees the future as a positive of prehistoric times and man-apes as negative of *Homo sapiens*. Kubrick shows to us that man-apes acquire intelligence when they evolve from just using sight as a sense perception, to using it to mentally produce and store images (as the camera does). This is Kubrick's metaphor of photography: he depicts the evolution of humanity as an evolution characterized by a photographic logic based on the relationship between negative and positive, or rather as if there always had been a human propensity to create a perpetual progression of negatives and positives. Human evolution is characterized by the varied repetition (positives) of an archetype (a negative). Kubrick conceives the evolution of humanity as an instinct to photography that occurs in prehistoric times with the transition from perception to a photographic memory. The film tells the invention and the destiny of pictures from Plato's cave to a future where we can see our life in a few minutes (as Bowman does in the Louis XVI room). The stylish and comfortable room is the evolution of the cave and consequently the camera obscura is the evolution of the primitive image production.

Chapter Eleven

The sublime in *2001: A Space Odyssey*

Rachel Walisko

Moving images have a unique way of eliciting emotions from their audience, and sometimes the feelings that arise in spectators while viewing a film are conflicting. I was first introduced to Stanley Kubrick's *2001* by my father when I was 7 years old. It was 1997 and DVDs had just been released. *2001* was the first one he purchased and we fittingly watched it on a computer. It was unlike anything I had ever seen in my life up to that point. I remember feeling confused and asking too many questions, which my father refused to answer; 'just watch', he would say. Yet even while trying to make sense of an unclear narrative, I was aware that I was observing something much bigger than myself. Watching *2001* was the catalyst for my first existential experience, brought about by my own conflicting feelings of uncertainty and awe.

When *2001* was first released, it received 'decidedly mixed reviews' from high-profile critics in New York who 'were in a quandary over the narrative, pace and significance of key events' (Kapferer 2014: 2). Penelope Gilliatt, of the *New Yorker*, wrote that this 'great film [is] funny without once being gaggy, but it is also rather harrowing' (1968: 150), while Renata Adler of the *New York Times* claimed it is 'somewhere between hypnotic and immensely boring' (1968: 58). Though it must be stressed that the film was received positively by a number of critics outside of New York as Peter Krämer has shown (2010: 92-93). This conflicting reception may be due to the inherent nature of the film, which elicits a divided sense of both fear and wonder in its audience. An object's ability to evoke these conflicting emotions is often characterized as sublime.

This chapter will argue that *2001* is a sublime film because it adheres to the four features of the sublime object identified by Cynthia Freeland in her article 'The sublime in cinema' (1999: 66–68); it creates a conflict between pain and pleasure, it is overwhelming and great, it evokes feelings of pain, which leads to pleasure and understanding, and it incites moral reflection. I will make this argument by explaining the sublime within the context of the Romantic movement and how the unknown American West became a vehicle for artists to express their fear and wonder of this unexplored land. I will then describe how space and technology became the subsequent frontiers of the twentieth century, and the subject of science-fiction films. I will analyse how the aesthetics of the special effects in *2001* convey a sense of greatness, and the way an anti-narrative storyline, believable effects, and minimal dialogue create feelings of fear and awe, leading to cognition. Finally, I will show how the monolith is used as a device to incite reflection in the audience.

There is significant scholarship written about the sublime and the films of Kubrick respectively, but few texts that merge the two subjects. Of those that do, the most notable is

Pezzotta's *Stanley Kubrick: Adapting the Sublime* (2013), which examines the key features of Kubrick's film adaptations and concludes that the sublime is the common thread running through all of these works. She also references Freeland's criteria of the sublime film while examining *2001*, and I will reference her analysis of the Star Gate sequence later on in this chapter. While Pezzotta writes about the sublime specifically in reference to Kubrick's adaptations, I will place *2001* within the context of American history, and the sublime artwork created to reflect the country's expansion and innovation.

Much of today's understanding of the sublime comes from the writings of Edmund Burke who, in 1957, published *A Philosophical Enquiry into the Origin of Our Ideas of the Sublime and Beautiful*. This text defines the sublime as:

> Whatever is fitted in any sort to excite the ideas of pain and danger, that is to say, whatever is in any sort terrible, or is conversant about terrible objects, or operates in a manner analogous to terror, is a source of the sublime; that is, it is productive of the strongest emotion which the mind is capable of feeling.
>
> (Burke 2008: 36)

Burke characterized the sublime as anything that can evoke a sense of terror, or overpowering emotion. Nicolas Brinded describes how this explanation of the sublime was 'at the time of its publication, the most in-depth study of the sublime to date and focused on the idea that the sublime is related to, or a direct consequence of, fear and terror' (2014: 225). Burke believed that in order for observers to experience the sublime, as opposed to simply absolute terror, they must view it through a degree of separation (2008: 37). Therefore, Brinded states, the sublime is 'something that is experienced through mediation, which allows for it to be presented through the arts' (2014: 225). Artists are able to take fearful subject matter and present it to an audience in an indirect form through representation. Scott Bukatman explains that in conjunction with Burke's influence and concept of mediation through art, 'painting became a new site for the instantiation of the sublime' (1999: 257). The characteristics of sublime, 'obscurity, privation, vastness, succession, uniformity, magnificence, loudness, suddenness and so on' (Wilton 1980: 30), can be seen 'in the dramatic landscapes of J. M. W. Turner and John Martin's apocalyptic vistas' (Brinded 2014: 226). Elizabeth Kessler describes how these nineteenth-century artists adhered to the aesthetics of Romanticism, which emphasizes 'the powerful forces of nature, strong compositions that convey great size and scale, dramatic lighting to heighten the intensity of the scene' (2012: 20). While the paintings of Turner and other Romantic landscape painters evoke a sense of fear and wonder in an audience, Freeland explains that the philosophy of the sublime was also applied to the work of 'Romantic poets, Gothic novelists, and composers like Beethoven' (1999: 65), which is a testament to the versatility of the sublime in the arts.

Even through the transition from the nineteenth century to twentieth, the Romantic aesthetic persevered through many different forms of creation, 'such as Ansel Adam's photographs, Hollywood westerns, Chesley Bonestell's space art, and science-fiction films'

(Kessler 2012: 55), which 'ensured a continued interest in representing features of the landscapes that dwarfed humanity with their size, scale, and power' (2012: 54). While many films exhibit the characteristics of Romanticism, Freeland argues, 'there are certain films best described as sublime and that this concept may facilitate more diverse descriptions of films as artworks' (1999: 65). Influenced by the writing of Immanuel Kant, Freeland identifies the four basic criteria of a sublime object as 'emotional conflict describable as "rapturous terror"' (1999: 69), 'greatness, cognition of the ineffable, and moral reflection' (1999: 70). I will argue that because of its adherence to these four characteristics, Kubrick's *2001* can be considered a sublime object.

First criteria: Pain and pleasure

Freeland's first and most important criterion of the sublime object is that 'it calls forth a characteristic conflict between certain feelings of pain and pleasure – it evokes what Burke labelled 'rapturous terror' (1999: 66). The sublime is the feeling of both terror and excitement, which is often elicited by the unknown. One embodiment of the mysterious is the frontier, which is defined as 'a border or an edge, a line between what is known and what remains beyond humanity's grasp. Along this line, two realms confront each other' (Kessler 2012: 210). The two territories that lay side by side along a frontier are the known and the unknown, and humanity's fear of the unfamiliar has facilitated the creation of artwork depicting the latter's landscapes. Kessler believes that the existence of a frontier is essential to creating the aesthetic experience of the sublime, as representing a limit 'that must be transcended' (2012: 210). During the westward expansion, the American frontier was an untamed wild, which painters like Thomas Cole tried to capture the essence of. Brinded explains how this unfamiliar landscape inspired a new genre of sublime:

> A distinctly American sublime arose mainly in the late-eighteenth and early-nineteenth centuries and was often linked to the land itself, which took on the characteristics of Kant's dynamical and mathematical sublime – its natural features were considered awe-inspiringly powerful and the size of the continent seemed to be impossibly large.
> (2014: 226)

The work of artists who painted the American frontier evoked a sense of terror by portraying the undomesticated landscape as a force beyond human control. It also elicited awe, by capturing the beauty and scale of a terrain that was completely unlike the land already inhabited by the majority of the population.

By the 1960s, the American West had been settled, but humanity was on the verge of exploring a new unknown. Kessler writes that, 'as a historical, metaphorical, and phenomological concept, the frontier is a consistent presence in the rhetoric that circulates around space exploration' (2012: 118). Humanity looked to the sky as the next territory to be conquered, and Kapferer describes 1968, the year *2001* was released, as 'the same year that Apollo 8 was launched, the first manned mission into outer space' and a 'time when humankind in its venture into space appeared to be embarking on a new era' (2014: 3). Humanity's focus now shifted to the colonization of space, propelled by the contexts of the Cold War and the Space Race. Kessler explains that, 'Burke considered the act of contemplating the stars to be a certain experience of the sublime' (2012: 470), bringing validity to the concept that viewing images of outer space brings about feelings of the sublime in most people. She goes on to write:

> Together the vast number of stars and their 'apparent confusion' gave rise to reflections on the infinite. Burke believed them so numerous and disordered as to make it impossible for us to become familiar enough to disrupt their sublimity.
>
> (2012: 47–48)

The universe evokes the same feelings of fear and wonder as the uninhabited American landscape of the West, due to its incomprehensible size, which results in an indeterminate number of scenarios and possibilities that can never be identified or predicted. As outer space was the new frontier of the mid-twentieth century, 'artist and filmmakers turned to the same Romantic model as the interest in space travel grew' (Kessler 2012: 57). Stanley Kubrick was one such artist who employed the Romantic aesthetic of the sublime to depict the space frontier.

With so much of the world's attention focused on the impending first venture into space, it is no wonder the subject also captured the imagination of artists and filmmakers. Brinded believes that humanity's intense fascination with 'outer space and the farthest reaches of the galaxy' is reflected 'in much twentieth and twenty-first-century cinema' (2014: 224). Science-fiction film usually features subject matter related to the forefront of human innovation at the time in which it is created, and this adherence to concepts of advancement is often evident through recurring themes, which include 'space, time, causality, consciousness, identity, agency, and other categories of experience' (Sanders 2008: 2). In addition to characteristic themes, most science-fiction films also have a cohesive look, of which Vivian Sobchack writes: 'the visual surface of all SF film presents us with a confrontation between and mixture of those images to which we respond as "alien" and those we know to be familiar' (1997: 87). Science-fiction film is marked by visuals that are familiar to an audience, juxtaposed to those that are unknown. An example of this aesthetic in *2001* is the scene on the Pan Am space plane carrying Dr. Heywood Floyd to a space station. The interior of the plane looks extremely similar to a commercial aircraft used to shuttle passengers from one location on Earth to another. However, this plane is flying through space, which means there is no gravitational pull. Zero gravity creates the unfamiliar sight on board in this context; a pen floating mid-aisle away from its sleeping owner, whose arm is buoying weightlessly up and down. Then enters the flight hostess, who uses Grip Shoes to walk methodically down the aisle to capture the pen and replace it in Dr. Heywood Floyd's pocket. The familiar visuals of the aircraft interior, coupled with the representation of zero gravity, create the signature aesthetic of familiar and unfamiliar distinct to the science-fiction genre.

Kessler links Sobchack's concept of the familiar and alien in the visuals of science-fiction film back to the sublime, writing, 'Sobchack's formulation recalls Kant's suggestion that the sublime involves a conflict between the imagination and reason, between what the senses cannot grasp and what reason can understand' (Kessler 2012: 59). Therefore, science-fiction films adhere to the characteristics of sublime aesthetics by appealing to a sense of the known, and unknown, which is also synonymous with the concept of the frontier. Bukatman states 'the precise function of science-fiction, in many ways, is to create the boundless and infinite stuff of the sublime experience, and thus to produce a sense of transcendence beyond human finitudes' (1999: 256). Science-fiction is an ideal vehicle for the sublime, as its subject matter often dwarfs humanity and encourages consumers of the genre to recognize the limitless potential of foreign environments, like space. Just as artists depicted their impressions of the wild American West through creative works, filmmakers are now able to portray their impressions of the outer space frontier through science-fiction film. For example, John Ford's 1962 epic, *How the West Was Won*, depicts the settlement of the United States through the narratives of pilgrims, outlaws, cowboys, Native Americans and soldiers, set against the backdrop of the western plains and mountains. Six years later, Kubrick released *2001*, initiating a new era of storytelling that exchanged the frontier of the West for outer space.

After collectively deciding to venture into space, humans were faced with the challenge of developing tools to facilitate this exploration. This meant that the late twentieth century became a time of developing and expanding new technologies (Bukatman 1999: 269), as space exploration was now combining 'the frontier as the physical movement into new territories with the acquisition of new knowledge' (Kessler 2012: 213). Rapid technological advancement became an additional frontline for humanity, who could not fully predict how it would develop or if it would surpass our own potential as human beings. Bukatman writes, 'it is technology that inspires the sensations characteristic of sublimity; therefore it is technology that alludes to the limits of human definition and comprehension' (1999: 251). The limitless capabilities of technology draw attention to the mortal inadequacies of human beings, and therefore arouse a sense of the sublime because of its endless possibility. Bukatman proclaims 'the might of technology, supposedly our own creation, is mastered through a powerful display that acknowledges anxiety but recontains it within the field of spectatorial power' (1999: 265). The capability of new technology has the potential to inspire both fear and awe in its creators, and this concept is conveyed through *2001*'s portrayal of the computer HAL.

HAL 9000 is the newest model in a series of super computers, and has a perfect rate of accuracy. He ('he' is given this pronoun due to his male voice) is placed onboard the Discovery One spacecraft to ensure things run as smoothly as possible on the voyage to Jupiter. HAL reports a faulty antenna, yet when astronauts Bowman and Poole bring it in for inspection, they find nothing wrong with it. After lip-reading a private conversation in which the two crewmembers discuss shutting him down due to potential error, HAL's helpful disposition rapidly disintegrates and he begins trying to kill off all humans on the ship. HAL manages to kill pool and the scientists who were hibernating on board, yet Bowman reaches his mainframe and disconnects his advanced processor. Kapferer writes:

> HAL could be conceived as operating from within the disingenuous position of the servant who participates in the sustaining of fictions that the other crew members (Poole and Bowman) also engage in and, who thus conspire in processes that may threaten their very existence.
>
> (2014: 64)

Kapferer implies that HAL could be a piece of technology that has evolved beyond the scope of human intention, and learned to fabricate false information. Of the strained relationship between humans and our technology, Jason Eberl describes how 'Kubrick's films present us with the struggle of humanity against artificial intelligence – a struggle that humanity has brought on itself and must endure' (2007: 242). He goes on to explain that humans typically assume that because we create something, we inherently have control over it. However, this is not always the case, and the dynamic between HAL and his human crew exemplifies how complex these relationships can become (2007: 242). The idea that artificial intelligence could have a will independent from those who created it, a sense of self-preservation and the ability to lie and murder, is most likely a terrifying thought to both original and contemporary viewers of the film.

Torben Grodal describes how 'space films often depict spaces and objects that are beyond normal interaction. In traditional aesthetics, experiences in which perception is dissociated from interaction are called sublime' (2009: 10). Science-fiction films, featuring astonishing scenes of space and technology have the potential to evoke a feeling of terror in an audience, who feels overwhelmed by far reaching concepts and an unknown future of space exploration. Kessler writes that Burke believed terror prompts a temporary loss of reason, and that 'pleasure arises not immediately but in terror's aftermath, in the delight experienced when the threat is relieved or recognized as only illusory' (2012: 47). Although being trapped in a spacecraft with a human-killing robot is an uncomfortable concept, which one might even describe as painful, this frightening idea is mediated in *2001* through the screen, which keeps the audience at a safe vantage point. Therefore, when terrifying moments are seen on a screen, the audience first feels terror, but then feels safe and is able to also feel pleasure. By evoking these two conflicting emotions, *2001* meets Freeland's first criteria of the sublime.

Second criteria: Greatness

Freeland's second criterion of the sublime object is 'something about it is "great" and astonishing […] the sublime object is vast, powerful and overwhelming' (1999: 67). In order for a film to be sublime, it must leave its audience with an impression of greatness. Although the titles of many science-fictions films, like *2001: A Space Odyssey*, *The Time Machine* (Pal, 1960), *The Day the Earth Caught Fire* (Guest, 1961) and *Fantastic Voyage* (Fleischer, 1966), often imply an object of 'spatiotemporal grandeur' (Bukatman 1999: 256), Freeland explains that a film's ability to move 'beyond beauty to the kind of grandeur we associate with the label sublime [is] partly due to its subject matter, but also to the film's treatment of this grand subject matter' (1999: 68). This notion is echoed by Rowe, who feels that many sequences of *2001* offer 'a direct expression of the Romantic sublime, not solely through the grandeur of their imagery but also as a result of their overt discordance with the film's narrative and logical-representational strategies of expression' (2013: 50). Treatment comes down to the aesthetic choices an artist makes in depicting a subject. In the genre of science-fiction, Bukatman believes that 'the special effects work of Douglas Trumbull is particularly distinctive and sustained in its evocation of the sublime' (1999: 250). Known for creating 'a sense of environmental grandeur' (1999: 258) through his aesthetics, Kubrick hired him as the special effects supervisor on *2001*. Trumbull's work elicits a sense of the sublime 'around a massive technological object or environment' (Bukatman 1999: 251) and in *2001* conveys the endless dimensions of outer space, which is epitomized in the Star Gate sequence.

The Star Gate sequence takes place in the film soon after the 'Jupiter and Beyond the Infinite' title card. Bowman directs his spacecraft towards Jupiter and enters another dimension, which features 'imagery from every pattern the mind's eye is capable of registering' (Walker et al. 190). This innovative scene is so visually striking that it has become one of the most memorable in *2001*. It was Trumbull who supervised the Star Gate sequence, and the scene is marked by the sublime aesthetics of his work, the first of which is that it 'features scarcely any objects: it emphasizes instead a continuum of spatiotemporal transmutations' (Bukatman 1999: 258). As Bowman is the sole subject in this scene, the audience's focus alternates between his figure and the expansive space of the environment, a trait common of the Romantic paintings of the American West. Just as 'nineteenth century artists used human figures to establish scale' (Kessler 2012: 40), so the Star Gate sequence uses Bowman to do the same. Both *2001* and Romantic paintings portray a massive sense of size, which 'propose that the natural world will overwhelm humanity by dwarfing us with its immensity' (2012: 40). By presenting Bowman as the only figure against the colossal backdrop of the Star Gate, Trumbull is able to convey the sublime through visuals that threaten to overwhelm the belittled human on screen.

Trumbull's second characteristic is that 'kinetic lights and amorphous shapes of Star Gate sequence' (Bukatman 1999: 260), intercut with close-ups of Bowman, 're-establish scale and re-emphasize the "otherness" of the sublime environment' (1999: 261), which allows for the presence of diegetic spectators to enhance 'the presentational aspect of the cinema, while also evoking the sublime' (1999: 261). In the Star Gate sequence, a feeling of the sublime is evoked through the audience's identification with Bowman and the camera. Empathy between Bowman and the camera in this scene develops in alignment with Christian Metz's theory of primary and secondary processes of identification. As the subject of the film, audience members first identify with Bowman as 'the character of the fiction' (Metz 2011: 23). Spectators then identify with the camera itself, as the point-of-view shots frame the expanse of space seen from Bowman's perspective (2011: 27). By cutting from images of Bowman's face to the abstract landscape, the audience sees the landscape through Bowman's eyes: as a foreign and unknown space. To create a heightened sense that Bowman is venturing through strange territory, the visual effects of the Star Gate are intercut 'with scenes from Monument Valley shown in psychedelic colors' (Kessler 2012: 59), which are images that resemble 'earthly geological and meteorological formations, especially as depicted in Romantic landscapes of the American West' (2012: 5). By intercutting footage of a scene that resembles the American West, the audience is able to make a direct connection between the environment Bowman is travelling through in *2001*, and the land depicted in the Romantic paintings of the West. Sobchack writes that in order to make us believe 'in the possibility, if not probability, of the alien things we see, the visual surfaces of the film are inextricably linked to and dependent upon the familiar' (1997: 88). Therefore, an audience accepts that the Star Gate exists in the film, because they recognize similarities between it and the western landscapes of America. Without a setting reminiscent of one they already know, viewers would have a more difficult time believing in the transcendental Star Gate of *2001*. The frontier emphasizes 'the knowledge of limits and borders' (Kessler 2012: 225) in this sequence, which 'not only creates distinction but also enables one to recognize continuity as it blurs the lines between the terrestrial and the celestial' (2012: 225). The *foreign* and the *unknown* are key traits of locations that evoke a sense of terror and awe; therefore, the Star Gate's unfamiliar environment, while alluding to the American West, links the frontiers of both land and space and conjures feelings of the sublime.

The third trait of Trumbull's sublime special effects is *luminism*, an aesthetic that emphasizes impersonal expression, horizontality, minute tonal gradations, intimate size, immobility and silence' (Bukatman 1999: 262). Luminism is also characterized as a style of landscape painting, which developed during the Romantic movement of the mid to late 1800s. Bukatman describes how, in *2001*, 'light's transformative power illustrates, embodies and enacts precisely the supersession of the human' (1999: 264). Luminism is used in the Star Gate scene to displace people on screen and belittle humanity, in a way similar to the work of the Romantic painters. This technique conveys the sheer magnitude and wildness of an environment, by removing or minimizing humanity's place in nature. The three features of Trumbull's Star Gate sequence (the emphasis on space, the portrayal of the environment as 'other', and the use of luminism) represent the overall aesthetic characteristics of his work in this film, with his treatment of the special effects in *2001* conveying a sense of greatness that meets Freeland's second criteria of the sublime object.

Third criteria: Pain and then pleasure

Freeland's third feature of the sublime 'is that it evokes ineffable and painful feelings, through which a transformation occurs into pleasure and cognition' (1999: 68). Building off the first and second features (a feeling of both pain and pleasure and an overall sense of greatness), the sublime object must then develop in a way that allows the audience to gain peace and understanding. Freeland goes on to explain, 'in Kant's view, the ineffability of the sublime object is tied to the overload on imagination or senses that it presents to us, hence its painfulness' (1999: 68). The overwhelming feeling that a sublime film evokes is due to its treatment of represented content, which is beyond the audience's comprehension. Bukatman describes the vast subject matter of *2001*:

> [...] the cosmic trajectories of *2001* are prefigured not only in the evocation of astronomical scale, but in the description of successive levels of macrocosmic order that ultimately yield to chaos that signals the very limits of our ability to comprehend the vastness of the universe.
> (1999: 256)

Much of outer space is beyond human understanding; its immense scale, function and purpose are still unknown to us. This content can make *2001* extremely overwhelming to an audience, as they experience physical discomfort upon recognizing the sheer size of space and humanity's insignificant role within it. Sublime objects present an audience with uncomfortable experiences, but the context 'forces us to shift into another mental mode, cognition, or thought' (Freeland 1999: 68). In sublime films, painful subjects are transformed into pleasure and cognition through context, or form. Kessler writes that, according to Kant, overwhelming experiences can cause pleasure, because 'the sublime set in motion the senses and reason, challenging the former and elevating the latter' (Kessler 2012: 20). Therefore, the aesthetic features of a sublime film are able to ignite a cycle in which the audience both accepts and questions their physical and mental reaction to what they see on screen. The discordance that occurs though the spectators' perception of the image on screen 'evokes the effect of the Kantian sublime upon the human faculties, pushing the spectator into new territories of cognition and comprehension' (Rowe 2013: 50). In *2001*, the way in which the overwhelming subject of space is visually represented is the key to audience comprehension of the sublime object, as 'the universe is without end – it confounds us; but the rhetoric of the sublime paradoxically permits an understanding of these sensory and conceptual limits' (Bukatman 1999: 256). This sets up a paradox in which the audience needs to experience the sublime in order to comprehend the content of the film, but also needs the content of the film to evoke the sublime.

By rejecting conventional narrative storytelling, *2001* disorients an audience and forces them to refocus on the imagery. This breaking of the classical mode of Hollywood narrative allows for an overall greater understanding:

> The way the usual time sequence of narrative cause and effect has been thrown out of the film is only the first of many things that unsettle a conventional audience. By demoting the story element, Kubrick restores tremendous power and importance to the image – and it is through images that the viewers have to make connections.
> (Walker et al. 1999: 172)

The 'anti'-narrative in *2001*, with its quiet, drawn out presentation of the cosmic subject matter, allows the audience time and space to mentally work through the intense visuals on screen, and ultimately reach a personalized understanding of the film dependent on their specific past and experiences. Trumbull's special effects are 'especially contemplative. If he desires to create effects "good enough to look at for a long period of time", then his sequences have encouraged precisely this kind of activity' (Bukatman 1999: 259). Because of the sophistication and believability of Trumbull's effects, the audience is able to engage with the imagery consistently for longer periods of time, and therefore spend more time considering the subject matter. In addition to being well crafted, 'the effects sequences unfold, if not in a reflective silence, then at least in the absence of language' (1999: 267). Specifically, there is less than 40 minutes of spoken word in the entire film and what dialogue there is does little to contribute to the exposition of the narrative (Walker et al. 1999: 172). This lack of diegetic language provides each member of the audience a space in which they can note, analyse and deliberate the images presented to them on screen. Through this process, spectators are able to find meaning in the film, which is achieved not through verbalization, but by 'feeling it in the images drawn from past and future time, in the involvement with the experience of space, and in apprehending what is happening rather than being fed cut-and-dry information' (Walker et al. 1999: 172). By minimizing on-screen dialogue, audience members are given more freedom to assign significance to the visuals on screen, without the interference of language telling them explicitly how to interpret what they are seeing. The sparse dialogue is Kubrick's way of 'experimenting with the power of images in *2001* to carry the multi-level import of the philosophical arguments he was trying to communicate' (Kapferer 2014: 37). While the slow pace and absence of spoken words are used as tools to facilitate thought about overwhelming subjects, Kubrick did not intend for the audience to come to a specific conclusion about what they saw on the screen; after all, '2001 does not "explain" its ultimate trip, and so denies its viewers the firm ground provided by cognitive comprehensibility' (Bukatman 1999: 271). Kubrick himself refused to be pressed as to the precise meaning of the film, stating in one interview that, 'You are free to speculate as you wish about the philosophical and allegorical meaning of *2001*' (Kapferer 2014: 2). Kubrick wanted his audience to reach cognition on an individual basis, which means that there are inevitably different interpretations of the subject matter.

Fourth criteria: Moral reflection

Freeland's fourth and final feature of the sublime 'is that it prompts moral reflection' (1999: 68), and in *2001* the monolith is that very sublime object that provokes such moral contemplation. Interestingly, monoliths are 'fantastic towers of rock' that are 'a common subject in the work of many painters and photographers' (Kessler 2012: 35):

Both today and in the nineteenth century, such harsh and isolating landscapes punctuated by immense towers and cavernous abysses signify the American West, and they evoke notions of strength, power, masculinity, even hostility.

(Kessler 2012: 37)

Monoliths have been a significant symbol throughout the history of the Westward expansion, often appearing in artwork and carrying associations of might and power. In the mid-1800s, American photographers were sent out to document the western part of the country so that the rest of the world could marvel at its dramatic landscapes. One of these early photographers, Carleton Watkins, often framed 'a single monolithic object' between trees, which 'presented an ideal version of the landscape – carefully balanced, silent, and grand' (Hyde 1993: 369). After the turn of the century, photographer Ansel Adams also fixated on monolithic structures in his images of Yosemite National Park, aptly naming one of his photographs of a vertical rock structure *Monolith, the Face of Half Dome* (1927). Both Watkins and Adams chose to capture monoliths in their work as a way to portray the strength and scale of the western landscapes, but also as a device to capture the attention of viewers. In *2001*, the monolith serves as a point of interest for audiences to focus their eyes on, helping to draw them into the imagery, which otherwise often contains only barren expanses of space.

The documentation of the monolith by photographers in the American West serves as a marker for the discovery and conquest of this new frontier. In *2001*, the monolith is a black structure that also marks the chapters of human advancement, but this time representing intellectual and technological development throughout the film. The monolith is described as a 'black oblong vertical standing structure which some critics interpret as mirroring the upright posture of human being. In other words the Monolith is Human Being in the fullness of its potential' (Kapferer 2014: 44). By reappearing during the milestones of human innovation, the monolith becomes synonymous with humanity's potential. It was originally intended by Kubrick and Arthur C. Clarke that the monolith would be used 'didactically, not mystically, by projecting onto it pictures teaching the apes how to use weapons and kill for meat' (Walker et al. 1999: 181) – a feature that remained in Clarke's novel. Even though Kubrick decided against a literal depiction, this fact illustrates the intended purpose of the monolith: to reflect human progress by showing our species the more technologically advanced version of their future selves. It is an idea that can be reinforced further if the monolith is considered as a mirror in which, 'the non-reflective blackness of its surface is integral to its agentive power, forcing Human Being into itself from out of which new consciousness and potential is born' (Kapferer 2014: 44). Once humans are able to recognize their future potential in the monolith, they come to identify the monolith as the device that facilitates this understanding, a concept of Kant's that can be summarized as follows:

The ineffability is both 'out there' in the great natural object and 'in us', in our depth of feeling about the object. He [Kant] regarded our awareness of the sublimity of an object outside ourselves as an awareness of the moral law and of certain moral duties.

(Freeland 1999: 69)

For Kant, the acknowledgement of the sublime in an object outside of ourselves is accompanied by the understanding of the moral responsibilities we are bound to as humans. Because it acts as a reflective surface in which humanity can foresee their own potential and consider the moral implications of these technological developments, the monolith is a sublime object.

In the final moments of the Star Gate sequence, Bowman arrives at a hotel prepared for him by the alien race responsible for creating the monolith. Bowman looks across the ornate room in which he inhabits, and sees an older version of himself. That older version sees an even older version, and so on. This continues until Bowman reaches an age so old that he is bedridden. The monolith appears before him and Bowman then transforms into the Star-Child, 'a planet-sized super intelligent foetus [that] continues to overwhelm audiences as one of the most sublime visions in all of cinema' (Abrams 2007: 248). Pezzotta explains that these last few moments of the Star Gate sequence, and even the film as a whole, 'can be interpreted through the concepts of the uncanny and the sublime' (2013: 169). She believes that the presentation of Bowman as a double, through different stages of life, is the main aspect of the uncanny in this scene (2013: 169). Bowman sees himself as the replication of his future self through the monolith, and is therefore able to understand his identity in a way impossible for any other human being. He recognizes himself as sublime object and comprehends his own morality, therefore evolving into the Star-Child.

While the audience watches Bowman experience the sublime on screen, they too have a sublime experience:

> What is great and terrifying is watching a man who sees himself aging quickly, who looks at his image reflected in a mirror to recognize his older self, and who is finally reborn into a Star-Child who has the power to travel in the universe. Also magnificent and horrifying is the idea that the future is not influenced by the present.
> (Pezzotta 2013: 170)

According to Pezzotta, seeing and comprehending the ideas exhibited in the Star Gate sequence evokes feelings of terror and wonder in the audience. Watching Bowman come face to face with his future selves, and then transform into an omniscient Star-Child, is beyond the realm of human possibility. Yet, by exposing spectators to these visuals, *2001* opens a door of potential and acts as a catalyst for feelings of the sublime. The effectiveness of the Star Gate sequence in helping the audience reach such 'an extradiegetic perspective' (Pezzotta 2013: 171) is a direct result of the aesthetic method used to tell the story. The Star Gate sequence 'displays its referentiality, breaking its narrative fluidity through several means' (2013: 171) one of which is exemplified as 'Bowman looks directly into the camera, addressing the spectators, in five shots and, in one of them, he even walks towards it' (2013: 171). Another moment in which this the film makes direct contact with the viewer is through 'the gaze of the Star-foetus', an allegory of 'the viewer's perception *vis-à-vis* the film itself' (Rowe 2013: 48). Through the reflexivity of the film in these moments, in which Bowman and the Star-Child break the fourth wall and look directly into the eyes of the audience, *2001* breaks with classical narrative modes and prompts the audience to consider the film itself as an object, crucial to the story it tells.

Just as the monolith serves as a mirror for the moral reflection of Bowman in *2001*, the film itself becomes a parallel platform for its audience. Kapferer argues that, 'technology, of which the monolith is the key totalizing symbol [demonstrates] the shifting contexts of humanity's relation to its own inventions' (2014: 95) and so allows human beings to realize their own potential. The film is a technological object that enables this same understanding in the audience. The content of *2001*, a science-fiction film set in the future, shows our potential as a race and our more than likely inevitable future:

> The Future cannot be known in advance. It is as yet undetermined, unlike the past. The Future is an open potential and this is its risk, but it is also that which makes the risk worthwhile. By taking the risk, Human Being has the opportunity to participate in its own determination.
> (Kapferer 2014: 90)

The future is sublime, because it is an unknown; it is the frontier constantly ahead of us that holds the potential for risk and reward, anxiety and gratification. A feeling of pain and terror is evoked in *2001*, through a specific portrayal of our future selves interacting with space and technology, yet we also receive pleasure in knowing the reality on screen has not yet happened, and we are still safe in the present of our time. Acknowledging what we like and do not like of our future selves in *2001*, and adjusting our actions as a result, is a direct result of moral reflection. The monolith and the film itself are technologies, which allows for humans to see their future potential and facilitate moral reflection, making them objects conforming to Freeland's final feature of the sublime.

Conclusion

By adhering to the four features of Cynthia Freeland's sublime object, *2001* can be considered a sublime film. The sublime is descriptive of something that evokes both a feeling of terror and pleasure, a characteristic that, while initially featured in the work of Romantic landscape painters, soon became a common feature of other arts, including film (Burke 2008). Freeland's first criterion of the sublime object is directly derived from Burke's text, as she states that a film must elicit a sense of fear and wonder. This feeling often comes from a sense of the unknown, which is a concept reflected in the Romantic paintings of the American frontier; the mysterious nature of the West was both foreboding and wonderful. In paintings, the landscape was portrayed as a massive force beyond human control, as well as unbelievably beautiful. Outer space, which became the next frontier of the twentieth century and the setting of Kubrick's *2001*, also evokes fear and wonder, because it is inhospitable, expansive and unfamiliar. As soon as humans designated space as the new frontier, they were challenged to develop tools to aid in its exploration. Technology became the next frontline of discovery, but the rapid pace of development evoked a sense of anxious uncertainty and awe of its potential. These feelings are conceptualized in the supercomputer HAL, who acts on his own will and murders the crew he is meant to be serving. Science-fiction films often feature these terrifying themes of space and technology, but because they are mediated through the screen, the audience is able to view them from a safe vantage point and also feel pleasure.

2001 meets Freeland's second criterion of the sublime, characterized by a sense of greatness, through the treatment of its content. The three features of the Star Gate sequence represent the overall aesthetic quality of Douglas Trumbull's special effects and the sublimity of his work. The film's emphasis on space, the portrayal of the environment as 'other', and the use of luminism convey a sense of greatness and sublime. Freeland's third feature of the sublime is that the overwhelming feelings of pain and terror eventually lead to pleasure and cognition. In *2001*, the subject matter of the universe, which is such a mystery to humanity and beyond comprehension, will overcome the audience with discomfort. However, the form in which this content is conveyed allows the audience to construct their own understanding of what they see on screen and reach cognition, which is achieved through the use of the anti-narrative storyline, believable effects and minimal dialogue. Freeland's fourth and final feature of the sublime is that it initiates moral reflection. The monolith featured in *2001* is a shiny black structure, which symbolically reflects human potential and allows the characters in the film to consider the moral implications of their technological developments. The film itself also becomes a platform for moral reflection, because it is also a technology that facilitates this same understanding in the audience. *2001* evokes terror through a specific portrayal of our future selves, exploring space and technology, while also eliciting pleasure, because the audience knows the film is fiction. The audience then engages in moral reflection, by acknowledging the strengths and weaknesses of our future selves, influencing their course of action. The sublime is a crucial component of experiencing *2001*, because instead of leaving us with a sense of our insignificance, it presents the universe as 'a place that we experience as both overwhelming *and* within our grasp' (Kessler 2012: 175). It justifies outer space as the next frontier, which is both daunting, while also holding the potential for significant opportunity and discovery. Through *2001*'s adherence to Freeland's criteria of the sublime object, this film can be categorized as a sublime film, and more broadly, a philosophical thought experiment that encourages its audience to consider ideas related to emotion, the unknown, outer space, technological development, intellectual cognition and moral responsibility.

Part Six

Production

Part six

The size of the production on *2001* was immense, with its budget having doubled by its completion. Kubrick was not a novice when it came to Hollywood epics however, having directed *Spartacus* with its mammoth battle scenes shot in Spain, with extras in the thousands. But the magnitude of what Kubrick was attempting on *2001* is perhaps best exemplified in the creation of the Discovery One spaceship's centrifuge, witnessed by journalist David Robinson who visited the set in the spring of 1966:

> The most staggering set constructed for the film is, however, the great centrifuge, designed and built for the film by Vickers Armstrong […] The wheel itself stands 36 feet high – half as tall again, roughly, as the rooftop of a reasonably sized two-storey house. The working areas of the set is the inner part of the wheel or drum, which can be rotated in either direction […] this operation is quite alarming. Movement is at all times heralded by a warning hooter of eerie pitch and piercing volume; and the wheel picks up speed with disconcerting muted creaks and grunts.
>
> (1966: 58)

To understand what Kubrick was trying to achieve, both as a producer negotiating and liaising with the studio and with a variety of external companies, and as a director that had to keep in mind the final vision of the complexity of the production, it is necessary to map out a chronological timeline of the production. Filippo Ulivieri's is the only chapter in this section, providing such a comprehensive chronology of *2001*, detailing the extensive work involved in realising the film and exploring the historical perspectives of *2001* within cinematic history and industrial contexts. The chronology reveals the collaborative nature of the production and, though grounded within the framework of auteur theory, demonstrates Kubrick's artistry and management abilities. Ulivieri's chapter draws on a range of sources, including trade journals, academic texts, memoirs and interviews, in order to provide a glimpse into the at times chaotic, but always collaborative nature of the production of *2001*.

Further reading

Piers Bizony's (2014) *The Making of 2001: A Space Odyssey* is the latest Taschen book that lavishly explores the details of the film production, including behind the scenes photographs and artwork, as well as including material from the Stanley Kubrick Archive. Meanwhile,

Michel Chion explores the impact of *2001* in cinema history in his *Kubrick's Cinema Odyssey* (2001), with his chapter 'Science-fiction cinema after *2001*', pp. 156–63, while Philip Strick (1985) examines the ways in which Arthur C. Clarke's work developed following his collaboration with Kubrick in, 'Ring round the moons: The Space Odyssey of Arthur C. Clarke', *Film Bulletin*, 1 January, p. 52.

Chapter Twelve

2001: A comprehensive chronology

Filippo Ulivieri

When Kubrick first started working on *2001* in 1964 he faced what was his most ambitious and complex work yet: thematically, he wanted to explore the first confrontation between humankind and intelligent extraterrestrial life (Musel 1968: 17); stylistically, he looked to create a majestic visual experience (Alpert 1966: 51). Kubrick's interest in a science-fiction film emerged fuzzily during the post-production of *Dr. Strangelove*.[1] Uncertain what to do for an encore, Kubrick pondered such important and contemporary issues as atomic warfare, the population explosion and questions of race and gender (Anon. 1964c).[2] Yet, it was science-fiction that eventually took a hold of his interest; after 'reading and reading and reading about it' (Anon. 1964a: 80) Kubrick found the ideal collaborator in writer and scientist Arthur C. Clarke, whose novels of space exploration and future philosophy had impressed him deeply. Kubrick and Clarke launched themselves into making 'the proverbial "really-good" science-fiction movie' (Krämer 2010: 18) and, although they worked exceptionally well together, the making of the film was a complex process that required more than four years. When *2001* opened in April 1968 it was met with mixed reviews, but most critics agreed that it was the singular vision of one artist.[3] But was it?

By cross-referencing published memoirs with those who participated in the film's production, alongside academic studies, newspaper articles, production documents and web resources, this chapter provides a comprehensive account of the lengthy creation of *2001*, achieving an almost day-to-day chronology of Kubrick's massive undertaking and the collaborative efforts involved. A production study of *2001* and how it was put together allows us to better understand the intricacy and seminal nature of the production; from Kubrick's production plan (or lack thereof), to the role of every company and artist that took part in it, and most importantly Kubrick's own role in imagining, developing, shaping and delivering what indeed proved to be a 'really good science-fiction film' (McAleer 1992: 192).

From the early 1970s, many authors have studied how *2001* was produced, mostly by interviewing those who participated in the making of the film. All these studies are organized thematically, with Arthur C. Clarke's *The Lost Worlds of 2001* (1972) and Daniel Richter's *Moonwatcher's Memoir* (2002) being the only accounts that have, in part at least, a chronological approach. I used all these works as sources for expanding the entries in my chronology. The only production calendar published to date is Carolyn Geduld's *Filmguide to 2001: A Space Odyssey* (1973).[4] Geduld's calendar features around 40 entries for the 1964–68 period, and only in half of the instances provides a full date (day, month, year), and without providing any references. A comparative study of the sources that have now become available has proven Geduld's calendar partially inaccurate as well.[5] What follows is therefore the first systematic attempt at reconstructing the entire chronology of Kubrick's endeavour. However, I would like to stress that this calendar is still partial without a thorough study of the immense amount of production documents held at the Stanley Kubrick Archive at the University of Arts London.

The dates and events in the following production calendar represent key moments and turning points within the four years of collective work, selected with the aim to illustrate the main threads of the technical and creative efforts put into the production, and their interconnection.

Production calendar

17 February 1964: During a lunch with Roger Caras, head of Columbia Pictures' Sales Department, Kubrick remarks he has been researching an idea for a serious science-fiction film. Caras suggests he should contact Arthur C. Clarke, in his opinion the best writer in the field. Approached via cable by Caras, Clarke quickly replies he is 'frightfully interested in working with enfant terrible' (McAleer 1992: 190–91).

31 March 1964: Reassured by Clarke's reply, Kubrick writes to ask to be able to 'discuss with you the possibility of doing the proverbial "really good" science-fiction movie' (Kubrick 1964b). Kubrick's interests lie in the discovery of intelligent extraterrestrial life, the impact (or lack of impact) of such a discovery, and the exploration of the Moon and Mars (McAleer 1992: 192).

8 April 1964: Clarke replies enthusiastically to Kubrick's invitation: 'I also feel, as you obviously do, that the "really good" science-fiction film is a great many years overdue' (Chapman and Cull 2013: 95).

9 April 1964: Uncertain whether Kubrick wants him to collaborate on an original idea or adapt one of his stories, Clarke suggests the overall narrative for a potential film could combine his short story 'The Sentinel' (1951), in which a mysterious artefact discovered on the Moon's surface hints at the existence of extraterrestrials, with the epic sweep of his best known novel, *Childhood's End* (1953), in which an alien civilization visits Earth and guides humankind towards the next stage in evolution (Krämer 2010: 26). Clarke's second letter also includes a visual suggestion that would prove seminal:

> I have thought of a nice opening for a space movie, which might give you some ideas. Opening: Screen full of stars. A completely black disc slowly drifts in from the left until it fills the centre of the screen, eclipsing the stars. Its right-hand edge lightens, the glow of the corona appears, and the sun rises… We realize we are looking down on the night side of the Moon.
>
> (Bizony 2014: 19)

22 April 1964: Kubrick and Clarke meet for lunch and then keep talking for eight solid hours, walking around New York's Central Park (McAleer 1992: 193–94). Clarke is struck at once by the director's 'pure intelligence: Kubrick grasps new ideas, however complex, almost instantly. He also appears to be interested in practically everything' (Clarke 1999: 261). Kubrick has already absorbed an immense amount of science fact and science-fiction, as Clarke recalls:

> Even from the beginning, he had a very clear idea of his ultimate goal […]. He wanted to make a movie about Man's relation to the universe – something which had never been attempted, still less achieved, in the history of motion pictures. Of course, there had been innumerable 'space' movies, most of them trash. Even the few that had been made with some skill and accuracy had been rather simpleminded, concerned more with the schoolboy excitement of space flight than its profound implications to society, philosophy, and religion.
>
> (Clarke 1972: 29)

At the end of the day, Kubrick proposes they write the story as a complete novel: this way they would generate more ideas and would give the project more body and depth (McAleer 1992: 195). For the next month, Kubrick and Clarke would talk 'on an average of five hours a day – at Stanley's apartment, in restaurants and automats, movie houses, and art galleries' (Clarke 1999: 261). They also watch numerous science-fiction films, with Kubrick being far more critical about them than Clarke (1999: 261).

1 May 1964: Kubrick meets Colin Low, the co-director of *Universe* (Kroitor and Low, 1960), a 29-minute educational documentary about the Solar System made by the National Film Board of Canada over seven years of work and at a cost of more than $60,000 (Kubrick 1964g; LoBrutto 1998: 273). Struck by the film's panning shots of slowly revolving planets, flying asteroids and expanding gas nebulas, Kubrick asks Low if he is interested in working as a designer for the special effects for his new film. Due to prior commitments, Low cannot accept, but Kubrick manages to hire *Universe*'s special effects designer Wally Gentleman (Glassman 1999: 29).

20 May 1964: A contract is signed that sees Kubrick's production company pay $10,000 for an option on six Arthur C. Clarke stories (McAleer 1992: 195–97).

28 May 1964: 'The Sentinel' is formally picked as the basis of the film, and Clarke signs an agreement to write a treatment for $30,000 (McAleer 1992: 197).

4 June 1964: Clarke starts writing, setting the story in 1987, 'when the colonization of the Moon is starting and the manned exploration of the Solar System is just getting under way' (Chapman 2013: 96).

20 June 1964: Clarke finishes the opening chapter, titled 'View from the Year 2000' (Clarke 1972: 33). With NASA spending over $10 million every day on the Gemini and Apollo space programmes, real space exploration seems closer and closer. Kubrick and Clarke have to create a story that will not be made obsolete by the events of the next few years – the dawn of the new Millennium seems a good date to choose (Bizony 2000: 6).

26 June 1964: Capitalizing on the great financial and critical success of *Dr. Strangelove*, Kubrick decides to refuse a two-picture deal proposed by Columbia Pictures, which he judges quite restrictive on his personal control over his films: 'I must have complete total final annihilating artistic control over the picture, subject only to approval of the budget, and approval of the two principal players' (Krämer 2015b: 50).

July 1964: In the first week of July, Clarke is averaging one or two thousand words a day. He notes in his diary, 'Stanley reads first five chapters and says, "We've got a best seller here"' (Clarke 1972: 33).

26 July 1964: Kubrick asks designer Ken Adam to work on the film, 'with preparation starting Octoberish-Novemberish' and a tentative start date around March 1965 (Frayling 2015: 11–12). Adam has just signed a contract for designing the new Bond film, *Thunderball* (Young, 1965), and cannot accept (Frayling 2015: 11–12).

6 August 1964: A female computer, named Athena after the Greek goddess of wisdom, is worked into the story at the suggestion of Kubrick. A few days later, the main hero is christened Alex Bowman (Clarke 1972: 33).

September 1964: At this stage, Clarke's typescript begins with the discovery of an alien artefact at a lunar base and follows the journey of a scientist from Earth to investigate it. The text stops before Bowman and the astronauts of the subsequent expedition encounter any alien. It is a fairly standard science-fiction narrative, heavy on space technology and explanatory dialogue (Poole 2015: 178).

26 September 1964: To obtain 'a smashing theme of mythic grandeur', Kubrick gives Clarke a copy of *The Hero with a Thousand Faces* (1949), a study of comparative mythology by Joseph Campbell (Clarke 1972: 34).

2 October 1964: Clarke has finished reading Robert Ardrey's *African Genesis* (1961), a popular science book about the origin of the human species (Clarke 1972: 34). Inspired by its ideas about cosmic-ray mutations helping the spark of life in the African continent, Clarke reworks his own story *Encounter in the Dawn* (1953) into a flashback sequence to be placed at the end of the astronauts' journey: it shows an alien character visiting Earth 100,000 years ago and interacting with a semi-human male, christened Moon-Watcher, thus giving rise to human evolution (Poole 2015: 179).

17 October 1964: Kubrick suggests the aliens create a 'Victorian' environment to put the astronauts at their ease at the end of their journey (Clarke 1972: 33).

21 November 1964: After a visit to the Natural History Museum where he talks to the Anthropology department, Clarke reads Louis Leakey's *Adam's Ancestors* (1960). 'Stan had a rather amusing idea. Our ETs arrive on Earth and teach commando tactics to our pacifistic ancestors so that they can survive and flourish' (Clarke 1972: 35).

24 December 1964: Clarke delivers the first complete draft of his treatment, a 251-page long typescript titled *Journey Beyond the Stars* (Krämer 2010: 29–31; Bizony 2014: 20). The ideas about human evolution have now formed a prologue in which a tribe of man-apes develop intelligence thanks to the teachings of a mysterious crystal cube (Poole 2015: 179–80). Part two of the story begins on 5 October 2001: Presidential Scientific Adviser Dr. Heywood Floyd takes a shuttle to an orbiting space station where he attends a high-level summit to discuss the puzzling discovery of a black pyramid on the Moon. The artefact is transmitting radio signals towards Jupiter, so a mission is arranged to send a manned spaceship to the planet. Following a long voyage, bedevilled by various incidents, the spaceship arrives in orbit around Jupiter where a mysterious hole is detected. Commander Bowman pilots a pod inside the hole and is transported to another solar system where he sees a vast city inhabited by eight-feet tall humanoids. Bowman is guided to a hotel suite, designed by the aliens to make him feel comfortable. A telephone rings and Bowman is assured he will be returned to his world 'without any ill effects'. A door opens and Bowman sees a transparent cube: is he about to evolve, like his ancestor did? At this point the narrative ends (Chapman 2013: 96). The text is no more than a rough draft and it stops at the most exciting point, but, reading it on Christmas Day, Kubrick says he is 'delighted with the last chapters and convinced that we've extended the range of science fiction' (Clarke 1972: 35).

Kubrick's lawyer, Louis Blau, delivers a copy to Robert O'Brien, President of Metro-Goldwyn-Mayer, inclusive of Kubrick's prospective production schedule and budget: two years and $6 million. Considering that the average budget of a Hollywood film at the time is approximately $1.5 million and that other noteworthy science-fiction films had earned less than $3 million collectively, *Journey Beyond the Stars* is clearly a very risky endeavour (Krämer 2010: 31; Bizony 2000: 13).

9 January 1965: Impressed by *Tetsuwan Atomu* (*Astro Boy*) (Tezuka, 1963–66), a Japanese TV series syndicated in the United States, Kubrick contacts its creator, cartoonist and animator Osamu Tezuka, to inquire if he would be interested in helping on the artistic direction or design of 'a very realistic science-fiction film' (Schodt 2007: 92). Being busy with his own manga, and put off by the idea of relocating abroad for one or two years, Tezuka declines the offer (Schodt 2007: 92).

14 January 1965: Betting on a rising space-film trend fuelled by the USA/USSR Space Race, and on Kubrick's name – he has just been awarded by the New York Film Critics the Best Director for *Dr. Strangelove*, Columbia's highest-grossing film in 1964, and debuted on *Variety*'s annual Big Rental Picture chart, with *Spartacus* and *Lolita* also in the paper's 'All-Time Top Grossers' list – Robert O'Brien authorizes funding for the science-fiction project (McAleer 1992: 201).

23 January 1965: Designer and illustrator Harry Lange and scientific consultant Frederick Ordway are introduced to Kubrick via Clarke. They spend the afternoon at Kubrick's apartment discussing their work. Kubrick is particularly impressed by some space vehicle concepts the two have designed for Wernher Von Braun at NASA. At the end of the day, they leave with a copy of the film treatment and a promise of some form of cooperation (Ordway 1982: 49).

2 February 1965: Kubrick writes again to Ken Adam asking for a list of recommended British art directors, which Adam provides on the 28 February (Frayling 2015: 12). This indicates Kubrick has now decided to shoot the film in England.

13 February 1965: Lange and Ordway are formally asked to join the production. Ordway is hired as the principal technical adviser and Lange maps out a range of detailed and realistic spaceship configurations. On 16 February, the pair signs an initial six-month contract to work in New York (Bizony 2000: 85).

21 February 1965: The *New York Times* reports Kubrick is co-writing with Arthur C. Clarke *Journey Beyond the Stars*, a science-fiction novel that will be adapted into a screenplay for a new Cinerama film for MGM, with production to commence 15 August on location in England, Africa, Switzerland, Germany and the United States, with interiors being shot at MGM's Elstree Studios near London. The story opens in the year 2001, when permanent bases have been established on the Moon and the entire Solar System has been explored, and follows the unexpected discovery of extraterrestrial intelligence. It is anticipated that the novel will be published in the near future, and the film should be ready for release in the autumn of 1966 (Weiler 1965: X9).

23 February 1965: A press release is issued by MGM. Drafted by Kubrick himself, it reads as an appraisal of the transformative potential that space exploration could bring about to human society, comparing it to 'the voyages of the Renaissance that brought about the end of the Dark Ages' (Bizony 2000: 10–11).

April 1965: During spring, the small production team expands to include (among others) Ray Lovejoy, assistant editor on *Dr. Strangelove* now working as Kubrick's assistant, executive producer Victor Lyndon, who was production associate on *Dr. Strangelove*, Roger Caras, who resigned as Columbia's national director of merchandising, artist Richard McKenna, hired to provide conceptual drawings, and art director Tony Masters (Ordway 1982: 50), whose name was in Ken Adam's list of suggestions (Frayling 2015: 15).

While Ordway and Lovejoy visit many NASA and other space installations to document the construction of the Apollo lunar module, Kubrick rents a corset factory where a young special effects company called Effects-U-All shoots high-velocity footage of drops of various chemicals reacting under oil and water, creating lava lamp-like effects that will be used for representations of deep space (Debert 1998).

24 April 1965: In an interview for the *New Yorker*, Kubrick explains what he's trying to do: 'About the best we've been able to come up with is a space odyssey – comparable in some ways to the Homeric *Odyssey*. It occurred to us that for the Greeks the vast stretches of the sea must have had the same sort of mystery and remoteness that space has for our generation' (Bernstein 1965: 38–39).

3 May 1965: Clarke delivers a new lengthy draft of the treatment. Despite being 'twice as long and ten times better' than *Journey Beyond the Stars*, nothing has changed in its ending

(Poole 2015: 180). The title on the typescript is *2001: A Space Odyssey*. 'As far as I can recall, it was entirely his idea' (Clarke 1972: 32).

June 1965: The pace of design work has accelerated, and by early June six major space vehicles have emerged from Lange's sketches: the Orion III Earth-to-orbit shuttle, the Space Station V orbiting around the Earth, the Aries 1B Earth-orbit-to-lunar-surface shuttle, the Rocket Bus for transporting men and material on the Moon's surface, and the Discovery One interplanetary spaceship with its Space Pods. Kubrick insists on knowing the purpose and function of each assembly and component, down to the logical labelling of individual buttons and the presentation on screens of plausible operating, diagnostics and other data. To get all the needed information, Ordway has toured the United States, visiting 65 companies, including General Electric, Bell Telephone, Whirlpool Corporation, Honeywell, and IBM (Ordway 1982: 51). Kubrick entices the companies into contributing ideas and designs to the film in return for having their corporate logos displayed – an avant la lettre product placement idea (LoBrutto 1998: 266).

11 June 1965: Kubrick contacts visionary graphic artist M. C. Escher asking his 'assistance in producing a four-dimensional film' (Campbell 2013). The request is not accepted and instead the art department and the special effects artists attempt visualizations of the alien worlds. By the end of June, most of the crew transfer to the MGM Studios in Borehamwood, north London (Bizony 2000: 97). Kubrick has found Lange and Ordway's assistance indispensable and asks them to follow the production to England (Ordway 1982: 53).

6 July 1965: The treatment evolves into a first screenplay, divided into four sections: A) The Dawn of Man, B) Floyd's journey to the Moon and investigation of the tetrahedron, C) the Discovery One expedition and D) Fantastic Voyage. It still reads mostly as a treatment, with dialogue only in section B, whilst an extensive voice-over narration is used to link sequences and provide background information (Kubrick 1965; Chapman 2013: 98).

9 July 1965: *Newsday* reports Kubrick has signed Keir Dullea for the lead role (Harris 1965: 2C). After more than a year away, Clarke returns to his home in Ceylon (Sri Lanka) (Clarke 1972: 37).

July 1965: Lester Novros, the president of Graphic Films, an independent Los Angeles based special effects company, is summoned to New York to discuss a possible cooperation. Kubrick is impressed by their documentary *To The Moon and Beyond* (Novros, 1964), shot for the 1964/65 New York World's Fair; it makes extensive use of multiple exposure and travelling mattes. Kubrick shows Novros a copy of the *2001* script, and they discuss both the special effects and how to design aliens, with Kubrick suggesting a possible inspiration in Alberto Giacometti's sculptures. Graphic Films is put under a year's contract to create storyboards and design lunar transportation and deep-space vehicles (Finch 1984: 104–12; Miller 2016).

21 July 1965: Kubrick and his family sails to England on the *Queen Mary* (Anon. 1965e). At the MGM complex in Borehamwood, nine stages are booked for *2001*. MGM's president,

Robert O'Brien, has promised Kubrick that their operating costs will not be charged to the *2001* budget (LoBrutto 1998: 271).

27 July 1965: IBM delivers a concept for the Athena computer – instead of a console, they think the complexity required to run a spaceship would ask for a huge computer 'into which men went' (Bizony 2014: 116). A couple of days later Kubrick, possibly knowing that NASA are pushing for a computer small enough to fit inside the lunar capsules, deems the design 'useless and totally irrelevant to our needs' (2014: 116).

3 August 1965: Novros and Con Pederson, the director of *To the Moon and Beyond*, ship concept sketches and copious, detailed notes on the draft script from Los Angeles, commenting on the scientific accuracy and plausibility of the narrative. On the matter of computers, Pederson writes:

> [They] will be reduced virtually to little featureless magic boxes in a decade or so. […] By the turn of the century, all computer systems will long have been taken for granted with not much room for change. So, to keep us in business, our first guideline is elegant simplicity.
>
> (Miller 2016)

4 August 1965: Ordway has concluded his research tour of the United States and sails to England, carrying 20 trunk loads of artwork and technical materials aboard the Oceanic liner S.S. France (Ordway, 1982: 53).

9 August 1965: Frustrated by the slow long-distance communication, Kubrick summons Pederson 'for two days discussion' over his 'provocative new and complicated ideas' (Miller 2016).

13 August 1965: Pederson arrives in London (Anon. 1965e). Upon his return to Los Angeles, he tells Novros he wants to leave Graphic Films to work exclusively for Kubrick. Meanwhile, Douglas Trumbull, a 23-year-old animation artist who has been working at Graphic Films for two years, phones Kubrick to ask if he can join his production. Much to Novros's chagrin, Graphic Films loses its best artists (Finch 1984: 113).

Throughout August, the special effects team is set with the employment of Wally Veevers, a veteran of model engineering and cinematography, and Tom Howard, Britain's leading optical effects man (Ordway 1982: 56). Artist Roy Carnon is hired to draw dramatized versions of Harry Lange's concepts (Ordway 1982: 56). Lange also assembles a team of model makers to turn his drawings into convincing three-dimensional objects. The personnel amounts to 105 people, coming from all kinds of specialized background: boat builders, architectural students, fine artists, sculptors, lithographers, metalworkers and even some scrimshaw carvers fresh off a whaling boat (Bizony 2014: 119).

Kubrick demands an extreme degree of realism both in the models and in the full-scale sets: no matter how close or in which direction the camera goes, everything must look perfectly detailed (Bizony 2000: 97–98; Peldszus 2015: 204). The process is further complicated by the presence of Clarke, back from Ceylon: his primary job is to polish the novel, but he becomes involved in all kinds of technical discussions with the artists and production staff, with his words and their design influencing each other (Clarke 1972: 37). Ordway's task is now 'always to keep in mind possible mismatches between what Kubrick [has] in mind for the picture, what Clarke [is] writing, and equipment and vehicular realities emerging from the Art Department' (Ordway 1982: 54). He also oversees the supervision of the construction of the helmets, spacesuits, controls, displays, etc. (1982: 54).

25 August 1965: Clarke is not satisfied with leaving what happens to Bowman entirely to the viewer's imagination. He proposes Bowman returns to Earth having gained knowledge of extraterrestrial science, linking his evolution to Moon-Watcher's, an idea he believes will solve the lack of cohesion in the story (Chapman 2013: 99).

10 September 1965: Clarke writes to a friend: 'This is no longer a 6 million dollar movie. I think the accounts department has thrown in its hand. The guess I heard was 10 million' (Bizony 2014: 120). During the course of September, Ordway starts travelling once more, this time across Europe, to acquire further information about the lunar surface from several observatories. He then returns to the United States, visiting NASA space centres in Texas, Alabama, Florida and its headquarters in Washington, D.C. (Ordway 1982: 57). According to Tony Masters, the joint work of every department has made them design in the same way: 'Just like "Georgian" or "Victorian" is a period, we designed *2001* as a period. We designed a way to live, right down to the last knife and fork. If we had to design a door, we would do it in our style' (Shay and Duncan 2001: 81).

25 September 1965: Top scientists from NASA visit the sets and, impressed by all the hardware and detailed documentation piling up everywhere, they dub Kubrick's offices 'NASA East' (Ordway 1982: 57). Due to its derivative design of the real space industry, *2001* becomes almost a speculative space program in itself (Peldszus 2015: 200). The *Los Angeles Times* reports Gary Lockwood has been signed to star in the film (Martin 1965: B8).

3 October 1965: During a telephone conversation, Clarke hits upon the right image for the ending: 'Bowman will regress to infancy, and we'll see him at the very end as a baby in orbit. Stanley called again later, still very enthusiastic' (Clarke 1972: 38).

15 October 1965: Despite Clarke spicing up the story of Discovery One's voyage to Jupiter with a series of accidents and hardware failures, by mid-October Kubrick has decided the story still lacks drama. He proposes the mission is to be veiled in secrecy because of a general assumption that the aliens might be hostile; only the ship's computer will know the true purpose of the mission, being instructed to conceal the information from the crew. This gradually results in an incompatible conflict and ultimately a sort of neurosis with murderous tendencies (Chapman 2013: 99). The bland Athena is upgraded and becomes the compelling HAL 9000. At the end of the story, all astronauts are killed but Bowman. Clarke notes in his diary, 'Drastic, but it seems right. After all, Odysseus was the sole survivor…' (Clarke 1972: 38). Caras and Ordway reassure

IBM that their corporate logo will not be associated with any malfunctioning hardware, and that HAL 9000 definitely will not be an IBM machine (Bizony 2014: 117; Chapman 2013: 102).

22 October 1965: *Variety* reports that Kubrick has pushed back principal photography until January (Archerd 1965b: 2).

December 1965: A week from the start of principal photography, Ordway notes that:

> [We are] continually facing difficulties of decision making at the Kubrick level. What U.S. industry comes up with does not always please Stanley, often placing us in a difficult position. And many design aspects of the vehicles in the film change regularly so that it becomes impossible at times to finalize anything. Moreover, we are faced with the fact that the screenplay has a definite tendency to change rather rapidly…
>
> (Ordway 1982: 58)

Lange echoes Ordway's concerns by saying that Kubrick 'would have you design for days, in order to show him that this is not what he wants to do. So it's a process of elimination' (Frayling 2015: 50). Everything has to be done to 'a hand-rubbed motorcar finish. If [Kubrick] spotted a nail head anywhere, that [is] impossible, because this [is] a story about the future, and there could be no imperfection' (Shay 2001: 81). Such imperfections force the art department into a constant process of revisiting their work (2001: 81).

17 December 1965: While the construction of the sets and models continues, Kubrick starts shooting 16mm footage that will be inserted in the spacecrafts' monitors (Anon. 1965d).

26 December 1965: Clarke finishes a revised version of the script, tightening up the narrative. The voyage sequence is described purely as a visual experience, 'a breathtakingly beautiful and comprehensive sense of different extraterrestrial worlds' (Chapman 2013: 99).

29 December 1965: Principal photography of *2001* has officially begun, not at MGM British Studios but at the nearby Shepperton Studios, where Kubrick has the vast Tycho Magnetic Anomaly 1 Moon set built. This involves the creation of a large trench incorporating 90 tons of carefully graded, washed and coloured coke (Bizony 2000: 110; Shay 2001: 86). Europe's second-largest shooting stage must be cleared by the first week of the new year, meaning Kubrick has only a few days to shoot 'the second crucial encounter between Man and Monolith' (Clarke 1972: 41–44).

The design of the monolith has undergone many changes. After discarding a tetrahedron for the risk of unnecessary association with the pyramids, and a transparent cube because it proved impossible to make one of the required size, Kubrick settles on a rectangular shape and obtains a two-ton slab of Lucite – the largest ever cast – onto which images would be projected, as the visual teaching machine is described by Clarke in his novel. Unfortunately, the plastic slab appears greenish and unconvincing when shot on camera and is replaced by a completely black slab of the same dimensions (Clarke 1972: 44; Bizony 2014: 182).

3 January 1966: Back at Borehamwood, Kubrick begins filming the scenes with Dr. Floyd travelling on the Aries and Orion spaceships, the stewards and the pilots on board, Floyd travelling on the Moon rocket bus, and Floyd speaking in the conference room (Anon. 1966b).

17 January 1966: Clarke has finished writing the last chapters of his novel, which now includes an orbiting 'baby', the eventual Star-Child. He feels that the end is in sight, but he cautions himself that this would be the third time he's felt that way (McAleer 1992: 208).

19 January 1966: Kubrick phones Clarke to say he is 'very happy with the last chapters and feels that the story is now "rock-hard"' (Clarke 1972: 45). *Variety* reports that Keir Dullea has arrived in London (Anon. 1966e: 18).

27 January 1966: *Variety* reports that the budget of the film is now $7 million (Archerd 1966a: 2). Compared to the inside rumour of $10 million, this indicates that either MGM is hiding the costs to the press, or Kubrick is hiding them from MGM. $75 million alone has been spent on the construction of a 40-ton, 38 feet in diameter rotating centrifuge devised to provide camera angles to simulate artificial gravity. The eight-feet-wide interior of the set is where most of the action with the two leading players will take place (Bizony 2000: 138). The centrifuge took six months to build, after Ordway signed off his blueprint in June 1965 (Ordway 1982: 92).

28 January 1966: Kubrick has finished shooting the scenes inside Space Station 5, and other 16mm inserts (Anon. 1966b). Roger Caras starts sending off letters to ask the world's leading scientists, theologians, astronomers and philosophers to contribute to a filmed prologue of edited interviews. Kubrick's idea is 'to help the audience realize that the basic subject matter of the film is not fantasy but possible if not probable fact' and overcome right from the start the general perception of science-fiction films as mere entertainment, assessing *2001* as a serious work of fiction (Frewin 2005b: 236).

4 February 1966: Clarke attends a screening of a demonstration reel in which Kubrick has spliced together the scenes shot so far to give the MGM executives an

> [...] idea of what's going on. He'd used Mendelssohn's *Midsummer Night's Dream* for the [artificial gravity] scenes, and Vaughan Williams's *Sinfonia Antartica* for the lunar sequence and the [early voyage] special effects, with stunning results. I reeled out convinced that we have a masterpiece on our hands – if Stan can keep it up.
> (Clarke 1972: 45–46)

Clarke returns to Ceylon but continues to provide narration and new scenes for another two months (1972: 46).

7 February 1966: After a week of tests and rehearsals, Kubrick begins shooting in the centrifuge with Keir Dullea and Gary Lockwood (Anon. 1966b). Kubrick directs the scenes from outside the centrifuge, with the aid of radio equipment and a television monitor (Anon. 1966f: 27). It is complex and slow work; all the cameras and lighting have to be rearranged for each new sequence, plus the 16mm films for projections of the eight monitors in the computer console have to be rewound. The rotation of the centrifuge also makes the spotlight bulbs explode, and falling objects have to be re-attached and the set cleaned or repaired (Lockwood 2001: 24–25).

16 February 1966: *Variety* reports that the production is expected to continue until the end of May, with the film tentatively set for release in early 1967 (Anon. 1966j: 25).

February 1966: Exasperated by Kubrick's 'absolute obsession with the finicky details of everything' (Shay 2001: 106) and by what he judged a huge waste of money, Wally Gentleman leaves the production. Douglas Trumbull takes over responsibility of the special effects work from Gentleman.

Kubrick hires a young photographer, Keith Hamshere, to take photos of the spacecraft models. At just 21 years old, he is given an entire studio, all the camera equipment he requests, five darkrooms and four people working under his supervision (Bizony 2000: 112). Hamshere has to find a way to photograph the models using a single light source to mimic the Sun yet achieve extreme deep focus, a complex process on the longest 54-feet Discovery One model. He experiments a lot, in a studio covered in black velvet, using very slow film shot on weekend-long exposures (Mawston 2016: 34–35; Bizony 2000: 115). The model makers, who have completed the models in full detail, are disappointed to see Kubrick choose only one side to film, using Hamshere's photographs as travelling mattes (Frayling 2015: 82). However, it proves an effective time-saving method for many secondary shots.

Andrew Birkin, a 21-year-old runner and tea boy, is promoted assistant to the art department. His first assignment is to help log the special effects and to locate a desert-like location in England suitable for the prehistoric 'The Dawn of Man' sequence; this is because Kubrick is not satisfied with a painted background in the studio (Bizony 2000: 129).

March 1966: Roger Caras shoots black-and-white interviews with the scientists for the prologue. For the next two months, he tours Europe, the United States and even Russia in order to realize the sequence (Frewin 2005b: 95).

2 April 1966: Clarke writes in his diary, 'As far as I'm concerned, it's finished' (Clarke 1972: 46).

7 April 1966: Shooting inside the centrifuge is almost complete. Kubrick begins filming the space weightlessness scenes (Anon. 1966b). Wiring actors and models to the ceiling and shooting them from below creates the illusion. It is once more long and tedious work: for each shot, the position of the actor and model has to be altered so that the camera appears to shoot them with different perspectives (Bizony 2000: 145). Tony Masters's crew has to rig a genuine air supply to each space suit to let the actor breathe and avoid steam on the helmet's visor. When the actors are suspended, Kubrick communicates with them only through two-way transmitters fixed inside their suits (Robinson 1966: 59).

8 April 1966: Kubrick writes to composer Carl Orff, whose *Carmina Burana* (1935–36) fascinates him. He asks Orff for the names of younger composers that he admires (McQuiston 2011: 146). It is possible Kubrick wants Orff to compose the score himself. Kubrick also contacts Bernard Herrmann, but the American composer asks for an extraordinary fee (Merkley 2007: 7). Kubrick has spent several weeks listening to almost every modern composition available on record in an effort to decide what style of music would fit the film (Bernstein 1966b: 98).

11 April 1966: Kubrick writes to Clarke saying he wants to see 'some magical enchantment both in the writing and ultimately in the filming' (Poole 2015: 184). He especially finds the alien 'teaching-machine' problematic, not only technically but in its didactic nature: he sees 'a kind of silly simplicity of which I think we are presently in danger' (Krämer 2010: 48). With the planned prologue of interviews with scientists, and the film's abundance of explanatory voice-overs, *2001* is shaping to be a very literal film designed to teach viewers lessons about human evolution, extraterrestrial intelligence, space exploration and intelligent machines (2010: 48–49). This is a turning point for Kubrick's perception of his film. After many months of accumulating careful scientific justifications for everything that is to appear on screen, the mystery he intended to convey is at risk of being pushed out of the picture (Bizony 2014: 182).

19 April 1966: Clarke returns to England and finds Kubrick is still shooting inside the centrifuge. Kubrick admits to him that the film is not going to be ready until late in 1967 or probably even 1968 (Clarke 1972: 46).

27 April 1966: At the annual meeting of Cinerama stakeholders, the president of the company reveals that *2001* will be ready in the spring of 1967. *Variety* notes this is the first indication of a slippage in production, for it had been hoped that the film would be ready for a Christmas release (Anon. 1966c: 14). As he did with the escalating cost, Kubrick keeps MGM executives in the dark; he has fed MGM snippets of the film to keep them distracted, and in the rare instances when executives visit the set, he has filled the walls of the offices with obscure and complex-looking charts and plans, never disclosing how much time is still needed to complete the film (Bizony 2000: 148).

May 1966: Shooting continues with Keir Dullea and Gary Lockwood (Anon. 1966b). Caras is in the United States filming interviews with scientists for the prologue (Frewin 2005b).

14 June 1966: *Variety* reports that Gary Lockwood has returned home to Los Angeles (Archerd 1966b: 2).

5 July 1966: Casting for the prehistoric sequence begins with a request for actors who do not 'top five feet, while six-foot-and-over artists are featured in the scenes of man's later development' (Anon. 1966a: 12). A test with a short performer wearing a neutering codpiece and a hairy hominid facemask does not look convincing (Poole 2015: 174).

July 1966: Director of photography Geoffrey Unsworth leaves the production to meet previous obligations. His assistant John Alcott takes on photographic duties (Bizony 2014: 330). Keir Dullea has completed his scenes (Anon. 1966b). Frederick Ordway also leaves the production (Ordway 1982: 102).

25 July 1966: The *Los Angeles Times* reports Martin Balsam has been signed to play the role of a computer (Anon. 1966h: C19). During the shooting, Kubrick himself at times feeds HAL 9000's lines to the actors (Bernstein 1966b: 104).

15 August 1966: MGM has slated *2001* to open in Easter 1967 (Anon. 1966g: 6).

26 August 1966: While Birkin travels around the United Kingdom to find a suitable desert, a second attempt is made at creating the man-ape characters in the 'The Dawn of Man' sequence: taller, slender performers, with extremely broad shoulders and narrow hips are dressed with a heavy monkey suit designed by Stuart Freeborn (Anon. 1966d: 18).

14 September 1966: Robert O'Brien publicly defends Stanley Kubrick, the director having now gone over budget by at least $1 million.

> Stanley is an honest fellow and he simply admitted to me that he hadn't anticipated the tremendous technical problems he's having with all the fantastic special effects he wanted. […] Why have Buck Rogers at $6 million, when you can have Kubrick at $7 million?
> (Anon. 1966i: 3)

With principal photography finished, special effect shooting is now fully underway. Kubrick is determined to have the effects footage as pristine looking as the live action shots. To achieve this 'first-generation look', he turns to the oldest cinematic tricks of all – hand-drawn mattes and in-camera multiple exposures. Models are shot while they slowly travel along Veevers' smooth rigs, then the film is rewound, the models blackened out except for the windows, onto which footage is projected via travelling projectors; a third passage along the rig is required for background stars (Finch 1984: 119–120). Different shots are photographed many months apart, with the undeveloped film tucked safely into refrigerators between takes (Bizony 2000: 119).

24 October 1966: Daniel Richter, a 28-year-old mime teacher, meets with Kubrick to discuss the 'The Dawn of Man'. After trying several kinds of costumes, and various stuntmen and dancers, Kubrick feels that a mime may be able to find a solution. Richter agrees it is essentially an acting problem. He undertakes a test wearing a black leotard filled with towels to alter his thin body in strategic places. Kubrick is impressed by Richter's interpretation of three different 'ape characters' and asks him to find and train a tribe of 30 man-apes. Richter accepts the task but admits it will take him months (Richter 2002: 1–8).

30 October 1966: Kubrick provides Richter with a number of books, articles and papers on the latest theories of human evolution. Richter begins discussions with Freeborn about the changes and development needed to make costumes and masks suitable for his performing style (Richter 2002: 10–15).

13 November 1966: Kubrick provides Richter with a 16mm film from National Geographic, as well as an 8mm camera with zoom and slow-motion to shoot footage of chimpanzees and gorillas at London Zoo (Richter 2002: 29).

November 1966: Birkin shoots aerial footage in the Outer Hebrides. The special effects team applies a colour-processing misalignment to this footage, creating an eerie alien landscape to be used for the Star Gate sequence (Bizony 2000: 131; 2014: 326).

2 January 1967: A new draft of the script for the 'The Dawn of Man' sequence is compiled. It is very close to being a shooting script and it incorporates suggestions from Richter (Richter 2002: 54).

January 1967: In the second week of January, Richter finds the key to develop credible hominid movements: he films a gibbon walking at half speed and trains his men to mimic it. Kubrick is enthusiastic about the result (Richter 2002: 64).

24 January 1967: *Variety* reports that MGM, 'for reasons unknown, has put back to October the opening dates of *2001*' (Anon. 1967c: 3).

January 1967: Douglas Trumbull shoots footage with his newly assembled slit-scan machine: prompted by Kubrick's idea that the camera should 'go through something' (Bizony 2000: 121) for the Star Gate sequence, Con Pederson suggests the key may lay in the work of filmmaker John Whitney, Sr., who experimented with controlled light streaks. Trumbull is convinced that a third dimension can be added to the effects displayed in Whitney's seminal short-film *Catalog* (Whitney, 1961), achieving an infinite tunnel of light. Kubrick gives the go-ahead and Trumbull spends several months building a special camera rig that takes up an entire studio (Bizony 2000: 121; Finch 1984: 123–24).

31 January 1967: The search for a suitable desert in the United Kingdom is deemed a failure. After scouting in Spain where *Lawrence of Arabia* (Lean, 1962) was shot, Andrew Birkin, production designer Ernie Archer, and a *Life* magazine photographer are sent to the Namibian Desert, in South-West Africa. 'The Dawn of Man' will instead be shot in the studio, with large-format transparency photographs of African skies and landscapes providing the backdrop (Richter 2002: 74; Bizony 2014: 326). However, the *Life* photographer has an accident and another photographer is sent to Namibia in his place, only to be fired a few days later. Keith Hamshere is eventually dispatched to replace him. Archer, Birkin and Hamshere stay in Africa until May (Bizony 2000: 132).

27 February 1967: Casting for the prehistoric sequence continues, with Richter having auditioned 2000 men without much result. He now begins auditioning boys (Richter 2002: 84).

March 1967: Freeborn has built extremely light undergarments from fine wool, with hair from horses, yaks and humans woven through the fibres. His masterpieces are the man-ape masks, involving magnets and a complex set of toggles to be operated by the performers with their tongues, enabling them to execute incredibly naturalistic facial expressions, like lips curling (Richter 2002: 78–83; Bizony 2014: 327).

17 March 1967: Richter has no luck in auditioning boys, young athletes and jockeys for his man-apes; he instead auditions dancers, but only a few pass his test (Richter 2002: 86–88).

24 March 1967: A second audition for dancers is crowded with people of all shapes and sizes, showing up only because MGM and Kubrick's names are involved in the advertisements. A few days later, Kubrick suggests to hire the cast of *The Young Generation*, a TV programme featuring teenage dancers, who prove to be perfect (Richter 2002: 90–91).

23 May 1967: The casting for the man-apes is complete. Stuart Freeborn is now able to produce costumes and masks to the dimensions of the performers (Richter 2002: 97).

5 June 1967: Richter begins training his cast of man-apes by taking them to London Zoo to observe the primates' group hierarchies, kinship relationships, etc. (Richter 2002: 98).

7 June 1967: The release date is now set for Easter 1968 following conflict with the release of *Far from the Madding Crowd* (Schlesinger, 1967) as a road show presentation, and a 70mm rerelease of *Gone with the Wind* (Fleming, 1939) (Anon. 1967b: 3).

28 June 1967: Kubrick and Ray Lovejoy begin editing the footage (Anon. 1967d). This is contrary to the common Hollywood procedure in which the film editor completes a first cut during shooting without the director. Lovejoy has only ever previously catalogued and filed the footage, not edited it (LoBrutto 1998: 307). Having so little dialogue to work with, Kubrick and Lovejoy use music from Kubrick's record collection to find the pace of the scenes (Bizony 2014: 427).

5 July 1967: Infant chimps are brought to the studio to familiarize themselves with the performers playing female roles in the 'The Dawn of Man'. Following Kubrick's requests, Freeborn has devised fake breasts filled with warm milk for the infants to drink (Richter 2002: 104).

19 July 1967: Stage 3, the largest at MGM, is being prepared for the sequence (Richter 2002: 108). The scenes will be shot by projecting the photographic plates taken in Africa onto a 40-by-90-foot screen covered with highly reflective material from the American company, 3M. This classic technique is perfected by Tom Howard (Finch 1984: 117). The desert set is built on a 90-foot-diameter rotating platform, so that different foreground scenery can be positioned in front of the reflective screen without having to move the delicate front-projection rig (Bizony 2014: 330).

July 1967: Kubrick hires British composer Frank Cordell to conduct excerpts of Mahler's *Symphony No. 3* (1893–96) (McQuiston 2011: 148). It is the first indication of Kubrick's intention to use pre-existing music for the film (Merkley 2007: 7).

2 August 1967: First day of shooting for the 'The Dawn of Man' sequence commences with the scene of Moon-Watcher's tribe foraging and attacking a neighbouring tribe at a muddy pool. After a week of shooting the cast is put on hold while Tony Masters and his art department construct the next set (Richter 2002: 115–19).

18 August 1967: Christiane Kubrick casually listens to a BBC radio broadcast of György Ligeti's composition *Requiem* (1965), which she thinks would be 'marvellous for the film'. Her enthusiasm is enough for Kubrick to start pursuing the music (McQuiston 2011: 148).

21 August 1967: The man-ape performers are back on Stage 3 where a cave set has been built (Richter 2002: 120). Kubrick uses the same rectangular monolith used on the lunar surface and in the hotel room. A single alien artefact provides cohesion in the story, and its black stillness conveys the sought-after sense of mystery.

1 September 1967: Over a small elevated rectangular platform built on a field on the back lot, Kubrick shoots Richter from an extremely low angle as he smashes bones on the ground and throws them in the air (Richter 2002: 132). 'The Dawn of Man' is now complete. Kubrick asks his associate Bob Gaffney, who has previously conducted second unit work on *Lolita*, to shoot scenes in Monument Valley for the 'Fantastic Voyage' sequence, to complement those shot in the Hebrides (LoBrutto 1998: 288).

5 September 1967: Richter's final duty on *2001* is an attempt to visualize an alien figure. With his body painted white and covered with small black polka dots, he is shot with high contrast film against a similarly dotted background. The effect is interesting but unsatisfactory (Richter 2002: 137). This is the last in a long line of attempts: if showing an alien in 'The Dawn of Man' was dismissed pretty quickly, efforts to visualize the encounter between Bowman and an extraterrestrial never decreased. Giacometti-inspired figures, small insect-like aliens, a humanoid character borrowed from Clarke's *Encounter in the Dawn*, lizard-like creatures, Devil-like beings as in Clarke's *Childhood's End*, bulky figures sculpted in clay by Christiane, elongated luminous figures created with anamorphic lenses, and finally shapes of pulsating light created by Trumbull using video feedback and the slit-scan machine – all have been discarded (Odino 2013). Ultimately, Kubrick decides that anything visible on screen and comprehensible to audiences would not, by definition, be 'alien' to them (Bizony 2014: 510). Once again, he believes that the suggestion is better than a literal visual interpretation.

25 September 1967: Kubrick hires Douglas Rain to provide the voice-over narration for the film (Chapman 2013: 103). A Shakespearean actor, Douglas was the narrator of *Universe*.

4 October 1967: After unsuccessfully trying to acquire the Ligeti tape from the BBC, and a trip to Vienna by his brother-in-law, Jan Harlan, to find the composer, Kubrick finally obtains a copy of *Requiem* from the publisher. Meanwhile he has pursued all avenues to hear as much of Ligeti's music as possible (McQuiston 2011: 149).

November 1967: Kubrick discusses with composer Gerard Schurmann a series of classical pieces he is thinking of using in the film: Schumann piano music, Chopin, Orff's *Carmina Burana*, Ligeti's *Atmosphères* (1961), and Johann Strauss's *The Blue Danube* waltz (1866) (Merkley 2007: 10–11). Around this time, Jan Harlan brings Kubrick samples of (much needed) music that is 'majestic and beautiful but which comes to an end' for Moon-Watcher's bone smashing scene. Among the many LPs Harlan provides is Richard Strauss's *Also Sprach Zarathustra* (1896) (Glintenkamp 2013b).

23 November 1967: Kubrick cables Clarke to say, 'As more film cut together it became apparent narration was not needed' (Chapman 2013: 103). *2001* is progressively taking shape as a non-verbal experience. Narrator Douglas Rain is employed to deliver HAL 9000's lines.

13 December 1967: MGM president Robert O'Brien admits the company failed to pay off any of its outstanding debt, a situation to which Kubrick's delays have contributed. Cost of *2001* has now reached $9,500,000–$3,500,000 over its original budget (Anon. 1967a: 5).

14 December 1967: Kubrick hires Alex North, who composed the score for *Spartacus* (McQuiston 2011: 150). Kubrick intends to use some of the classical and contemporary pieces he has selected and asks North to compose music to substitute Ligeti's compositions whose rights he may not be able to obtain. North accepts, but insists in composing all of the music for the film (Merkley 2007: 12).

15 January 1968: North records his music, which covers approximately the first third of the film (Anon. 1968a). Some of his cues bear obvious structural resemblances to the pre-selected tracks. Kubrick attends the recording and is very complimentary of the results, but admits some of the music 'doesn't suit my picture' (Merkley 2007: 23). North's cue for the space station docking sequence, intended as a substitute for Mendelssohn's *Scherzo* from *A Midsummer Night's Dream* (1826), prompts in Kubrick the idea of using a waltz. Trying out various possibilities at the Movieola with Lovejoy, Kubrick finds *The Blue Danube* appropriate and recuts the sequence to match it (Merkley 2007: 23–25).

17 January 1968: *Variety* reports that *2001* will have its premiere on 2 April 1968 at the Uptown Theatre in Washington (Anon. 1968c: 3).

22 January 1968: Kubrick tells Alex North no more music is needed and that he is going to use breathing effects for the remainder of the film (McQuiston 2011: 151; Agel 1970: 199). The situation with the music is still so unclear that MGM is notified the souvenir booklet may go to press without mentioning any (McQuiston 2011: 150).

25 January 1968: Kubrick contacts the conductor of a recent recording of Ligeti's *Requiem* to obtain permission to use it, which is finally granted in February (Heimerdinger 2011: 130).

2 February 1968: The rights to use Ligeti's *Atmosphères* are cleared with an agreement between MGM and the music company (Glintenkamp 2013b).

19 February 1968: Kubrick obtains the rights to use Ligeti's *Lux Aeterna* (1966) from his publisher. The necessary agreements for a third piece by Ligeti he has selected, *Aventures* (1962), are still pending (McQuiston 2011: 151).

7 March 1968: With the last effects shots delivered days, if not hours, before (Anon. 1968d), Kubrick leaves for the United States on board the *Queen Elizabeth* (Anon. 1968b). A separate cabin is equipped with an editing desk so that he can work on the film while at sea (Bizony 2014: 413). Arriving in New York, Kubrick then leaves for Los Angeles, continuing to cut the film on the train (Lockwood 2001: 154).

16 March 1968: Arriving in Culver City, California, Kubrick continues cutting and mixing the film at the MGM Studios. The department is working around the clock, utilizing 31 persons in sound and editing facilities (Anon. 1968f: 2; Cocks 2000: xiv). Following the first screening for MGM executives, Kubrick cuts the prologue interviews with the scientists (Agel 1970: 27).

27 March 1968: Rights for the use of *Aventures* are finally cleared (McQuiston 2011: 151–52). However, it is not possible to change the end credits of the film and the composition is not listed. O'Brien tells *Variety* Kubrick is 'precisely on schedule ever since the Easter-holiday release was set months ago' (Anon. 1968f: 2). The final cut runs two hours, 40 minutes, 30 seconds and is spooled on nineteen reels (1968f: 2).

1 April 1968: At a preview screening in New York, Alex North is shocked to discover none of his music has been used in the film (McQuiston 2011: 151).

2 April 1968: *2001*'s world premiere takes place at the Uptown Theatre in Washington, DC. Kubrick, Clarke, O'Brien, Dullea and Lockwood are in attendance (Anon. 1968e: E6). The audience is made up mostly of politicians and top industry figures. The atmosphere is extraordinarily tense (Cocks 2000: xvi).

3 April 1968: In its advance review, *Variety* writes:

> *2001* lacks dramatic appeal to a large degree [...] leaving interpretation up to the individual viewer. To many this will smack of indecision or hasty scripting. Despite the enormous technical staff involved in making the film, it is almost entirely one man's conception and Kubrick must receive all the praise and take all the blame.
>
> (Frederick 1968: 3)

The audience at the Loew's Capitol Theatre for the New York opening night with cast and crew, mostly executives over the age of 50, is puzzled, bored, restless, derisive and finally hostile (Cocks 2000: xv). Later, an MGM delegation arrives at the hotel where Kubrick is staying and rails against him and the film (Bizony 2014: 413).

4 April 1968: *Newsday* movie critic Joseph Gelmis writes that *2001* is 'one of the most bizarre films ever made [...] by conventional standards of drama, this new film is, I suppose, a spectacular, glorious failure' (Gelmis 1968: 3A). Renata Adler, of the *New York Times*, writes that the film 'is somewhere between hypnotic and immensely boring' (1968: 58). Kubrick does not read the reviews or the press reaction and spends the entire day sleeping. The invitational premiere in Los Angeles, which Kubrick does not attend, is again met with mixed reactions, though much of the younger Hollywood crowd is impressed (Cocks 2000: xv; Lockwood 2001: 140).

5 April 1968: Charles Champlin, in the *Los Angeles Times*, calls the film an 'epic achievement […] [*2001*] is the picture which science-fiction enthusiasts of every age and in every corner of the world have prayed that the industry might one day give them' (1968: E18). Kubrick begins the process of re-editing *2001* in an MGM basement, trimming 19 minutes, and adding an insert with the Monolith before Moon-Watcher's climactic bone smashing scene, along with two additional title cards (Agel 1970: 170). Reaction to the film is turning, however, and audiences are beginning to line up around the block to see the film (Bizony 2014: 416).

Conclusion

This production calendar clearly demonstrates – and defines – the title card 'Produced and Directed by Stanley Kubrick'. Kubrick conceived the film, he developed it with a writer, he secured a budget, he managed it, he picked a group of creative talents, he pushed them beyond their limit, he chose the actors, he directed them, he edited the footage, he struggled over musical choices and he solved countless other problems during the course of the four years he spent producing *2001*.

The artistic process Kubrick went through was not a mere execution of a plan, but involved a constant trial-and-error, organic approach, in every field and even in a far less linear way than the above calendar suggests, especially as far as the writing and the technical solutions were concerned.[6] As Tony Masters noted, the artists never had a schedule or a script, but worked through the movie guided by ideas that were changed on a daily basis: 'We just sort of made it up as we went along' (Shay 2001: 94). Speaking to Alexander Walker, Kubrick said that:

> Making a film is a process of discovery, of figuring out what you think about the material – you think you know about it before you begin, but however much you prepare it, you never have a chance to explore it with as much concentration and detail as when you are actually making the film. I think it is a process that a lot of artists share. You start something because you are interested in it, but you actually do it to find out about it.
> (Walker 1970)

What led to the continual delaying of the film's completion was not merely the complexity of the production, or the multitude of technical issues, but rather the need for artistic contemplation and exploration.

At the same time, the calendar shows that *2001*, as much as it was imbued with Kubrick's vision, was a colossal collaborative effort to which many creative minds brought their best and achieved what was initially thought impossible. The special effects artists arguably provide the best accounts of Kubrick's directing style. For instance, according to Douglas Trumbull, Kubrick was not afraid to delegate responsibility and stand by his collaborators, even to the point of never letting them be hassled by the MGM management (Finch 1984: 126). As Trumbull has explained, 'we enjoyed the luxury of an open-ended budget. It wasn't our business how much things cost; we simply were told to get the job done, no matter how long it took' (Thomas 1972: 18). However, he realized Kubrick 'wants to totally run everything. He has to see absolutely everything you're doing, he has to understand everything that's going on, and he'll be the one to say yes or no. He's in total control all the time' (Delson 1978: 10).[7] This is just one of the many apparent contradictions in Kubrick's personality. Trumbull found him to be

> [...] a sort of contrary character, determined to do things another way. Even if somebody's done something a certain way for 2,000 years because that's the way to do it, he just rejects that idea out of hand and says 'we're going to do something else'.
> (Chapman and Chapman 1982: 61)

The technical perfection achieved with the help of veterans of the business – Gentleman, and especially Veevers and Howard – provided *2001* with an authenticity and realism, but it was Kubrick's will to explore 'new areas where answers do not yet exist' (Thomas 1972: 18) that pushed Pederson, Trumbull, Richter and the group of flexible youngsters to achieve something new and different. Kubrick's open-minded control – to coin a phrase – gave *2001* both its radical distinctness and strong coherence.

In conclusion, rather than the product of a solipsistic author, *2001* is the work of an inspired, always searching, indefatigable artist who drove his talented collaborators relentlessly. It is, in short, the work of a brilliant director. Kubrick summarized incisively what he thought was his role when he said 'the director must always be the arbiter of esthetic taste' (Weinraub 1972: 26). If one wishes to consider Kubrick an auteur, I suggest this is how the concept should be tailored to suit him. A film – and especially one of such complexity and ambition as *2001* – is made by a long series of creative and technical decisions. Kubrick knew that 'it's the director's job to make the right decisions as frequently as possible' (Gelmis 1970: 408). Fifty years from its original theatrical distribution, the enduring influence of *2001* attests that Kubrick made them in abundance.

Appendix One: Stanley Kubrick Filmography

Day of the Fight (1951), USA: RKO Radio Pictures.

The Seafarers (1951), USA: Seafarers International Union.

Fear and Desire (1953), USA: Joseph Burstyn Inc.

Flying Padre (1953), USA: Radio Pictures.

Killer's Kiss (1955), USA: Minotaur Productions.

The Killing (1956), USA: United Artists.

Path of Glory (1957), USA: United Artists.

Spartacus (1960), USA: Universal.

Lolita (1962), UK/USA: Seven Arts/Metro-Goldwyn-Mayer.

Dr. Strangelove or: How I Learned to Stop Worrying and Love the Bomb (1964) UK/USA: Columbia Pictures.

2001: A Space Odyssey (1968), UK/USA: Metro-Goldwyn-Mayer.

A Clockwork Orange (1971), UK/USA: Warner Bros.

Barry Lyndon (1975), UK/USA: Warner Bros.

The Shining (1980), UK/USA: Warner Bros.

Full Metal Jacket (1987), USA: Warner Bros.

Eyes Wide Shut (1999), USA: Warner Bros.

Appendix Two: *2001: A Space Odyssey* Film Credits

Produced and Directed by Stanley Kubrick
Screenplay by Stanley Kubrick and Arthur C. Clarke

Cinematographer: Geoffrey Unsworth
Additional photography on 'The Dawn of Man' by John Alcott
Editor: Ray Lovejoy
Associate Producer: Victor Lyndon
Unit Publicist: Roger Caras

Distributed by Metro-Goldwyn-Mayer
Made at MGM British Studios Ltd. Borehamwood, England
Production Companies: MGM, Polaris Productions Inc. and Hawk Films Ltd.
Running time: 142 minutes
Release dates: 3 April 1968 (USA), 15 May 1968 (UK)

Cast

Keir Dullea as David Bowman
Gary Lockwood as Frank Poole
William Sylvester as Heywood Floyd
Daniel Richter as Moon-Watcher
Leonard Rossiter as Andrei Smyslov
Margaret Tyzack as Elena
Robert Beatty as Ralph Halvorsen
Sean Sullivan Roy Michaels
Douglas Rain as the voice of HAL 9000

Notes

Introduction

[1] For further details on the cinematic influence of *2001* see David Hughes' (2000) *The Complete Kubrick*, pp. 149–53 and James Howard's (1999) *Stanley Kubrick Companion*, pp. 115–16.

[2] On 24 August 1964, Kubrick's Polaris Productions registered the title *Journey beyond the stars* with the MPAA. The Title Registration Report listed similar titles, mostly registered between 1952 and 1962, including Columbia's 'Journey into the unknown', Paramount's 'Reach for the stars', Charles H. Schneer's 'Journey into the unknown', and 'Journey to the end of space' (MPAA 1964). Kubrick himself scrawled further title ideas, including 'The hot blue giant', 'Journey beyond the galaxy', 'Across the space frontiers', 'The conquest of the stars', 'Life in space', 'Life in the universe', 'The dark galaxy', 'Two million light years', 'Exploring the universe', 'Conquering the universe' and many more (Kubrick n.d.a).

[3] One only needs to think of the now infamous anecdote of Kubrick's terse relationship with classical Hollywood cinematographer, Lucien Ballard, on the set of *The Killing*. Despite his relative youth and anonymity within the industry, Kubrick asserted his control over Ballard, as documented by both Baxter (1997: 80–81) and LoBrutto (1997: 119–20).

[4] Ligeti himself was not initially made aware that Kubrick had obtained the rights to use his music in *2001*. It was only recently that, following the discovery of letters from Ligeti by the German scholar Julia Heimerdinger, that we know his reaction, calling *2001*, 'a piece of Hollywood shit' (Ross 2013). See also Heimerdinger (2011).

[5] See the special issues of *Historical Journal of Film, Radio, and Television* (Fenwick, Hunter and Pezzotta 2017a) and *Cinergie* (Fenwick, Hunter and Pezzotta 2017b) for a fuller account of this New Kubrick Studies.

[6] For more on Kubrick's cult auteur status see David Church (2006), and I. Q. Hunter (2016).

[7] The British Film Fund Agency recorded the total production staff as follows: 495 production staff, 48 actors, actresses and musicians, 55 other artistes, 754 other staff, including scenery craftsmen, electricians and seamstresses (Anon. 1968).

[8] *Stanley Kubrick: A Retrospective* took place from 11 to 13 May 2016 at De Montfort University, Leicester. It ran parallel to an academic exhibition, *Stanley Kubrick: Cult Auteur*, held at De Montfort University's Heritage Centre, displaying items from the Stanley Kubrick Archive, loaned by the University of Arts London.

Chapter One

[1] As a matter of fact, the short story 'The Sentinel' (Clarke 1951), often referred to as the source of *2001*, is hardly a story to be 'obsessed' or to 'fall in love' with. Arthur C. Clarke said, 'I am continually annoyed by careless references to "The Sentinel" as the story on which *2001* is based; it bears about as much relation to the movie as an acorn to the resultant full-grown oak' (Clarke 1983: 88). Moreover, Clarke sold Kubrick the rights for other five short stories (later bought back by Clarke) that also influenced the plot; see Bizony (2014: 18–20).

[2] For accounts of Kubrick's multiple interests see Joyce (2008), Clarke (1999: 261) and Frewin (2005a; 2005b: 28–29).

[3] Kubrick first mentions his interest in Arthur Schnitzler's works about jealousy and sexual fantasies in 1961 (Ginna 1961); the 1926 novel *Traumnovelle* (also known as *Rhapsody* or *Dream Story*) would fascinate him for the rest of his career, until he finally adapted it into *Eyes Wide Shut*. Filippo Ulivieri identified at least seven 'romance' projects that Kubrick was interested in, on several levels, in the late 1950s-60s. See Ulivieri (2017).

[4] For more on this issue see Macklin (1965), McAvoy (2015), Krämer (2014: 22–23, 38, 50, 65–73, 88–89, 97).

[5] For a good overview see Mayhew (2014: 183–212).

[6] Kubrick was ahead of his time: the recognized masterpieces of this genre would be published only in coincidence with the rise of the environmental movement. For an exhaustive list and a discussion on how the topic has been treated in science fiction, see Westfahl (2005: 574–76) and Heise (2003: 74–77; 2008: 71).

[7] Email correspondence between the author and Ian Watson, 13 January 2016.

[8] In comparison, today only five nations have officially admitted to possessing nuclear weapons capability, whilst four more are believed to have acquired them or are in the process of doing so (Kristensen and Norris 2016).

[9] For a detailed description of Orion, see Dyson (2002). For more thematic links see Krämer (2010: 18–28; 2014: 24, 26–28, 42, 59, 100).

[10] Perhaps not coincidentally, *Dr. Strangelove* won a United Nations sponsored award in 1965, the 'United Nations Award for the best Film embodying one or more of the principles of the United Nations Charter' (LoBrutto 1998: 100; Case 2014: 121).

[11] For a detailed account on how the two met and started to work together, see McAleer (1992: 195-97) and Clarke (1999: 259–63).

[12] See Case (2014: 127–31). The movie has recently been broadcast for the first time in almost 50 years and is available on Youtube: https://www.youtube.com/watch?v=xhQri14A0LU. Accessed 10 May 2016. See Hadley (2008) for an account of the TELSUN project.

[13] It is interesting to note that a different brand of Europans appear in Arthur C. Clarke's sequel books to *2001*, *2010: Odyssey Two* (1982); *2061: Odyssey Three* (1987); and *3001: The Final Odyssey* (1997).

[14] [...] where the benign alien Overlords are revealed, halfway through the novel, to be demon-looking creatures at the service to an even greater and mysterious alien entity they call the Overmind. Kubrick wanted again to use this theme during the development of 2001, as reported by Clarke in an entry in his diary dated 25 May 1965 (Clarke 1972: 37). The same

narrative device was used in the contemporary comic *El Eternauta* (1957–59). The premise of *Shadow* bears an obvious debt to Fred Hoyle's *The Black Cloud* (1957), and H. G. Wells' *The War Of The Worlds* (1898) is even explicitly referenced by the main characters.

[15] Some of the scenes that Kubrick commented or highlighted ('SEVERAL SPACE SHIPS LANDING'; 'there are more than enough good scenes among the people reacting'; spaceships hovering over Hampstead 'eating' people [Kubrick n.d.]) on his breakdown of the plot suggest he had an interest in the 'invasion' theme of the plot and in its visual appeal; again, shades of *Childhood's End*?

[16] See Brian Aldiss and Ian Watson in Joyce (2008); see also (Frewin 2005a).

[17] There is an anecdote that Alexander Walker has recalled on many occasions: at the end of the 1950s, several Japanese science-fiction reels were being unloaded from a truck into Kubrick's New York apartment. Walker has recounted at least four versions of the anecdote; the event is likely to have happened during the pre-production of *Dr. Strangelove* or even later. See Baxter (1997: 199–201), Ciment (1999: 37), Walker (1988: 286; 2000) and Walker et al. (2000: 361).

[18] The book Kubrick was referring to was *Habitable Planets for Man* (1964) written by Stephen H. Dole and published for the US Government contractor RAND Corporation; it was adapted later in the year in a hardbound edition by Isaac Asimov. Published at the height of the Space Race, this 'extraordinarily detailed and prescient book' (Scharf 2011) has been mentioned by Kubrick in several other instances. RAND was the world's first think tank and Kubrick had met or made contact with several of its most prominent members during the pre-production of *Dr. Strangelove*. See Smith (2007: 402–31) and Broderick (2016).

[19] The construction of the Berlin Wall (August 1961) and the Cuban missile crisis (October 1962) took place in the period when Kubrick was finishing *Lolita* and starting researching for *Dr. Strangelove*. See Bernstein (1966a).

[20] See Krämer (2014: 12, 22–23, 103–06). Nathan Abrams has recently suggested that Kubrick's moral 'search for meaning' could be related to his Jewish upbringing and cultural heritage; in this regard, the Yiddish term *mensch* (a decent, upstanding, ethical and responsible person) and *menschlikaty* (the yiddish expression for ethical responsibility and social justice) seem to fit the profile of a socially conscious director. See Abrams (2015) for further reading.

Chapter Two

[1] A detailed discussion on the early reception and commentary on Stanley Kubrick's film can be found in R. Barton Palmer's '2001: The Critical reception and the generation gap' published in *Stanley Kubrick's 2001: A Space Odyssey* (2006) edited by Robert Kolker (13–27). Kolker's introduction to the book also discusses the general status of the film and its various interpretations (it also touches upon the film's relationship with Clarke's novel).

[2] Patterson's essay 'Music, structure and metaphor in Stanley Kubrick's 2001: A Space Odyssey' (2004) brings in ideas from Clarke's novel at certain places to explain the uses of musical patterns and filmic metaphors in Kubrick's film. Sofia's essay 'Exterminating Fetuses: Abortion, Disarmament, and the Sexo-Semiotics of Extraterrestrialism' points out certain differences between the film and the novel in order to explain the foetal imagery in the film. Both of these essays acknowledge the differences, yet looks to the novel for explanations of the film.

[3] In *Of Grammatology*, Derrida displaces the centrality of speech given by Saussure's system, and argues that writing is not only a substitution for speech or the presence of the speaker, but also a supplement that completes or improves communication. In French, he coins the term 'differance' which is indistinguishable from 'difference' unless written down, to point at not only the differential relationship between the signifiers, but also the continual deferral of the signified within the network of linguistic signs. 'Differance' also indicates the supplemental nature of writing, which creates new network of differential relations unavailable to speech. However, I argue, in spite of this 'loss' or 'slippage' of signification, between speech and writing, the experience fundamentally remains linguistic. While substituting one system of signs for another, despite loss and misdirection of meanings, the majority of the significations crosses over.

[4] Clarke attributes this in his 'Author's Note' in *2010* (1982) mainly to the new information on Jupiter and its moons made available by the discoveries of the Voyager space craft in 1979.

[5] The theme of evolution and the transformation into maturity from childhood is a recurrent theme in Clarke's novels, most famously explored in *Childhood's End* (1953).

[6] This theme is also a recurrent one in Clarke, notably in the Rama series: *Rendezvous with Rama* (1972), *Rama II* (1989), *Garden of Rama* (1991), *Rama Revealed* (1993).

Chapter Three

[1] This is admittedly a simplified description of their collaboration, which is more fully detailed in Clarke's *The Lost Worlds of 2001*. A key passage: 'In theory, therefore, the novel would be written (with an eye on the screen) and the script would be derived from this. In practice, the result was far more complex; toward the end, both novel and screenplay were being written simultaneously, with feedback in both directions. Some parts of the novel had their final revisions after we had seen the rushes based on the screenplay based on earlier versions of the novel [...] and so on. After a couple of years of this, I felt that when the novel finally appeared it should be "by Arthur Clarke and Stanley Kubrick; based on the screenplay by Stanley Kubrick and Arthur Clarke" – whereas the movie should have the credits reversed. This still seems the nearest approximation to the complicated truth' (1972: 31).

[2] Consideration of these sequel comics are regrettably beyond the scope of this chapter, though I do intend to analyse them in a future publication.

[3] See Simon Garfield, *Just My Type: A Book about Fonts* (2011: 9–21) for a nuanced appraisal and historicization of Comic Sans.

[4] It's worth noting that the cover of the comic introduces it not as a novelization but rather as 'an official adaptation of the MGM/Stanley Kubrick production.' As Johannes Mahlknecht's essay 'The hollywood novelization: Film as literature or literature as film promotion?'(2012) makes clear, the language used on cover images is significant and often indicates the extent to which a given book is being positioned as an autonomous work or as a mere marketing paratext for the film. In the case of Marvel's *2001: A Space Odyssey*, the cover image bears little visual similarity to the aesthetics of the film, suggesting that the combination of Marvel and *2001* is the primary lure for potential readers. (In fact, Kirby's name does not appear anywhere on the cover, casting doubt on the extent to which his authorship functioned as a draw at the time.)

[5] Jack Kirby is effectively the poster child for exploitative treatment by the comic book industry, with fan furore over Marvel's refusal to fairly credit and compensate him (and, since his death, his heirs) for his creative work resulting in myriad lawsuits, boycotts and a movement in the industry toward creator-owned (rather than company-owned) intellectual properties. See, for instance, Cavna 2012.

[6] While comic book versions of popular films were common as far back as the 1930s, Marvel only came to embrace the practice in the 1970s as a response to lagging sales. As part of a larger effort to build relationships with Hollywood studios – to whom they ultimately hoped to license their original characters for film adaptations – Marvel purchased the adaptation rights for a variety of existing properties, including 'Hanna-Barbera cartoons, science-fiction films (*Logan's Run* and *2001*), *Godzilla*, Edgar Rice Burroughs characters (*Tarzan* and *John Carter, Warlord of Mars*), and even a real-life costumed stuntman from Montreal (*The Human Fly*)' (Howe 2012: Kindle loc. 3375). The contract between MGM and Kubrick available at the Stanley Kubrick Archive specifically indicates that MGM 'shall have the right to publish in any medium and form and use, vend and otherwise dispose of (and authorize others to do so) in advertising and exploiting the Photoplay, excerpts, dialogue, summaries, serializations and novelizations of the Work, the Screenplay or the Photoplay (including sequels and/or continuations)' (1965: 3).

[7] Ro does not provide citations for such claims, but his most likely source is Mark Evanier, Kirby's longtime assistant.

[8] To depict the Negative Zone, Kirby would resort to photocollage, inserting his cartoon figures into photographic and occasionally abstract landscapes – a technique that he also draws upon at various points in his adaptation of *2001*.

[9] The text in these comics is presented in italics and all capital letters, using bold text for selective emphasis. For the sake of readability, I will reproduce the italics/bolding conventions but use traditional capitalization.

[10] Later Marvel comics would explicitly tie these threads together, identifying the monoliths seen in Kirby's *2001: A Space Odyssey* comics as the source of the Celestials' power. See, for example, *Earth X* (Krueger and Leon 1999), a limited series that integrates aspects of Kirby's *2001*, *The Eternals* and the overarching Marvel Universe into a single narrative storyworld.

[11] Priest adapted the film *eXistenZ* (Cronenberg, 1999), among others, under the pseudonym John Luther Novak.

[12] As a representative example, the first ten issues of Lee and Kirby's *The Fantastic Four* – nearly 250 pages altogether – contain only *one* textless panel.

[13] Indeed, Kirby often drew what Jonathan Letham describes as 'movie-monster' comics (2004: 7), the comic book equivalent to exactly the kind of low-brow sci-fi that Kubrick sought to avoid with *2001*.

Chapter Four

[1] Email correspondence between the author and Jean Barbour of The American Mime Theatre, 10 February 2017.

[2] Email correspondence between the author and The American Mime Theatre, 10 February 2017.
[3] On the West Coast, the San Francisco Mime Troupe was also pioneering new forms of expression with their mime, one based on radicalism and satire. This reflected the growing counter-cultural, anti-establishment politics of the city. The Troupe began giving free performances in Golden Gate Park and became actively involved in the anti-Vietnam War movement. See Michael William Doyle (2002).
[4] Following *2001*'s completion, Richter found himself at the heart of New York's countercultural scene in the 1960s. He lived and worked with John Lennon and Yoko Ono in 1969, and undertook photography for Lennon's *Imagine* (1971).
[5] Mike Wilson was a friend, colleague and fellow adventurer of Arthur C. Clarke. He introduced Clarke to deep-sea diving, with one of their adventures in Ceylon captured in Clarke's *The Treasure of the Great Reef* (1964). Jeremy Bernstein, profiling Clarke in the *New Yorker*, described their relationship as follows: 'He [Clarke] has summarized his feeling about Ceylon in *The Treasure of the Great Reef*, his most recent book on deep-sea diving. In it he describes the discovery and salvage of a seventeenth-century treasure ship that was sunk on the Great Basses Reef, off the south coast of Ceylon – an enterprise he undertook with Mike Wilson, a former British paratrooper, frogman, film producer, and professional diver, who introduced Clarke to diving and has been his partner in underwater explorations ever since' (Bernstein 1969). Dan Richter was also a friend of Wilson, and so through the mutual contact of Arthur C. Clarke, Wilson introduced him to Stanley Kubrick.
[6] The 1960s saw a turn in psychology and studies of human behaviour towards aggression; nearly two decades on from the end of Second World War, and as scholarly work on the Holocaust mounted, there was a 'rush of studies of aggression in human society' (Poole 2015: 184), as well as around authority and obedience. Perhaps one of the most notorious experiments from this period was Stanley Milgram's 1963 experiment, *Obedience to Authority: An Experimental View* (1974).
[7] The narrative of 'The Dawn of Man' was eventually written with the intention that Moon-Watcher leads a species of dying man-ape that, similar to Robert Ardrey's work, sees them transformed 'into a carnivorous primate [after] a chance genetic mutation' – in *2001*, this would be the man-apes' encounter with the monolith (Ardrey cited in Poole 2015: 189).

Chapter Five

[1] Translation by the author.
[2] Michel Chion describes HAL's voice as a 'Voice-I' (Chion 2005: 240), a voice that resonates in us like our own inner voice, while other characters have a 'voice-he' – a voice whose exteriority can be heard. More specifically, in *2001* men's voices are often filtered by microphones (from Floyd's daughter to Bowman and Poole's conversations through their helmets' radios).
[3] This expression is used by Richard Rushton (2012) to define Gilles Deleuze's concept of the Time-Image.

Chapter Six

[1] In this chapter, I quote Ninian Mellamphy's translation of *Du mode d'existence des objets techniques* entitled *On the Mode of Existence of Technical Objects*, University of Western Ontario, 1980 (cf. 'References'). This text, which was published as a 'typescript' with a preface written by John Hart, only contains the translation of the introduction and of the first part of Simondon's work. The quotes that were not translated by Ninian Mellamphy but by the translator and are marked in the chapter with a (*). In order to keep coherence, the references in parenthesis refer to the French text published by Aubier.

[2] We can consider the horse and its jockey as a technically prepared, trained and shaped ensemble; the subsets (horse and jockey) constitute one whole when put together through the intervention of other subsets (saddle, stirrups, bit, etc.). In the same way, the ensemble is working only if this layout allows a state of meta-stability and internal coherence (the equipment that links the horse to the jockey doesn't slow the animal down or make the jockey fall for example).

[3] André Leroi-Gourhan explains in his book *L'Homme et la Matière* (*Man and Matter*) (Leroi-Gourhan 1943) that the *homo faber* 'is a theoretical creature that would only have the possession of tools as a human characteristic' (1943: 10). Indeed, the *homo faber* is less a paleontological reality, as it is a philosophical concept mainly theorised by Henri Bergson in his book *L'Évolution Créatrice* (*Creative Evolution*) (Bergson 1907).

Chapter Seven

[1] *2001: A Space Odyssey* (DVD, 2007) commentary.

Chapter Eight

[1] It is important to note that 2001 does not have a conventional film-music score. It was going to have one but Kubrick rejected it (Scheurer). Bearing in mind the suggestion that 'all musicians [...] are faggots in the parlance of the male locker room' (Hubbs 2000: 390), the unorthodox musicality of *2001* could, in itself, be considered queer (Brett 1994: 18).

[2] Marriage at this time was exclusively a heterosexual institution, so Clarke's comment is about his sexuality, rather than his attitude to long-term relationships.

[3] Kubrick's eye for past perversion when casting Dullea in 2001 can be compared with his selection of Murray Melvin to play the effeminate Rev. Runt in *Barry Lyndon*, bearing in mind that Melvin had first come to prominence playing Geoffrey, a camp gay youth, in Shelagh Delaney's play, A Taste of Honey, a role he reprised in the film version of 1961 (Richardson UK). A further point of comparison is with the casting of Tom Cruise in *Eyes Wide Shut*, particularly in relation to the sequence in which he 'cruises' the streets late at night, in the course of which he is taunted and accused of being a 'faggot'. Stefan Mattessich has suggested that Kubrick was deliberately playing on recent rumours concerning the star's sexuality.

[4] See also Sofia (1984: 49).

[5] To put this situation into context, it is important to emphasize that a series of iconic New York high-rise buildings had been pictured in earlier sf narratives, as, for instance, was the

case with the Metropolitan Life Assurance Building in the decade after its completion in 1908 (Yablon).

Chapter Nine

[1] Translation by the author.

Chapter Ten

[1] Philippe D. Mather has conducted extensive research into the photographic career of Kubrick and of his time at *Look* magazine. See Mather (2006, 2013).
[2] The mistakes are faithfully reproduced from the Kubrick/Clarke screenplay.
[3] It is possible to read a detailed analysis of the HAL 9000 panel at this website http://www.therpf.com/f9/hal-9000-panel-2001-space-odyssey-pg-119324/.
[4] First published online in 1999 in a Google Group named alt.movies.kubrick in which Katharina answered the question put to her a by Kubrick fan. The interview is available also at the www.archiviokubrick.it.

Chapter Twelve

[1] Kubrick's interest for science-fiction predates *2001*: an early draft of *Dr. Strangelove* included a science-fiction framing story featuring extra-terrestrial beings. See Krämer (2010: 18).
[2] For a detailed analysis of this period, see Odino's chapter in this volume.
[3] Cf. Watters 1968: 'once again, as so rarely happens in film history, an individual talent has widened and exalted the art of the film by his vision, dedication and uncompromising creative approach to the medium'; and Thomas 1968: '[The film is] a one man job. Seldom since *Citizen Kane* has a major film so identified was the work of one man as has *2001: A Space Odyssey*'. This concept was stressed during the making of the film as well: a reporter who visited the set described the film as 'a multimillion dollar vote of confidence by MGM in the talents of one man. At 37 Kubrick is in danger of being more interesting than the stars he employs' (Musel 1965: 6).
[4] Geduld's calendar has been reprinted in excerpts in Schwam (2000).
[5] Merkley (2007) used excerpts of Geduld's calendar in his study of Alex North's work, pointing out she specified a wrong year for North's involvement.
[6] See Clarke (1972), Poole (2015) and Chapman (2013) for the process of devising a plot, and Shay (2001) for an account of the numerous dead ends the technical department often found itself.
[7] It is interesting to note how age played a substantial part in the artists' experience with Kubrick. Wally Gentleman, a 39-year-old well-experienced cinematographer, couldn't stand the director's excesses, and his 'autocratic methods [...] I learned that one doesn't work with Kubrick – one only works for him – and I found that rather difficult' (Shay 2001: 106). On the contrary, Con Pederson, 31, had no objection to the fact that Kubrick 'was always concerned about every corner of the film [...] Stanley always looked through the camera and always made changes, and was making sure that his sense for the film was coming

through' (Debert 1998). The praise for Kubrick becomes even more pronounced with the youngest. Keith Hamshere, 21, found that 'people were allowed to blossom and Stanley encouraged it' (Mawston 2016: 36). Douglas Trumbull, 23, termed the production 'a real education' (Thomas 1972: 18). Dan Richter, 28, realized 'that older, more experienced movie professionals often search out safe ground and do things the way they have always been done. On *2001*, Stanley values our young imagination, creativity, and boldness, as well as our ability to do hard work over long hours' (Richter 2002: 12).

Bibliography

Abbott, S. (2009), 'Arthouse SF film', in M. Bould, A. M. Butler, A. Roberts and S. Vint (eds), *The Routledge Companion to Science Fiction*, London: Routledge, pp. 463–67.
Abrams, J. J. (2007), 'Introduction', in J. J. Abrams (ed.), *The Philosophy of Stanley Kubrick*, Lexington: University Press of Kentucky, pp. 1–6.
—— (2007), 'Nietzsche's overman as posthuman Star-Child in *2001: A Space Odyssey*', in J. J. Abrams (ed.), *The Philosophy of Stanley Kubrick*, Lexington: University Press of Kentucky, pp. 247–65.
Abrams, N. (2015a), 'An alternative New York Jewish intellectual: Stanley Kubrick's cultural critique', in T. Ljujič, P. Krämer and R. Daniels (eds), *Stanley Kubrick New Perspectives*, London: Black Dog Publishing, pp. 62–79.
—— (2015b), 'Becoming a macho mensch: Stanley Kubrick, *Spartacus* and 1950s Jewish masculinity', *Adaptation*, 8:3, pp. 283–96.
Adams, V. (1964a), '6 dramas on U.N. planned for TV: Xerox to underwrite costs – Celebrities to waive fee', *New York Times*, 9 April, p. 63.
—— (1964b), 'Serling play to begin U.N. TV series', *New York Times*, 18 August, p. 63.
Addams, C. (1947), *Addams and Evil: An Album of Cartoons*, New York: Random House.
Adler, R. (1968), 'The screen: '2001' is up, up and away: Kubrick's Odyssey in space begins run', *New York Times*, 4 April, p. 58.
Agel, J. (1970), *The Making of Kubrick's 2001*, New York: New American Library.
Aldiss, B. (1968), *Supertoys Last All Summer Long*, New York: St Martin's Press.
Alexander, J. P. (2001), 'Graffiti on the monolith: Kirby vs. Kubrick', *The Jack Kirby Collector*, 31, pp. 53–57.
Alpert, D. (1964), 'What makes Kubrick laugh? It's the bomb', *Los Angeles Times*, 9 February, p. 34.
Alpert, H. (1966), 'Is it Strangelove? Is it Buck Rogers? Is it the future? Offbeat director in outer space', *New York Times Magazine*, 16 January, pp. 14–15, 40–41, 43, 46, 51.
Anon. (1952), 'Zero hour minus X years', *Astounding Science Fiction* (US edition), September, pp. 82–90.
Anon. (1960), 'Stanley Kubrick movie maker', *The Observer*, 4 December, p. 21.
Anon. (1964a), 'Direct hit', *Newsweek*, 3 February, pp. 79–80.
Anon. (1964b), 'Show selects 100 directors', *Show Magazine*, April 1964, p. 88.

Anon. (1964c), 'Hollywood's Man Stanley', *McCall Magazine*, February, SK/11/6/22, London: Stanley Kubrick Archive (SKA), University of the Arts London (UAL).

Anon. (1964d), 'Production notebooks', March, SK/12/2/8, /Creative Evolution SKA, UAL.

Anon. (1965a), 'Modern art museum show five Kubrick pictures', *Boxoffice*, 2 August, 87:15, p. E3.

Anon. (1965b), 'Production notes', 1 June–18 June, SK/12/2/7, /Creative Evolution SKA, UAL.

Anon. (1965c), 'Cunard lines sticker', Sant'Angelo in Theodice, Italy: Emilio D'Alessandro Archive.

Anon. (1965d), 'Sheets in script order number – Television monitor material', 17 December–20 April, SK/12/3/4/2, Sant'Angelo in Theodice (FR), Italy SKA, UAL.

Anon. (1965e), 'Who's where', *Daily Variety*, 13 August, p. 2.

Anon. (1965–68), 'Backstage photographs', SK/12/9/1/3, Sant'Angelo in Theodice (FR), Italy SKA, UAL.

Anon. (1966a), 'Casting in new film is called A Space Odyssey', *Kingsport Times*, 5 July, p.12.

Anon. (1966b), 'Continuity reports in scene order', 3 January–30 June, SK/12/3/4/3, Sant'Angelo in Theodice (FR), Italy SKA, UAL.

Anon. (1966c), 'C'rama annual meeting so quiet, stockholders can hear losses fall', *Variety*, 4 May, p. 14.

Anon. (1966d), 'Display ad: MGM requires males, any age...', *The Stage*, 26 August, p. 18.

Anon. (1966e), 'International soundtrack: London', *Variety*, 19 January, p. 18.

Anon. (1966f), 'International soundtrack: London', *Variety*, 16 February, p. 27.

Anon. (1966g), 'MGM lists 28 features for release covering year through July 1967', *Boxoffice*, 15 August, p. 6.

Anon. (1966h), 'Poe buys McCoy novel', *Los Angeles Times*, 25 July, p. C19.

Anon. (1966i), 'Some MGM European features burst budgets but O'Brien holds boxoffice potential justifies', *Variety*, 14 September, p. 3.

Anon. (1966j), '"Space Odyssey" to meld facts with fiction', *Variety*, 16 February, p. 25.

Anon. (1966k), 'Paul Curtis's mime', *Back Stage*, 18 March, 7: 11, p. 16.

Anon. (1967a), 'Debt Payoff awaits inventory playoff; metro leans on Kubrick's "Odyssey"', *Variety*, 13 December, p. 5.

Anon. (1967b), 'Kubrick's "2001" for Easter, 1968', *Variety*, 7 June, p. 3.

Anon. (1967c), 'Metro delays "2001" for fall opening', *Variety*, 25 January, p. 3.

Anon. (1967d), Post-production, 28 June–4 November, SK/12/4, Sant'Angelo in Theodice (FR), Italy SKA, UAL.

Anon. (1968a), '*2001* music: Alex North/Henry Brant correspondence etc.', December 1967–26 February 1968, SK/12/8/1/42, Sant'Angelo in Theodice (FR), Italy SKA, UAL.

Anon. (1968b), 'Koffer labels', 21 July 1965–31 May 1968, SK/1/2/1/1, Sant'Angelo in Theodice (FR), Italy SKA, UAL.

Anon. (1968c), 'MGM-Kubrick "Odyssey", four years a-making, Preems April 2 in D.C.', *Variety*, 17 January, p. 3.

Anon. (1968d), 'Special effects progress charts – A-C', 17 March 1967–6 March 1968, SK/12/3/2/3, Sant'Angelo in Theodice (FR), Italy SKA, UAL.

Anon. (1968e), 'Washington', *Boxoffice*, 8 April, p. E6.

Anon. (1968f), 'Work round clock editing "Odyssey" for Tuesday program', *Daily Variety*, 27 March, p. 2.

Bibliography

Anon. (1968g), 'Letter from Bromhead, Foster & Co Chartered Accountants to Mr. Davies of the board of trade', 23 April, BT 335/28, London: National Archives, Kew.

Anon. (1968h), '*2001: A Space Odyssey*', *The Independent Film Journal*, 13 April, 61:10, p. 52.

Anon. (1968i), 'Pictures: "2001" As Grist for Coffee Cup Debate', *Variety*, 24 April, 250:10, p. 29.

Anon. (2002), 'La figlia di Kubrick risponde ai fan', http://www.archiviokubrick.it/testimonianze/persone/katharina.html. Accessed 13 October 2016.

Anon. (2010), 'Jane Goodall', http://www.janegoodall.org.uk/jane-goodall. Accessed 30 April 2015.

Anon. (n.d.), 'Letter sent to Allan, Foster, Ingersoll and Weber for advertising purposes', SK/12/5/14, London: SKA, UAL.

Aragay, M. (2005), *Books in Motion: Adaptation, Intertextuality, Authorship*, Amsterdam and New York: Rodopi.

Archer, E. (1964), 'How to learn to love world destruction', *New York Times*, 26 January, p. X13.

Archerd, A. (1965a), 'Just for variety', *Daily Variety*, 27 August, p. 2.

—— (1965b), 'Just for variety', *Daily Variety*, 22 October, p. 2.

—— (1966a), 'Just for variety', *Daily Variety*, 27 January, p. 2.

—— (1966b), 'Just for variety', *Daily Variety*, 14 June, p. 2.

Ardrey, R. (1961), *African Genesis: A Personal Investigation into the Animal Origins and Nature of Man*, New York and London: Collins.

Azulys, S. (2011), *Stanley Kubrick, une odyssée philosophique*, Chatou: Les éditions de la transparence, Cinéphilie.

Baetens, J. (2005), 'Novelization, a contaminated genre?', *Critical Inquiry*, 32:1, pp. 43–60.

—— (2010), 'Expanding the field of constraint: Novelization as an example of multiply constrained writing', *Poetics Today*, 31:1, pp. 51–79.

Banerjee, S. (2001), 'Literature and cinema: Some observations', *Literature and Criticism*, 1:1, pp. 154–59.

Baron, C. and Carnicke, S. M. (2008), *Reframing Screen Performance*, Ann Arbor: University of Michigan Press.

Barone, D. (1996), 'Klaatu was no angel: A historical-contextual analysis of *The Day the Earth Stood Still*', *Studies in the Humanities*, 23:2, pp. 202–12.

Barthes, R. (2003), *La camera chiara: Nota sulla fotografia* (trans. R. Guidieri), Turin: Einaudi.

Barton, C. (1949), *Africa Screams*, USA: United Artists.

Baudrillard, J. (1987), *L'autre par lui-même: habilitation, Collection Débats*, Paris: Editions Galilée.

—— (1981), *Simulacres et simulation, Débats*, Paris: Galilée.

Baxter, J. (1997), *Stanley Kubrick: A Biography*, New York: Carroll & Graf.

Bazin, A. (2008), 'Ontologia dell'immagine fotografica', in A. Bazin (ed.), *Che cos'è il cinema?* (trans. A. Aprà), Milan: Garzanti, pp. 3–10.

Bean, R. (1963), 'How I learned to stop worrying and love the cinema', *Films and Filming*, June, p. 12.

Beckett, S. (1957), 'Acts without words I', *Samuel Beckett: The Complete Dramatic Works*, London: Faber and Faber, pp. 201–06.

—— (1960), 'Acts without words II', *Samuel Beckett: The Complete Dramatic Works*, London: Faber and Faber, pp. 207–11.

Benjamin, W. (1936), *The Work of Art in the Age of Mechanical Reproduction*, New York: Schocken Books, 1969.

Bereday, G. Z. F. and Lauwerys, J. A. (eds) (1965), *World Yearbook of Education 1965: The Education Explosion*, London: Evan Brothers.

Bernstein, J. (1965), 'Beyond the stars', *New Yorker*, 24 April, pp. 38–39.

—— (1966a), 'Interview with Stanley Kubrick', in A. Castle (ed.), *The Stanley Kubrick Archives*, Cologne: Taschen, 2005 [CD].

—— (1966b), 'Profiles: How about a little game?', *New Yorker*, 12 November, pp. 70–110.

—— (1969), 'Out of the ego chamber', *The New Yorker*, 9 August, http://www.newyorker.com/magazine/1969/08/09/ego-chamber. Accessed 7 October 2016.

Bianucci, P. (2015), *Vedere, guardare. Dal microscopio alle stelle, viaggio attraverso la luce*, Novara: UTET.

Biel, S. (2012), *Down with the Old Canoe: A Cultural History of the Titanic Disaster*, rev. ed., New York: W. W. Norton.

Bishop, R. (2008), 'Several exceptional forms of primates: Simian cinema', *Science Fiction Studies*, 35:2, pp. 238–50.

Bizony, P. (1994), *2001: Filming the Future*, 1st ed., London: Aurum Press.

—— (2000), *2001 Filming the Future*, 2nd ed., London: Aurum Press.

—— (2014), *The Making of Stanley Kubrick's 2001: A Space Odyssey*, Cologne: Taschen.

Blakeney, G. (1961), *Shadow on the Sun*, script, uncatalogued boxes, London: SKA, UAL.

Bliss, M. (2014), *Invasions USA: The Essential Science Fiction Films of the 1950s*, London: Rowman & Littlefield.

Bloom, A.B. (2010), *The Literary Monster on Film: Five Victorian Novels and Their Cinematic Adaptations*, Jefferson: McFarland.

Bluestone, G. (1957), *Novels into Film*, Baltimore: Johns Hopkins University Press.

Booker, M.K. (2005), 'English dystopian satire in context', in B. W. Shaffer (ed.), *A Companion to the British and Irish Novel, 1945–2000*, Malden: Blackwell, pp. 32–44.

Bould, M. (2010), 'Stanley Kubrick (1928–99)', in M. Bould, A. M. Butler, A. Roberts and S. Vint (eds), *Fifty Key Figures in Science Fiction*, Routledge: London, pp. 126–31.

Boylan, J. H. (1985), 'HAL in *2001: A Space Odyssey*: The lover sings his song', *Journal of Popular Culture*, 18:4, pp. 53–56.

Bozung, J. (2014), '*2001: A Space Odyssey* interview series: Brian Johnson', *TVStore Online*, http://blog.tvstoreonline.com/2014/08/2001space-odyssey-interview-series.html. Accessed 17 October 2016.

Bradbury, R. (1950), *The Martian Chronicles*, New York: Doubleday.

Braden, G. (2009), 'Spartacus and the second part of the soul', in J.J. Abrams (ed.), *The Philosophy of Stanley Kubrick*, Lexington: University Press of Kentucky, pp. 167–82.

Brett, P. (1994), 'Music, essentialism and the closet', in P. Brett, E. Wood and G. C. Thomas (eds), *Queering the Pitch: The New Gay and Lesbian Musicology*, New York: Routledge, pp. 9–26.

Brinded, N. (2014), 'Exceptionalist discourse and the colonization of sublime spaces: Alfonso Cuarón's *Gravity*, Ridley Scott's *Prometheus* and Thomas Cole's *The Oxbow*', *European Journal of American Culture*, 33:3, pp. 223–36.

Broderick, M. (2017), *Reconstructing Strangelove: Inside Stanley Kubrick's 'Nightmare Comedy'*, London and New York: Wallflower.

Bruno, M. W. (1999a), *Stanley Kubrick*, Rome: Gremese Editore.

—— (1999b), 'L'osso e l'astronave. Il montaggio intellettuale in Kubrick', *Close Up*, 7, pp. 49–56.

Bukatman, S. (1993), *Terminal Identity: The Virtual Subject in Postmodern Science Fiction*, Durham: Duke University Press.

——— (1999), 'The artificial infinite: On special effects and the sublime', in A. Kuhn (ed.), *Alien Zone II: The Spaces of Science-Fiction Cinema*, London: Verso, pp. 249–75.

Bull, P. (1965), *I Say, Look Here! The Rather Random Reminiscences of a Round Actor in the Square*, London: P. Davies.

Burgess, A. (1962a), *A Clockwork Orange*, London: Heinemann.

——— (1962b), *The Wanting Seed*, London: Heinemann.

Burke, E. (2008), *A Philosophical Enquiry into the Origin of Our Ideas of the Sublime and Beautiful*, Oxford: Oxford University Press.

Butler, J. (1993), *Bodies That Matter: On the Discursive Limits of 'Sex'*, New York: Routledge.

Campbell, C. (2013), *M.C. Escher's Letters to Canada, 1958–1972*, Ottawa: National Gallery of Canada.

Campbell, J. (1949), *The Hero with a Thousand Faces*, New York: Pantheon Books.

——— (1954), 'Window to tomorrow', *Astounding Science Fiction*, British ed., April, p. 2.

Caras, R. (1965a), 'Letter from Roger Caras to Arthur Pincus', 21 December, SK/12/6/8, London: SKA, UAL.

——— (1965b), 'Memo from Roger Caras to Stanley Kubrick', 20 July, SK/12/8/5, File 13 of 14, London: SKA, UAL.

——— (1966), 'Extra-terrestrial larder, request for using food brands', SK/2/3/7, London: SKA, UAL.

Carpenter, E. ([1914] 2007), *Intermediate Types Among Primitive Folk*, London: Forgotten Books.

Caruso, D. J. (2008), *Eagle Eye*, USA: Dreamworks.

Casarino, C. (1997), 'The sublime of the closet; or, Joseph Conrad's secret sharing', *Boundary*, 224:2, pp. 199–243.

Case, G. (2014), *Calling Dr. Strangelove: The Anatomy and Influence of the Kubrick Masterpiece*, Jefferson: McFarland & Company.

Cavna, M. (2012), 'CREATORS' RIGHTS: How the Jack Kirby case caused acclaimed ROGER LANGRIDGE to quit DC and Marvel', *The Washington Post*, https://www.washingtonpost.com/blogs/comic-riffs/post/creators-rights-how-the-jack-kirby-case-caused-acclaimed-roger-langridge-to-quit-dc-and-marvel/2012/05/19/gIQAvKA0ZU_blog.html. Accessed 28 January 2017.

Champlin, C. (1968), '"Space Odyssey" at Warner Cinerama', *Los Angeles Times*, 5 April, p. E18.

Chapman, D. and Chapman, R. (1982), 'Close encounter with the master of illusion: An afternoon with Douglas Trumbull', *Technology Review*, 85:2, February/March, pp. 60–64.

Chapman, J. and Cull, N. (2013), *Projecting Tomorrow: Science Fiction and Popular Cinema*, London: I. B. Tauris.

Charlet, A. (1984), 'Theatre reviews: American Mime Theatre', *Back Stage*, 23 November, 25:48, p. 6a.

Chion, M. (2001), *Kubrick's Cinema Odyssey*, London: British Film Institute.

——— (2005), *Stanley Kubrick: l'humain, ni plus ni moins*, Paris: Cahiers du cinéma.

——— (2006), *Stanley Kubrick. L'umano, né più né meno* (trans. S. Angrisani), Turin: Lindau.

Church, D. (2006), 'The "Cult" of Kubrick', *Offscreen*, 10:5, http://offscreen.com/view/cult_kubrick. Accessed 12 November 2014.

Church, M. (2004), 'Dear weekend over to you', *The Guardian*, 3 April, p. 12.
Ciment, M. (ed.) (1997), *Stanley Kubrick, La Biennale di Venezia*, Venice: G. Mondadori.
—— (1999), 'Entretien avec A.Walker, 'Une recherche de l'infallibilité?', *Positif*, 464, October, p. 37.
—— (2001), *Kubrick: The Definitive Edition* (trans. G. Adair), New York: Faber and Faber.
—— (2004), *Kubrick*, Paris: Calmann-Lévy.
Clarke, A.C. ([1951] 2000), 'The Sentinel', Glasgow: Voyager.
—— (1953a), *Childhood's End*, New York: Ballantine Books.
—— (1953b), *Expedition to Earth*, London: New English Library, 1983.
—— (1964), 'Letter from Arthur C. Clarke to Stanley Kubrick', 8 April, SK/12/8/1/12, London: SKA, UAL.
—— (1968), *2001: A Space Odyssey*, New York: New American Library.
—— (1972), *The Lost Worlds of 2001*, New York/London: Signet/Sidgwick and Jackson.
—— (1975), *Imperial Earth*, London: Victor Gollancz.
—— (1979), *The Lost Worlds of 2001*, Boston, MA: Gregg.
—— (1982), *2010: Odyssey Two*, New York: Ballantine.
—— (1983), *The Sentinel: Masterworks of Science Fiction and Fantasy – Arthur C. Clarke*, New York: Barkley Books.
—— (1986), *The Songs of Distant Earth*, London: Grafton.
—— (1987), *2061: Odyssey Three*, London: Grafton Books.
—— (1997), *3001: The Final Odyssey*, London: Voyager.
—— (1999), 'Son of Dr. Strangelove', in I. MacAuley (ed.), *Greetings, Carbon-Based Bipeds!: Collected Essays 1934–1998*, London: Voyager, pp. 259–63.
—— ([1968] 2000), *2001: A Space Odyssey*, New York: Roc Books.
—— (n.d.), 'Handwritten note', Clarkives MSS 005 *2001: A Space Odyssey* General Notes, Box 103, Folder 4, Washington DC: Arthur C. Clarke Collection, National Air and Space Museum, Smithsonian Institution.
Cochrane, L. (2014), '2001: Space Odyssey – The fashion power of designer Hardy Amies', *The Guardian*, https://www.theguardian.com/fashion/fashion-blog/2014/nov/28/2001-space-odyssey-the-fashion-power-of-designer-hardy-amies. Accessed 20 May 2017.
Cocks, H. (2001), 'Calamus in Bolton: Spirituality and Homosexual Desire in Late Victorian England', *Gender and History*, 13:2, pp. 191–223.
Cocks, J. (2000), 'SK', in S. Schwam (ed.), *The Making of 2001: A Space Odyssey*, New York: Modern Library, pp. xi–xviii.
Cocteau, Jean (1946), *La Belle et la Bête*, France: DisCina.
Cohen, K. (1979), *Film and Fiction: The Dynamics of Exchange*, New Haven and London: Yale University Press.
Collins, B. R. and Cowart, D. (1996), 'Through the looking glass: Reading Warhol's Superman', *American Imago*, 53:2, pp. 107–37.
Comstock, W. R. (1975), 'Myth and contemporary cinema', *Journal of the American Academy of Religion*, 43:3, pp. 598–600.
Cooke, J. B. (1997), 'Jack Kirby's infinite & beyond', *The Jack Kirby Collector*, 15, pp. 38–39.

Bibliography

Cooper, D. L. (2007), 'Who killed the legend of Spartacus? Production, censorship, and reconstruction of Stanley Kubrick's epic film', in M. M. Winkler (ed.), *Spartacus: Film and History*, Oxford: Blackwell, pp. 14–55.

Cooper, M. and Schoedsack, E. (1933), *King Kong*, USA: Radio Pictures.

Corliss, R. (1994), *Lolita*, London: British Film Institute.

Cornea, C. (2007), *Science Fiction Cinema: Between Fantasy and Reality*, Edinburgh: Edinburgh University Press.

Coyle, W. (1980), *Stanley Kubrick: A Guide to References and Resources*, Boston: G.K. Hall & Co.

Creed, B. (1993), 'Dark desires: Masochism in the horror film', in S. Cohan and I. R. Hark (eds), *Screening the Male: Exploring Masculinities in Hollywood Cinema*, London: Routledge, pp. 118–33.

Cronenberg, D. (1999), *eXistenZ*, Canada: Alliance Atlantis.

Daniels, D. (1960), '2001: A new myth', *Film Heritage*, 3:4, pp. 1–11.

Darius, J. (2013), *The Weirdest Sci-Fi Comic Ever Made: Understanding Jack Kirby's 2001: A Space Odyssey*, Edwardsville: Sequart Research & Literacy Organization.

Dart, R. (1953), 'The predatory transition from ape to man', *International Anthropological and Linguistic Review*, 1, pp. 201–19.

Davies, S. (2016), 'Towards HAL-ography', *Stanley Kubrick: A Retrospective*, 11–13 May, De Montfort University, Leicester.

Davin, E.L. (2006), *Partners in Wonder: Women and the Birth of Science Fiction, 1926–1965*, Oxford: Lexington.

De Bernardinis, F. (2006), *L'immagine secondo Kubrick*, Turin: Lindau.

Debert, A. (1998), '*2001: A Space Odyssey*: A discussion with Con Pederson', *VFX HQ*, http://www.vfxhq.com/spotlight98/9804c.html. Accessed 13 January 2014.

Deleuze, G. (2010a), *L'immagine-movimento* (trans. J.-P. Manganaro), Milan: Ubulibri.

────── (2010b), *L'immagine-tempo* (trans. L. Rampello), Milan: Ubulibri.

Delson, J. (1978), 'A definitive interview with the outspoken Douglas Trumbull', *Fantastic Films*, August, pp. 6–27.

Derrida, J. (2001), 'Of grammatology', in V. B. Leitch (ed.), *The Norton Anthology of Theory and Criticism*, New York: W. W. Norton, pp. 1822–30.

Desbarats, C. (2013), 'Philosopher avec Kubrick, 1/4: *2001 A Space Odyssey*', *Les Nouveaux chemins de la connaissance*, Radio Programme, 93:5, France Culture.

Dickens, C. (1850), 'A child's dream of a star', *Household Words*, 1, pp. 25–26.

Dorson, R.M. (1965), 'The career of "John Henry"', *Western Folklore*, 24:3, pp. 155–63.

Douglas, G. (1954), *Them!*, USA: Warner Bros.

Doyle, M.W. (2002), 'Staging the Revolution: Guerrilla Theater as a Countercultural Practice, 1965-1968', in M.W. Doyle and P. Braunstein (eds), *Imagine Nation: The American Counterculture of the 1960s and 70s*, New York: Routledge.

Dubois, P. (2009), *L'atto fotografico* (trans. B. Valli), Urbino: QuattroVenti.

Duffy, J. C. (2001), 'Gay-related themes in the fairy tales of Oscar Wilde', *Victorian Literature and Culture*, 29, pp. 327–49.

Dumont J. P. and Monod J. (1970), *Le Foetus Astral, Essai d'analyse structurale d'un mythe cinématographique*, Paris: Christian Bourgois Éditeur.

Dundy, E. (1963), 'Stanley Kubrick and Dr. Strangelove', in G. D. Phillips (ed.), *Stanley Kubrick Interviews*, Jackson: University Press of Mississippi, pp. 9–15, 2001.

Dyson, G. (2002), *Project Orion – The Atomic Spaceship 1957–1965*, London: Penguin.

Eberl, J. (2007), '"Please make me a real boy": The prayer of the artificially intelligent', in J. J. Abrams (ed.), *The Philosophy of Stanley Kubrick*, Lexington: University of Kentucky Press.

Ehrlich, P. R. (1954), *The Population Bomb*, New York: Ballantine Books.

Eichhorn, B. (2007), 'Branding 2001', in *Stanley Kubrick*, Frankfurt am Main: Deutsches Filmmuseum, pp. 120–25.

Erb, C. (1998), *Tracking King Kong: A Hollywood Icon in World Culture*, Detroit: Wayne State University Press.

Falsetto, M. (2001), *Stanley Kubrick: A Narrative and Stylistic Analysis*, Santa Barbara: Greenwood.

Fawell, J. (1990), 'Sound and silence, image and invisibility in Jacques Tati's Mon Oncle', *Literature/Film Quarterly*, 18:4, pp. 221–29.

Fay, G. (1963), 'Kubrick's strange love', *The Guardian*, 5 June, p. 5.

Fellini, F. (1960), *La Dolce Vita*, Italy: Pathé Consortium Cinéma.

Fenwick, J. (2017a), 'The Eady Levy, "the envy of most other European nations": Runaway Productions and the British Film Fund in the early 1960s', in I. Q. Hunter, J. Smith and L. Porter (eds), *The Routledge Companion to British Cinema History*, London: Routledge, pp. 191–99.

—— (2017b), '"Freddie, can you talk?": The Ethics of Betrayal in Frederic Raphael's Memoir *Eyes Wide Open* (1999)', *anglistik & englischunterricht*.

—— (2017c), 'Curating Kubrick: Constructing "New Perspective" Narratives in Stanley Kubrick Exhibitions', *Screening the Past*, http://www.screeningthepast.com/2017/09/curating-kubrick-constructing-new-perspective-narratives-in-stanley-kubrick-exhibitions/.

Fenwick, J., Hunter, I.Q., Pezzotta, E. (2017a), 'The Stanley Kubrick Archive: A Dossier of New Research', *Historical Journal of Film, Radio and Television*, 37:3, pp. 367–72.

—— (2017b), 'Stanley Kubrick: A Retrospective', special issue, *Cinergie*, 12, https://cinergie.unibo.it/issue/view/648.

Filz, W. (2004), *Das Reden der Rechner (On Computer's Talking)*, radio feature, Cologne: German public radio WDR.

Finch, C. (1984), *Special Effects: Creating Movie Magic*, New York: Abbeville Press.

Flannery, M.C. (2009), 'Building biology', *The American Biology Teacher*, 64:1, pp. 64–69.

Fleischer, R (1966), *Fantastic Voyage*, USA: Twentieth Century Fox.

Fleming, V. (1939), *Gone with the Wind*, USA: Selznick International Pictures.

Florey, R. (1932), *Murder in the Rue Morgue*, USA: Universal Pictures

Ford, John (1962), *How the West Was Won*, USA: Metro-Goldwyn-Mayer.

Foucault, M. (2008), *Surveiller et punir: naissance de la prison*, Paris: Collection TEL Gallimard.

Foster, T. (2009), 'SF and queer theory: Butler vs. Suvin', *Science Fiction Studies*, 36:3, pp. 390–92.

Frayling, C. (2014), 'Intelligent design: The creation of *2001: A Space Odyssey*', *Sight and Sound*, 24:12, December, pp. 18–24.

—— (2015), *The 2001 File: Harry Lange and the Design of the Landmark Science Fiction Film*, London: Reel Art Press.

Frederick, R. (1968), 'Review: "2001: A Space Odyssey"', *Daily Variety*, 3 April, pp. 3–4.
Freeborn, S. (1967), 'Dawn of man makeup research', SK/12/8/1/33, London: SKA, UAL.
Freedman, C. (1998), 'Kubrick's *2001* and the possibility of a science fiction cinema', *Science Fiction Studies*, 25, pp. 300–18.
—— (2001), 'Superman among the Stars: Review, Leonard F. Wheat, Kubrick's 2001: A Triple Allegory', *Science Fiction Studies*, 28:2, pp. 296–99.
Freeland, C. A. (1999), 'The Sublime in Cinema', in C. Plantinga and G. M. Smith (eds), *Passionate Views: Film, Cognition, and Emotion*, Baltimore: The Johns Hopkins University Press.
Freud, S. (1913), *Totem and Taboo: Resemblances Between the Mental Lives of Savages and Neurotics*, Boston: Beacon Press.
—— ([1919] 2003), *The Uncanny*, London: Penguin.
Frewin, A. (2005a), 'Stanley Kubrick and the search for extraterrestrial intelligence', in A. Castle (ed.), *The Stanley Kubrick Archives*, Cologne: Taschen, p. 378.
—— (2005b), *Are We Alone? The Stanley Kubrick Extraterrestrial Interviews*, London: Elliot and Thompson.
Friedman, T. (2005), *Electric Dreams: Computers in American Culture*, New York: New York University Press.
Fritscher, J. J. (1968), 'Stanley Kubrick's *2001: A Space Odyssey*: A sleep and a forgetting', *Journal of Popular Culture*, 2:1, pp. 167–71.
Gabbard, K. (1997), 'The circulation of sado-masochistic desire in the Lolita texts', *PysArt*, http://www.clas.ufl.edu/ipsa/journal/articles/art_gabbard01.shtml. Accessed 3 December 2009.
Garber, E. and Paleo, L. (1990), *Uranian Worlds: A Guide to Alternative Sexuality in Science Fiction, Fantasy and Horror*, Boston: G.K. Hall.
Garber, S. (2002), 'Introduction: Apollo 30th anniversary', *NASA History Office*, https://history.nasa.gov/ap11ann/introduction.htm. Accessed 19 January 2017.
Garfield, S. (2011), *Just My Type: A Book About Fonts*, New York: Gotham Books.
Geduld, C. (1973), *Filmguide to '2001: A Space Odyssey'*, Bloomington: Indiana University Press.
Gehman, G. (1986), 'Paul Curtis talks about his theories of mime', *The Morning Call*, http://articles.mcall.com/1986-07-06/entertainment/2544009_1_lux-sooamerican-mime-theatre.html. Accessed 1 May 2015.
Gelmis, J. (1968), '"Space Odyssey" fails most gloriously', *Newsday*, 4 April, p. 3A.
—— (1970), *The Film Director as Superstar*, New York: Doubleday.
—— (1974), *The Film Director as Superstar*, London: Pelican Books.
Géraud, N. (1999), 'Amitié d'étoiles', *Positif*, 464, October, pp. 76–78.
Gilliatt, P. (1968), 'After Man', *The New Yorker*, http://www.newyorker.com/magazine/1968/04/13/after-man. Accessed 12 April 2015.
Ginna, R.E. (1961), 'Kubrick uncovered, Part II', *The Guardian*, https://www.theguardian.com/film/1999/jul/16/stanleykubrick1.html. Accessed 15 October 2016.
Glassman, M. and Wise, W. (1999), 'A filmmaker of vision: Take one's interview with Colin Low, Part I', *Take One*, spring, pp. 18–31.
Glintenkamp, P. (2013a), 'The Stanley Kubrick Archive Oral History Project: Finding and Developing the Story', https://www.youtube.com/watch?v=Lx49KEJxUF0.html. Accessed 15 October 2016.

—— (2013b), 'The Stanley Kubrick Archive Oral History Project: Music', https://youtu.be/ptTYShYyOL4. Accessed 6 September 2016.

Godard, J. L. (1965), *Alphaville*, France: Athos Films.

Goodall, J. (2015), 'Jane Goodall', http://www.biography.com/people/jane-goodall-9542363. Accessed 1 May 2015.

Goodwin, A. and Simonson, W. (1979), *Alien: The Illustrated Story*, London: Titan Books.

Grant, B. K. (2006), 'Of men and monoliths: Science fiction, gender and 2001: A Space Odyssey', in R. Kolker (ed.), *Stanley Kubrick's 2001: A Space Odyssey, New Essays*, Oxford: Oxford University Press, pp. 69–86.

Grodal, T. (2009), 'Subjective aesthetics in film', *Embodied Visions: Evolution, Emotion, Culture and Film*, Oxford: Oxford University Press, pp. 229–49.

Guest, V. (1961), *The Day the Earth Caught Fire*, UK: Universal International Pictures.

Hadley, M. (2008), 'The UN goes to the movies', http://www.tvparty.com/fall-un.html. Accessed 15 October 2016.

Hall, C. S. (1962), 'Out of a dream came the faucet', *Psychoanalytical Review*, 49, pp. 113–16.

Harlan, J. (2001), *Stanley Kubrick: A Life in Pictures*, UK/USA: Warner Bros.

Harris, R. (1965), 'Merrick didn't laugh-might cost too much', *Newsday*, 9 July, p. 2C.

Harvey, J. (1995), *Men in Black*, London: Reaktion.

Hatfield, C. (2012), *Hand of Fire: The Comics Art of Jack Kirby*, Jackson: University Press of Mississippi.

Heidegger, M. (1954), 'The question concerning technology', *The Question Concerning Technology and Others Essays* (trans. W. Lovitt), New York and London: Garland Publishing.

Heimerdinger, J. (2011), '"I have been compromised. I am now fighting against it": Ligeti vs. Kubrick and the music for *2001: A Space Odyssey*', *Journal of Film Music*, 3:2, pp. 127–43.

Heise, U. (2003), 'The virtual crowds: Overpopulation, space and speciesism', in M.P. Branch and S. Slovic (eds), *The ISLE Reader: Ecocriticism, 1993–2003*, Athens and London: University of Georgia Press, pp. 72–101.

—— (2008), *Sense of Place and Sense of Planet: The Environmental Imagination of the Global*, London: Oxford University Press.

Heller, J. (1964), 'Stanley Kubrick and Joseph Heller: A conversation', unpaginated transcript, SK/1/2/8, London: SKA, UAL.

Hersey, G. (1999), *The Monumental Impulse: Architecture's Biological Roots*, Cambridge: MIT Press.

Heymann, D. ([1987] 2005), 'Le Vietnam de Stanley Kubrick', in A. Castle (ed.), *The Stanley Kubrick Archives*, Cologne: Taschen, pp. 476–79.

Hoch, D. G. (1971), 'Mythic patterns in 2001: A Space Odyssey', *Journal of Popular Culture*, 4:4, pp. 961–65.

Howard, J. (1999), *Stanley Kubrick Companion*, London: B.T. Basford.

Howe, S. (2012), *Marvel Comics: The Untold Story*, New York: Harper.

Howells, R. (2012), *The Myth of the Titanic*, 2nd ed., London: Palgrave Macmillan.

Hubbs, N. (2000), 'A French connection: Modernist codes in the musical closet', *GLQ*, 6:3, pp. 389–412.

Hughes, D. (2000), *The Complete Kubrick*, London: Virgin Books.

Hunter, I.Q. (2013), 'From adaptation to cinephilia: An intertextual Odyssey', in T. V. Parys and I.Q. Hunter (eds), *Science Fiction Across Media: Adaptation/Novelization*, Canterbury: Gylphi Limited, pp. 43–63.
—— (2015), 'Introduction', *Adaptation*, 8:3, pp. 277–82.
—— (2016), *Cult Film as a Guide to Life: Fandom, Adaptation and Identity*, London: Bloomsbury.
Hutcheon, L. (2006), *A Theory of Adaptation*, New York: Routledge.
Hyams, P. (1984), *2010: The Year We Make Contact*, USA: Metro-Goldwyn-Mayer.
Hyde, A. F. (1993), 'Cultural filters: The significance of perception in the history of the American West', *Western Historical Quarterly*, 24:3, pp. 351–74.
Janes, D. (2010), 'Seeing and tasting the divine: Simeon Solomon's homoerotic sacrament', in P. di Bello and G. Koureas (eds), *Art, History and the Senses: 1830 to the Present*, Farnham: Ashgate, pp. 35–50.
—— (2011), 'Clarke and Kubrick's 2001: A queer Odyssey', *Science Fiction Film and Television*, 4:1, pp. 57–78.
Jenkins, G. (1997), *Stanley Kubrick and the Art of Adaptation: Three Novels, Three Films*, Jefferson: McFarland & Co.
Jonas, G. (2008), 'Arthur C. Clarke, premier science fiction writer, dies at 90', *The Gay Recluse*, 18 March, http://thegayrecluse.com/2008/03/18/on-thesearch-for-gay-obituaries-arthur-c-clarke-the-times-version. Accessed 2 January 2009.
Jones, D. (2009), *Moon*, UK: Liberty.
Joyce, P. (2008), *The Last Movie: Stanley Kubrick and Eyes Wide Shut*, USA: Warner Bros.
Kagan, N. (1972), *The Cinema of Stanley Kubrick*, New York: Holt, Rinehart and Winston.
Kapferer, B. (2014), *2001 and Counting: Kubrick, Nietzsche, and Anthropology*, Chicago: Prickly Paradigm Press.
Kant, I. (1996), *Kant: The Metaphysics of Morals*, Cambridge: Cambridge University Press.
Kaplan, M. (2007), 'Kubrick: A Marketing Odyssey', https://www.theguardian.com/film/2007/nov/02/marketingandpr. Accessed 2 July 2016.
Kavanagh, K. (1964), 'Letter from Kevin Kavanagh to Jack Schwartzamn', 2 October, uncatalogued boxes, London: SKA, UAL.
Kennedy, J. F. (1962), 'Address at Rice University on the Nation's Space Effort', *John F Kennedy Presidential Library and Museum*, https://www.jfklibrary.org/AssetViewer/MkATdOcdU06X5uNHbmqm1Q.aspx. Accessed 9 October 2016.
Kessler, E. A. (2012), *Picturing the Cosmos: Hubble Space Telescope Images and the Astronomical Sublime*, Minneapolis: University of Minnesota Press.
Kilgore, De W. D. (2008), 'Queering the coming race? A utopian historical imperative', in: W. G. Pearson, V. Hollinger and J. Gordon (eds), *Queer Universes: Sexualities in Science Fiction*, Liverpool: Liverpool University Press, pp. 233–51.
Kincaid, J. R. (1992), *Child Loving: The Erotic Child and Victorian Culture*, New York: Routledge.
—— (1998), *Erotic Innocence: The Culture of Child Molesting*, Durham: Duke University Press.
King, S. (1977), *The Shining*, New York: Doubleday.
Kirby, J. (1972), *New Gods*, New York: DC Comics.
—— (1976a), *2001: A Space Odyssey*, New York: Marvel Comics.

―――― (1976b), *The Eternals*, New York: Marvel Comics.
Köhler, A. (2010), 'To think human out of the machine paradigm', *Integrative Psychological & Behavioral Science*, 44:1, pp. 39–57.
Köhler, C. ([1968] 2000), 'Stanley Kubrick raps', in S. Schwam (ed.), *The Making of 2001: A Space Odyssey*, New York: Modern Library, pp. 245–57.
Köhler, W. (1925), *The Mentality of Apes*, New York: Liveright, 1976.
Kolditz, G. (1970), *Signale – Ein Weltraumabenteuer* (*Signals: A Space Adventure*), GDR/Poland: DEFA.
Kolker, R. (2006) (ed.), *Stanley Kubrick's 2001: A Space Odyssey: New Essays*, New York: Oxford University Press.
―――― (2000), *A Cinema of Loneliness: Penn, Stone, Kubrick, Scorsese, Spielberg, Altman*, 3rd ed., New York: Oxford University Press.
―――― (2011), *A Cinema of Loneliness*, 4th ed., New York: Oxford University Press.
―――― (2017a), *The Extraordinary Image: Orson Welles, Alfred Hitchcock, Stanley Kubrick and the Reimagining of Cinema*, New Brunswick: Rutgers University Press.
―――― (2017b), 'The Legacy of Stanley Kubrick and the Kubrick Archives', https://blog.oup.com/2017/07/stanley-kubrick-archives/. Accessed 15 September 2017.
Kraft, D. A. (1976), '2001: A space retrospective', in J. Kirby (ed.), *2001: A Space Odyssey*, New York: Marvel Comics, pp. 73–82.
Krämer, P. (2009), '"Dear Mr. Kubrick": Audience responses to *2001: A Space Odyssey* in the late 1960s', *Participations*, 6:2, pp. 240–59.
―――― (2010), *2001: A Space Odyssey*, London: British Film Institute.
―――― (2014), *Dr. Strangelove or: How I learned to Stop Worrying and Love the Bomb*, London: British Film Institute.
―――― (2015a), '"A film specially suitable for children": The marketing and reception of *2001: A Space Odyssey* (1968)', in N. Brown and B. Babington (eds), *Family Films in Global Cinema: The World Beyond Disney*, London: I. B. Tauris, pp. 37–52.
―――― (2015b), '"Complete total final annihilating artistic control": Stanley Kubrick and post-war Hollywood', in T. Ljujič, P. Krämer and R. Daniels (eds), *Stanley Kubrick New Perspectives*, London: Black Dog Publishing, pp. 48–61.
―――― (2016), 'The legacy of Dr. Strangelove: Stanley Kubrick, science fiction blockbusters, and the future of humanity', in K. Ritzenhoff and A. Krewani (eds), *The Apocalypse in Film: Dystopias, Disasters, and Other Visions about the End of the World*, Lanham: Rowman & Littlefield, pp. 45–60.
Kramer, S. (1959), *On the Beach*, USA: United Artists.
Kristensen, H. M. and Norris, R. S. (2016), 'Status of world nuclear forces', https://fas.org/issues/nuclear-weapons/status-world-nuclear-forces/. Accessed 20 October 2016.
Kroitor, R. and Low, C. (1960), *Universe*, Canada: National Film Board of Canada.
Krueger, J. and Leon, J. P. (1999), *Earth X*, New York: Marvel Comics.
Kuberski, P. (2008), 'Kubrick's Odyssey: Myth, technology, gnosis', *Arizona Quarterly*, 64:3, pp. 51–73.
―――― (2012), *Kubrick's Total Cinema: Philosophical Themes and Formal Qualities*, London: Bloomsbury.

Kubrick, S. (1964a), 'Letter from Stanley Kubrick to Harlod Mirisch', 6 April, SK/11/9/19, London: SKA, UAL.

—— (1964b), 'Letter from Stanley Kubrick to Arthur C. Clarke', 31 March, SK/12/8/1/65, London: SKA, UAL.

—— (1964c), 'Letter from Stanley Kubrick to Edgar Rosenberg', 16 April, SK/11/9/107, London: SKA, UAL.

—— (1964d), 'Letter from Stanley Kubrick to Edgar Rosenberg', 16 July, SK/11/9/107, London: SKA, UAL.

—— (1964e), 'Letter from Stanley Kubrick to unknown', 22 April, SK/11/9/101, London: SKA, UAL.

—— (1964f), 'Letter from Stanley Kubrick to Herbert Biberman', 20 July, SK/11/9/8, London: SKA, UAL.

—— (1964g), 'Telegram to Colin Low', 30 April, SK/11/9/20, SKA, UAL.

—— (1966), 'Letter from Stanley Kubrick to Roger Caras', 11 July, SK/12/8/5, File 3 of 14, London: SKA, UAL.

—— (n.d.), 'Notes and plot breakdown for *Shadow on the Sun*', uncatalogued boxes, London: SKA, UAL.

—— (n.d.a), 'Handwritten notes by Stanley Kubrick for title ideas for *2001: A Space Odyssey*', SK/11/9/124, File 1 of 2, London: SKA, UAL.

Kubrick, S. and Clarke, A. ([1964] 2014), '*Journey Beyond the Stars*: A film story', in P. Bizony (ed.), *The Making of Stanley Kubrick's 2001: A Space Odyssey*, Cologne: Taschen, pp. 1–2.

—— (1965a), '*2001: A Space Odyssey* (draft script)', October–December, SK/12/1/2/1, London: SKA, UAL.

—— (1965b), '*2001: A Space Odyssey* screenplay', http://www.archiviokubrick.it/opere/film/2001/script/2001-originalscript. Accessed 4 October 2016.

—— (1965c), '*2001 – A Space Odyssey* (Athena Text)', 6 July, SK/12/1/2/1, London: SKA, UAL.

—— (1965–66), '*2001: A Space Odyssey* (Other HAL screenplay)', SK/12/1-4, London: SKA, UAL.

—— (1967), '*2001: A Space Odyssey* script supplement', 2 Jan, SK/12/1/2/5, London: SKA, UAL.

—— (2001), *2001: A Space Odyssey, Screenplay and Arthur C. Clarke 2001 Diary*, Utrecht: Stichting De Roos.

Labarre, N. (2014), '*Alien* as a comic book: Adaptation and genre shifting', *Extrapolation*, 55:1, pp. 75–94.

Lang, W. (1957), *Desk Set*, USA: Twentieth Century Fox.

Larbalestier, J. (2002), *The Battle of the Sexes in Science Fiction*, Middletown: Wesleyan University Press.

Lasseter, J. (1995), *Toy Story*, USA: Pixar Animation Studios/Walt Disney Pictures.

Leakey, L. (1960), *Adam's Ancestors: The Evolution of Man and His Culture*, New York: Harper Torchbooks.

Lean, D. (1964), *Lawrence of Arabia*, UK/USA: Columbia Pictures.

Lee, S. and Kirby, J. (1961), *The Fantastic Four*, New York: Marvel Comics.

Le Guin, U. K. (1969) *The Left Hand of Darkness*, New York: Ace Books.

Leitch, T. (2008), 'Adaptation studies at a crossroads', *Adaptation*, 1:1, pp. 63–77.

Leroi-Gourhan, A. (1943), *L'Homme et la Matière*, Paris: Albin Michel, College Sciences d'Aujourd'hui.

Letham, J. (2004), 'The return of the king, or, identifying with your parents', in S. Howe (ed.), *Give our Regards to the Atomsmashers! Writers on Comics*, New York: Pantheon Books, pp. 2–22.

Ligeti, G. (1961), *Atmosphères*, Germany: SWF Symphony.

Lightman, H. (1968), 'Filming *2001: A Space Odyssey*', *American Cinematographer*, June, pp. 412–14, 442–44, 446–47.

Linden, G. W. (1977), 'Dr. Strangelove and erotic displacement', *Journal of Aesthetic Education*, 11:1, pp. 63–83.

Lippi, G. (2008), *2001 Odissea nello spazio. Dizionario ragionato*, Recco: LeMani Microart's.

LoBrutto, V. (1997), *Stanley Kubrick*, London and New York: Faber and Faber.

Lockwood, G. (2001), *2001 Memories: An Actor's Odyssey*, Boca Raton, FL: Cowboy Press.

Losey, J. (1963), *The Servant*, UK: Elstree Studio Films.

Lothe, J. (2000), *Narrative in Fiction and Film: An Introduction*, Oxford: Oxford University Press.

Lott, T. (1999), *The Invention of Race: Black Culture and the Politics of Representation*, Hoboken: Wiley-Blackwell.

Loughlin, G. (2004), *Alien Sex: The Body and Desire in Cinema and Theology*, Oxford: Blackwell.

Lovejoy, R. (1964), 'Letter from Ray Lovejoy to Kevin Kavanagh', 15 October, uncatalogued boxes, London: SKA, UAL.

Lucas, G. (1977), *Star Wars*, USA: LucasFilm/Twentieth-Century Fox.

Lucas, J. M. (1968), 'The ultimate computer', *Star Trek*, 8 March, USA: Paramount.

Luckhurst, R. (2009), 'Remembering Eve Sedgwick', *Science Fiction Studies*, 36:3, http://www.depauw.edu/sfs/abstracts/a109.htm. Accessed 3 March 2010.

Lumet, S. (1964), *Fail Safe*, USA: Columbia.

Lust, A. (2003), *From the Greek Mimes to Marcel Marceau and Beyond: Mimes, Actors, Pierrots, and Clowns*, Lanham: Scarecrow Press.

Macklin, F. A. (1965), 'Sex and Dr. Strangelove', *Film Comment*, 3:3, pp. 55–57.

Mahlknecht, J. (2012), 'The Hollywood novelization: Film as literature or literature as film promotion?', *Poetics Today*, 33:2, pp. 137–68.

Malone, C.K. (2002), 'Imagining information retrieval in the library: *Desk Set* in historical context', *IEEE Annals of the History of Computing*, July–September, pp. 14-22.

Man, G. (1994), *Radical visions: American Film Renaissance, 1967–1976*, Westport: Greenwood.

Mankiewicz, J. L. (1964), *A Carol for Another Christmas*, USA: American Broadcasting Corporation.

Marcelli, A. (1964), 'Hollywood dissepolta', *L'Europeo*, 19 April, pp. 42, 55–57.

Martin, B. (1965), 'Annakin to Pen Auto Saga', *Los Angeles Times*, 25 September, p. B8.

Martino, C. (2016), 'Pictures of *2001: A Space Odyssey* in the Stanley Kubrick archive', *Photography and Culture*, 9: 1, pp. 79-87.

Marton, A. (1965), *Crack in the World*, USA: Paramount.

Mateus, M. (2001), 'Reading HAL: Representation and Artificial Intelligence', in R. Kolker (ed.), *Stanley Kubrick's 2001: A Space Odyssey: New Essays*, Oxford: Oxford University Press, pp. 103–125.

Mather, P. (2006), 'Stanley Kubrick: Photography and film', *Historical Journal of Film, Radio and Television*, 26:2, pp. 203–14.

—— (2013), *Stanley Kubrick at Look Magazine: Authorship and Genre in Photojournalism and Film*, Bristol: Intellect.

Mattessich, S. (2000), 'Grotesque caricature: Stanley Kubrick's *Eyes Wide Shut* as the allegory of its own reception', *Postmodern Culture*, 10:2, http://muse.jhu.edu/journals/postmodern_culture/v010/10.2.r_mattessich.html. Accessed 28 June 2010.

Mawston, M. (2016), 'Keith Hamshere: A Still-Life Portrait', *Cinema Retro*, 12: 34, pp. 32–37.

Mayhew, R.J. (2014), *Malthus: The Life and Legacies of an Untimely Prophet*, Cambridge: Harvard University Press.

McAleer, N. (1992), *Odyssey: The Authorized Biography of Arthur C. Clarke*, London: Victor Gollancz.

McAvoy, C. (2015), '"Gentlemen, You can't fight in here!": Gender symbolism and the end of the world in *Dr. Strangelove* and *Melancholia*', in K. Ritzenhoff and A. Krewani (eds), *The Apocalypse in Film: Dystopias, Disasters, and Other Visions About the End of the World*, Lanham: Rowman & Littlefield. pp. 61–69.

McCaffery, L. and Williamson, J. (1991), 'An interview with Jack Williamson', *Science Fiction Studies*, 18:2, pp. 230–52.

McCloud, S. (1993), *Understanding Comics: The Invisible Art*, New York: HarperPerennial.

McFarlane, B. (1996), *Novel to Film: An Introduction to the Theory of Adaptation*, Oxford: Clarendon.

McFarling, T. (1986), 'Computerised edit suite opens at TPV in London', *Screen International*, 1 March, 537, p. 10.

McGrady, M. (1964), 'Stanley Kubrick: A Filmmaker obsessed', *Newsday*, 11 February, p. 3c.

McLeod, K. (2003), 'Space oddities: Aliens, Futurism and meaning in popular music', *Popular Music*, 22:3, pp. 337–55.

McQuiston, K. (2011), '"An effort to decide": More Research into Kubrick's Music Choices for *2001: A Space Odyssey*', *Journal of Film Music*, 3:2, pp. 145–54.

Merkley, P. (2007), '"Stanley hates this but I like it!": North vs. Kubrick on the music for *2001: A Space Odyssey*', *The Journal of Film Music*, 2:1, pp. 1–34.

Metro-Goldwyn-Mayer (1965), 'Financing agreement between MGM and Polaris Productions', 22 May, SK/12/2/5, London: SKA, UAL.

Metz, C. (2011), 'Loving cinema; identification mirror; disavowal, fetishism', in T. Corrigan, P. White and M. Mazaj (eds), *Critical Visions in Film Theory*, Boston: Bedford/St. Martin's.

Meyer, R. (2008), '"Artists sometimes have feelings"', *Art Journal*, 67:4, pp. 38–55.

Miller, B. (2016), 'Graphic films and the inception of *2001: A Space Odyssey*', *Sloan Science & Film*, http://scienceandfilm.org/articles/2656/graphic-films-and-the-inception-of-2001-a-space-odyssey. Accessed 24 February 2016.

Miller, M. C. (2006), '2001: A cold descent', in G. Cocks, J. Diedrick and G. Perusek (eds), *Depth of Field: Stanley Kubrick, Film and the Uses of History*, Madison: University of Wisconsin Press, pp. 122–45.

Morrow, J. (2008), 'Dreaming feminisms', *Cultural Critique*, 1:1, http://ccjournal.cgu.edu/past_issues/janell_morrow.html. Accessed 3 November 2010.

Mosca, U. (1998), 'Finché c'è corpo c'è speranza', *Stanley Kubrick – Garage*, 12, pp. 75–87.
Moskowitz, G. (1965), 'Sci-fi snob: Call me Disney', *Variety*, 239:10, 28 July, pp. 7, 16.
MPAA (1964), '*Journey beyond the stars*, Title Registration Report', 24 August, SK/11/9/124, File 1 of 2, London: SKA, UAL.
Murray, P. and Schuler, J. (2007), 'Rebel without a cause: Stanley Kubrick and the banality of the good', in J. Abrams (ed.), *The Philosophy of Stanley Kubrick*, Lexington: The University Press of Kentucky, pp. 133–48.
Musel, R. (1965), 'Space worlds to be shown scientifically in pictures', *The Anderson Herald*, 8 October, p. 6.
—— (1968), 'Sophisticated science fiction', *Ottawa Journal Weekend Magazine*, 20:18, pp. 14–19.
Nabokov, V. (1955), *Lolita*, Paris: Olympia Press.
Naito, J. T. (2008), 'Writing silence: Samuel Beckett's early mimes', *Beckett san frontiers (Borderless Becket)*, 19, pp. 393–402.
Naremore, J. (1988), *Acting in the Cinema*, Berkeley: University of California Press.
—— (2000), *Film Adaptation*, London: Athlone.
—— (2007), *On Kubrick*, London: British Film Institute.
Nelson, T. A. (2000), *Kubrick: Inside a Film Artist's Maze*, 2nd ed., Bloomington, IN: Indiana University Press.
Neumann, K. (1950), *Rocketship X-M*, USA: Lippert Pictures.
Nolan, C. (2014), *Interstellar*, USA/UK: Warner Bros.
Nordern, E. (1968), '*Playboy* Interview: Stanley Kubrick', in G. D. Phillips (ed.), *Stanley Kubrick Interviews*, Jackson: University Press of Mississippi, pp. 47–74.
Novros, L. (1964), *To the Moon and Beyond*, USA: Graphic Films Corporation.
Oakes, P. (1965), 'Somebody up there likes me, I hope', *Sunday Times*, 3 October, p. 15.
Oboler, A. (1951), *Five*, USA: Columbia.
Odino, S. (2013), '2001: The aliens that almost were', *2001 Italia*, http://www.2001italia.it/2013/10/2001-aliens-that-almost-were.html. Accessed 17 October 2013.
Ohi, K. (2005), *Innocence and Rapture: The Erotic Child in Pater, Wilde, James and Nabokov*, Basingstoke: Palgrave Macmillan.
Ordway, F. (1982), '*2001: A Space Odyssey* in retrospect', in E. Emme (ed.), *Science Fiction and Space Futures: Past and Present*, San Diego: Univelt, pp. 47–105.
Pal, G. (1960), *The Time Machine*, USA: Metro-Goldwyn-Mayer.
Pantenburg, V. (2015), 'The cinematographic state of things', in V. Pantenburg (ed.), *Cinematographic Objects, Things and Operations*, Berlin: IKKM Books, pp. 9–21.
Patterson, D. W. (2004), 'Music, structure and metaphor in Stanley Kubrick's *2001: A Space Odyssey*', *American Music*, 22:3, pp. 444–74.
Patureau, A. (1964), 'UN specials rounding up a world of talent', *Newsday*, 9 April, p. 5C.
Pearson, W. G. (2009), 'Queer theory', in M. Bould, A. M. Butler, A. Roberts and S. Vint (eds), *The Routledge Companion to Science Fiction*, London: Routledge, pp. 298–307.
Peldszus, R. (2015), 'Speculative systems: Kubrick's Interaction with the aerospace industry during the production of *2001*', in T. Ljujič, P. Krämer and R. Daniels (eds), *Stanley Kubrick: New Perspectives*, London: Black Dog Publishing, pp. 198–217.

Perry, F. (1962), *David and Lisa*, USA: Continental Distributing.
Peucker, B. (2001), 'Kubrick and Kafka: The corporeal uncanny', *Modernism/Modernity*, 8:4, pp. 663–74.
Pezzotta, A. (1998), 'L'occhio di *Look*. Dalla fotografia alla regia', *Stanley Kubrick – Garage*, 12, pp. 5–11.
Pezzotta, E. (2013), *Stanley Kubrick: Adapting the Sublime*, Jackson: University Press of Mississippi.
Philips, G. D. (1999), *Major Film Directors of the American and British Cinema*, Cranbury: Associated University Press.
Pink, F. (1971), *Meddle*, London: Harvest Records.
Plank, R. (1977), 'Sons and fathers in A.D. 2001', in J. D. Olander and M. H. Greenberg (eds), *Arthur C. Clarke*, Edinburgh: Paul Harris Publishing, pp. 121–48.
Plotnick, J. (2014), *Space Station 76*, USA: Rival Pictures.
Poole, R. (2015), '*2001: A Space Odyssey* and "The Dawn of Man"', in T. Ljujič, P. Krämer and R. Daniels (eds), *Stanley Kubrick New Perspectives*, London: Black Dog Publishing, pp. 174–97.
Powell, A. (2007), *Deleuze, Altered States and Film*, Edinburgh: Edinburgh University Press.
Preminger, O. (1965), *Bunny Lake is Missing*, UK: Columbia.
Proyas, A. (2004), *I Robot*, USA: Twentieth Century Fox.
Pryor, T. (1951), 'Young man with ideas and a camera: Angel Bait', 14 January, p. 5, http://www.nytimes.com/1951/01/14/archives/young-man-with-ideas-and-a-cameraangel-bait.html?nytmobile=0. Accessed 18 April 2017.
Renaud, W. (1968), 'Entretien avec Stanley Kubrick', in M. Ciment (ed.), *Stanley Kubrick, La Biennale di Venezia*, Venezia: G.Mondadori, pp. 44–55, 1997.
Richter, D. (2000), 'Pictures from *Moonwatcher's Memoir*', http://www.danrichter.com/2001 MMPix/DOM%20Pix1.htm. Accessed 15 September 2017.
——— (2002), *Moonwatcher's Memoir: A Diary of 2001: A Space Odyssey*, New York: Carroll and Graf Publisher.
Ro, R. (2004), *Tales to Astonish: Jack Kirby, Stan Lee, and the American Comic Book Revolution*, New York: Bloomsbury.
Robinson, D. (1966), 'Two for the Sci-fi', *Sight and Sound*, 35:2, spring, pp. 57–61.
Robinson, W. R. and McDermott, M. (1972), '2001 and the literary sensibility', *The Georgia Review*, 26:1, pp. 21–37.
Rohwetter, M. (2011), 'Jäger und Trolle, *Die Zeit*', 37:8, September, p. 38.
Ronson, J. (2016), *Lost At Sea: The Jon Ronson Mysteries*, London: Picador.
Ross, A. (2013), 'Space is the place', *New Yorker*, https://www.newyorker.com/magazine/2013/09/23/space-is-the-place. Accessed 21 January 2017.
Rowe, C. (2013), 'The romantic model of *2001: A Space Odyssey*', *Canadian Journal of Film Studies*, 22:2, pp. 41–63.
Rushton, R. (2012), *Cinema After Deleuze (Deleuze Encounters)*, London and New York: Continuum.
Rydell, M. (1967), *The Fox*, USA: Claridge Pictures.
Sagolla, L. J. (2007), 'American Mime Theatre turns 55', *Back Stage East*, 13 September, 48:37, p. 21.

Sanders, S. M. (2008), *The Philosophy of Science Fiction Film*, Lexington: The University Press of Kentucky.

Sarris, A. ([1962] 1979), 'Notes on the Auteur theory in 1962', in G. Mast and M. Cohen (eds), *Film Theory and Criticism: Introductory Readings*, 2nd ed., Oxford: Oxford University Press, pp. 650-665.

―――― ([1968] 1996), *The American Cinema: Directors and Directions 1929-1968*, New York: Da Capo Press.

Saussure, F. de (2001), 'Course in general linguistics', in V. B. Leitch (ed.), *The Norton Anthology of Theory and Criticism*, New York: W. W. Norton, pp. 960-77.

Schaffner, F. J. (1968), *Planet of the Apes*, USA: Twentieth Century Fox.

Schaller, G. (1963), *The Mountain Gorilla: Ecology and Behaviour*, Chicago: University of Chicago Press.

Scharf, C. (2011), 'The habitable planets', http://blogs.scientificamerican.com/life-unbounded/the-habitable-planets/. Accessed 10 October 2016.

Schenk, R. (2015), 'Das schöne Spielzeug. Zur Entstehungsgeschichte des deutsch-polnischen Gemeinschaftsfilms Signale – Ein Weltraumabenteuer', in B. Braun, A. Dębski and A. Gwóźdź (eds), *Unterwegs zum Nachbarn. Deutsch-polnische Filmbegegnungen*, Trier: Wissenschaftlicher Verlag, pp. 97-114.

Scheurer, T. E. (1998), 'Kubrick vs. North: The Score for 2001: a space Odyssey', *Journal of Popular Film and Television*, 25, pp. 172-82.

Schlesinger, J. (1967), *Far From the Madding Crowd*, UK: Metro-Goldwyn-Mayer.

Schodt, F. (2007), *The Astro Boy Essays: Osamu Tezuka, Mighty Atom, and the Manga/Anime Revolution*, Albany: Stone Bridge Press.

Schrader, P. (1972), *Transcendental Style in Film: Ozu, Bresson, Dreyer*, Berkeley: University of California Press.

Schulman, J. (1969), 'The American Mime Theatre', *Back Stage*, 31 January, 10:5, p. 16.

Schwam, S. (2000), *The Making of 2001: A Space Odyssey*, New York: Modern Library.

Scott, Ridley (1979), *Alien*, UK/USA: Twentieth Century Fox.

―――― (1982), *Blade Runner*, USA/Hong Kong: Warner Bros.

Shantoff, J. (1968), 'A gorilla to remember', *Film Quarterly*, 22:1, p. 62.

Shaw, D. (2007), 'Nihilism and freedom in the films of Stanley Kubrick', in J. J. Abrams (ed.), *The Philosophy of Stanley Kubrick*, Lexington: The University Press of Kentucky, pp. 221-34.

Shay, D. and Duncan, J. (2001), '2001: A time capsule', *Cinefex*, 85, April, pp. 73-117.

Simondon, G. (1958), *Du mode d'existence des objets techniques*, Paris: Aubier.

―――― ([1958] 1980), *On the Mode of Existence of Technical Objects* (trans. N. Mellamphy), London, Ont: University of Western Ontario.

―――― (1961), 'Psychosociologie de la technicité', in N. Simondon (ed.), *Sur la technique (1953-1983)*, Paris: Presses Universitaires de France, pp. 23-128.

―――― (1965), *Imagination et Invention (1965-1966)*, Chatou: Les éditions de la transparence, Coll, Philosophie.

―――― (1968), 'Entretien sur la mécanologie, with Jean Lemoyne', in N. Simondon (ed.), *Sur la technique (1953-1983)*, Paris: Presses Universitaires de France, pp. 405-45.

—— (1982), 'Réflexions sur la techno-esthétique', in N. Simondon (ed.), *Sur la technique (1953-1983)*, Paris: Presses Universitaires de France, pp. 379–96.
Sklar, R. (1988), 'Stanley Kubrick and the American film industry', *Current Research in Film*, 4, pp. 114–24.
Smith, P. D. (2007), *Doomsday Men: The Real Dr. Strangelove and the Dream of the Superweapon*, New York: St. Martin's Press.
Sobchack, V. C. (1987), *Screening Space: The American Science Fiction Film*, New York: Ungar.
—— (1997), *Screening Space: The American Science Fiction Film*, 2nd ed., New Brunswick, NJ: Rutgers University Press.
Sofia, Z. (1984), 'Exterminating fetuses: Abortion, disarmament, and the sexo-semiotics of extraterrestrialism', *Diacritics*, 14:2, pp. 47–59.
Southern, T. ([1962] 2005), 'An Interview with Stanley Kubrick Director of *Lolita*', in: A. Castle (ed.), *The Stanley Kubrick Archives*, Cologne: Taschen, pp. 340–43.
—— ([1963] 2004), 'Check-up with Doctor Strangelove', in D. Wallis (ed.), *Killed: Great Journalism Too Hot to Print*, New York: Nation Books, pp. 25–44.
Spielberg, S. (1977), *Close Encounters of the Third Kind*, USA: Columbia Pictures.
Stang, J. (1958), 'Film Fan to Film Maker', *New York Times Sunday Magazine*, 12 October, p. SM34.
Starck, N. (2009), 'Sex after death: The obituary as erratic record of proclivity', *Mortality* 14:4, pp. 338–54.
Tarkovsky, A. (1972), *Solyaris* (*Solaris*), Russia: Mosfilm.
Tati, J. (1958), *Mon Uncle* (*My Uncle*), France/Italy: Gaumont.
—— (1967), *Playtime*, France: Gaumont.
—— (1971), *Trafic* (*Traffic*), France: Les Films Corona.
Telotte, J. P. (1995), *Replications: A Robotic History of the Science Fiction Film*, Urbana: University of Illinois Press.
Tenner, E. (1997), *Why Things Bite Back: Technology and the Revenge of Unintended Consequences*, New York: Vintage.
—— (2003), *Our Own Devices: How Technology Remakes Humanity*, New York: Vintage.
Tezuka, O. (1963–66), *Tetsuwan Atomu* (*Astro Boy*), Japan: Fuji TV.
Thackeray, W. M. (1844), *The Luck of Barry Lyndon*, http://www.gutenberg.org/files/4558/4558-h/4558-h.htm. Accessed 20 October 2016.
Theweleit, K. (1997), *Male Fantasies*, 2 vols (trans. S. Conway), Cambridge: Polity Press.
Thomas, B. (1968), 'Kubrick puts Mark on futuristic film', *The Newark Advocate*, 8 April, p. 24.
—— (1972), 'First feature: Douglas Trumbull', *Action*, May/June, pp. 16–20.
Thorpe, R. (1961), *The Honeymoon Machine*, USA: Metro-Goldwyn-Mayer.
Thron, E. M. (1977), 'The Outsider from the Inside: Clarke's Aliens', in J. D. Olander and M. H. Greenberg (eds), *Arthur C. Clarke*, Edinburgh: Paul Harris Publishing, pp. 72–86.
Toles, G. (2006), 'Double minds and double blinds in Stanley Kubrick's fairy tale', in R. P. Kolker (ed.), *Stanley Kubrick's 2001: A Space Odyssey: New Essays*, Oxford: Oxford University Press, pp. 147–76.
Tully, D. (2010), *Terry Southern and the American Grotesque*, Jefferson: McFarland.

Ulivieri, F. (2017), 'Waiting for a miracle: A survey of Stanley Kubrick's unrealized projects', *Cinergie*, November, https://cinergie.unibo.it/article/view/7349/7318.
Utterson, A. (2011), *From IBM to MGM: Cinema at the Dawn of the Digital Age*, London: Palgrave Macmillan.
Vadim, R. (1968), *Barbarella*, FR/IT: Paramount Pictures.
Van Parys, T. (2011), 'A fantastic voyage into inner space: Description in science-fiction novelizations', *Science Fiction Studies*, 38:2, pp. 288–303.
Walker, A. (1964), 'How Mr. Kubrick learned to stop worrying', *Evening Standard*, 11 December, p. 8.
—— (1970), 'Transcript of interview recorded at Abbots Mead', 25 May, Gemona, Italy: Cineteca del Friuli.
—— (1972), *Kubrick Directs*, London: Davis-Poynter.
—— (1988), *It's Only a Movie, Ingrid*, London: Headline.
—— (2000), *Stanley Kubrick ricordato da Alexander Walker*, http://www.archiviokubrick.it/testimonianze/persone/walker.html. Accessed 15 October 2016.
Walker, A., Taylor, S. and Ruchti, U. (1999), *Stanley Kubrick, Director: A Visual Analysis*, New York: W. W. Norton.
—— (2000), *Stanley Kubrick, Director: A Visual Analysis*, London: Weidenfeld & Nicolson.
Ward Baker, R. (1967), *Quatermass and the Pit*, UK: Hammer Film Productions.
Warren, J. (2012), 'Stanley Kubrick's favorite films', *Criterion Collection*, https://www.criterion.com/lists/106755-stanley-kubrick-s-favorite-films. Accessed 12 May 2017.
Watson, I. (2000), 'Plumbing Stanley Kubrick', http://www.ianwatson.info/plumbing-stanley-kubrick. Accessed 15 October 2016.
Watters, J. (1968), 'Feature review: *2001: A Space Odyssey*', *Boxoffice*, 8 April, p. 10.
Webster, P. (2011), *Love and Death in Kubrick: A Critical Study of the Films from Lolita Through Eyes Wide Shut*, Jefferson: McFarland.
Weiler, A. H. (1962), 'The east: Kubrick's and Sellers' new film', *New York Times*, 6 May, p. 149.
—— (1965), 'Beyond the blue horizon', *New York Times*, 21 February, p. X9.
Weinraub, B. (1972), 'Kubrick tells what makes "clockwork orange" tick', *New York Times*, 4 January, p. 26.
Westfahl, G. (ed.) (2005), *The Greenwood Encyclopedia of Science Fiction and Fantasy: Themes, Works, and Wonders*, vol. 2, Westport: Greenwood Press.
—— (2011), 'The endless Odyssey: The *2001* saga and its inability to predict the future', in G. Westfahl, W. K. Yuen and A. Kit-sze Chan (eds), *Science Fiction and the Prediction of the Future: Essays on Foresight and Fallacy*, Jefferson: McFarland & Co., pp. 135–70.
Wheat, L.F. (2000), *Kubrick's 2001: A Triple Allegory*, Lanham: Scarecrow Press.
White, L. (1955), *Clean Break*, New York: Signet.
White, S. (2006), 'Kubrick's obscene shadows', in R. P. Kolker (ed.), *Stanley Kubrick's 2001: A Space Odyssey: New Essays*, Oxford: Oxford University Press, pp. 127–46.
Whitney, J. (1961), *Catalog*, USA: Motion Graphics Incorporated.
Wilcox, F. M. (1956), *The Forbidden Planet*, USA: Metro-Goldwyn-Mayer.
Williams, D. E. (1984), '*2001: A Space Odyssey*: A warning before its time', *Critical Studies in Mass Communication*, 1:3, pp. 311–22.

Willoquet-Maricondi, P. (2006), 'Full-metal jacketing, or masculinity in the making', in G. Cocks, J. Diedrick and G. Perusek (eds), *Depth of Field: Stanley Kubrick, Film and the Uses of History*, Madison: University of Wisconsin Press, pp. 218–41.

Wilton, A. (1980), *Turner and the Sublime*, Chicago: University of Chicago Press.

Wise, R. (1951), *The Day the Earth Stood Still*, USA: Twentieth Century Fox.

—— (1979), *Star Trek: The Motion Picture*, USA: Paramount Pictures.

Wood, N. (2002), 'Creating the sensual child: Paterian aesthetics, pederasty, and Oscar Wilde's fairy tales', *Marvels and Tales: Journal of Fairy-Tale Studies* 16:2, pp. 156–70.

Yablon, N. (2004), 'The metropolitan life in ruins: Architectural and fictional speculations in New York, 1909–19', *American Quarterly*, 56:2, pp. 309–47.

Young, T. (1965), *Thunderball*, UK/USA: United Artists.

Zeller, O. (2011), *Immersive Cocoon*, USA: NAU.

Index

A
Abrams, Jerold J., 101
Abrams, Nathan, 11
Academy Awards. *See also* 2001: A Space Odyssey (film), 10
Adam, Ken, 206, 208
Adams, Ansel, 184, 193
Adler, Renata, 183, 222
Agel, Jerome, 8, 35
A.I. Artificial Intelligence. See also Aldiss, Brian, 97
Alcott, John, 66, 178, 216
Aldiss, Brian, 22, 27, 31, 97
Alien, 48–49, 56
Alphaville. See also science fiction, 5
Also Sprach Zarathustra. See Thus Spoke Zarathustra, 38, 107, 144, 160, 220
American Mime Theatre, The. *See* Curtis, Paul J., 61, 66–70, 73–74, 76–77
American Mime School, The. *See* Curtis, Paul J., 68
Amies, Hardy, 131
Apollo Program (1961–72), 3–4, 6, 205, 208
Apple (business), 155
  iPad, 155
Archer, Ernie, 217
Ardrey, Robert, 70, 206
Aries (spacecraft), 136, 209, 213
Armstrong, Neil. *See* Apollo Program, 3
Artificial intelligence, 28, 39, 57, 97, 117, 123, 126–127, 154, 188
Asimov, Isaac, 22

Astronauts, 53–54, 84, 87, 89, 131, 140, 154–161
  sexuality, 139, 153
Australopithecus africanus. *See* man-apes, 70
auteur theory. *See also* Kubrick, Stanley, 9–10, 15, 65, 199

B
Balsam, Martin, 216
Barry Lyndon, 76–77, 86, 92, 110, 137, 145, 178
Barthes, Roland, 177
BBC, 26–28, 219
Benjamin, Walter, 170, 176
Berenson, Marisa, 76
Bernstein, Jeremy, 35
Birkin, Andrew. *See* Dawn of Man, The, 66–67, 214, 216–217
Blade Runner, 140, 156
Blakeney, Gavin, 26–28
Blau, Louis C., 207
Blue Danube, The. See Strauss, Johann, 4, 38, 81, 136, 220
Bogarde, Dirk, 138
Borehamwood Studios, 7, 209, 213
Boulat, Pierre, 169
Bowie, David, 149, 158
Bowman, Dave. *See* Dullea, Keir
  as dehumanised, 84, 86–93, 109, 119, 131
  HAL, 121, 124–126, 153, 187
  Frank Poole, 156
  influence, 158

monolith, 141, 176
sexuality, 138–140, 144–145, 148, 157
Star Child, 102, 112, 146, 161, 211
Star Gate, 5, 40–41, 51, 56, 177–180, 189–190, 194
technology, 155
2001: A Space Odyssey (novel), 38
2010: The Year We Make Contact, 8, 158
Bradbury, Ray, 5
Brahms, Penny, 67, 82–83
Brahe, Tycho. See TMA–1, 172
Brando, Marlon, 24
British cinema, 5–7
British Film Fund Agency, 7
Bruno, M.W., 175
Bukatman, Scott, 35
Burgess, Anthony. See *Clockwork Orange, A*, 22
Burke, Edmund, 184, 186, 188

C
Campbell, Joseph, 206
Caras, Roger, 5, 20, 67, 69–70, 148, 204, 208, 211, 213–215
Carnon, Roy, 210
Childhood's End, 26, 38, 136, 148, 204, 219
Chion, Michel, 81, 87, 109, 111, 140, 157, 200
Ciment, Michel, 92
Cinema Technology, 3, 9, 65, 97, 104, 108, 110, 121, 165, 223
Cinerama, 165, 208, 215
Clarke, Arthur C.
    monoliths, 141–142
    Planet of the Apes, 65–66
    primatology, 70–71
    scientific accuracy, 44
    sequel novels, 5
    sexuality, 131, 135–139, 144–147, 156–157
    Sri Lanka, 209, 211
    Stanley Kubrick, 20, 22–25, 27–30, 37, 67, 73, 135, 200, 203–205, 207–208, 215

2001: A Space Odyssey (novel), 35, 41–43, 47, 213–214
2001: A Space Odyssey premiere, 221
Classical Hollywood, 5, 8
Clavius Base, 171, 173, 175
Clean Break, 6
Clockwork Orange, A. See Burgess, Anthony, 20, 22, 24, 30, 40, 50, 76, 110, 131
Close Encounters of the Third Kind. See Spielberg, Steven, 7, 140
Cold War, 3, 5, 21, 85, 141
Cole, Thomas, 185
Columbia Pictures. See also *Dr. Strangelove*, 204, 206–207
communism, 5
Conrad, Joseph, 145
Cordell, Frank, 218
Corliss, Richard. See *Lolita*, 10
counter culture, 8, 144, 149
Coward, Noel, 139
Crack in the World, 118
Cruise, Tom. See *Eyes Wide Shut*, 76, 110
Curtis, Paul J. See American Mime School, The, 61, 66, 68–70, 73–75, 77

D
Darius, Julian. See Marvel Comics, 47, 54
Dart, Raymond. See man-apes, 70
Dawn of Man, The
    ape costumes, 65, 67
    Daniel Richter, 61, 70, 74, 76
    front projection, 66, 169, 173
    human evolution, 23, 71, 82
    location shooting, 214, 216
    man apes, 83, 104
    mime, 68–69, 74–75
    monoliths, 178
    Moon-Watcher, 175, 219
    Stuart Freeborn, 218
    writing of, 73, 81, 206, 217
Day of the Fight, 6
Day the Earth Caught Fire, The, 118, 189
Day the Earth Stood Still, The, 5, 118

Index

DC Comics. *See also* Marvel Comics, 50–51, 57
Deleuze, Gilles, 174
Desk Set, 118–120
Discovery One, 81–84, 86–89, 92–93, 119, 124, 159–160
   centrifuge, 154
   HAL, 187
   and Jupiter Mission, 42, 120, 125, 153, 176
   nuclear weapons, 24
   special effects, 108, 155, 209, 214
Douglas, Kirk, 6–7
Dr. Strangelove, 7, 15, 19–21, 25–26, 29–30, 104, 110, 119, 131, 137, 140, 142, 203, 206–208
Dullea, Keir. *See* Bowman, Dave, 84, 86, 91, 139–140, 153, 158, 209, 213, 215–216, 221

E

Eagle Eye, 123
Escher, M.C., 209
European cinema, 5, 8, 57
Expedition to Earth/Encounter in the Dawn, 65, 206, 219
evolution, 38–40, 42, 44, 52–54, 81–82, 87, 92, 102–108, 114, 170, 174–175, 178–180, 211, 215
   anthropology, 70–71, 76
   Darwinian, 66, 179
   extinction, 23, 30
   killer-ape theory, 70
   primatology, 70–73, 76, 206
Eyes Wide Shut, 76, 104, 110

F

Fail Safe, 119
Falsetto, Mario, 61
Fantastic Voyage, 189
Fear and Desire, 6
Five, 118
Floyd, Dr. Heywood. *See* Sylvester, William, 27, 38, 81–83, 85–86, 119, 141, 158, 160, 171–173, 175, 186, 207, 213

Fluxus art movement, 169
Flying Padre, 6
Forbidden Planet, The, 5, 118–119
Ford, John, 165, 187
Foucault, Michel, 89
Frayling, Chris, 3, 10
Freeborn, Stuart. *See also* man-apes, 66–67, 71, 216–218
Freeland, Cynthia, 183–185, 188–192, 195–196
Freud, Sigmund, 170
   Freudian, 39, 142
Frewin, Anthony, 27
Full Metal Jacket, 40, 61, 76, 97, 104, 110, 131, 137, 140, 142, 147

G

Gaffney, Bob, 219
Garber, S, 3
Geduld, Carolyn, 203
Gelmis, Joseph, 10, 221–222
Gentleman, Wally, 205, 214, 223
Gilliatt, Penelope, 183
Godard, Jean-Luc, 5
Goodall, Jane. *See* man-apes, 70–71, 74–75
Graphic Films, 209–210

H

HAL 9000, 8, 39–40, 43, 57, 61, 81, 83, 86, 102, 109, 119, 120, 135, 155, 160, 176, 179, 187–188, 196, 211–212, 216, 219–220
   death of HAL, 88, 90–91, 117, 124–127, 160
   gaze, 89–90, 93, 111, 120, 159, 176
   homosexuality, 138–139, 157, 161
   as human, 87, 117, 121–122, 124, 126, 153–154, 156
   malfunction, 109–110, 156
   as monster, 88, 97, 111, 117, 121, 123
Hamshere, Keith. *See* man-apes, 67, 214, 217
Harlan, Jan, 219–220
Harris-Kubrick Pictures Corporation, 6–7
Harris, James B., 6–7
Hayden, Sterling, 25

Heidegger, Martin, 101
Hermann, Bernard, 215
hetronormativity, 136
Hollywood
   independent filmmaking, 6
   industrial contexts, 6
   post-classical, 8
Homer, 37
   Odyssey, 37, 40, 208
Homo sapiens. *See* man-apes, 175, 179
Honeymoon Machine, The, 120
How the West Was Won (1962). *See* Ford, John, 165, 187
Howard, Tom, 210
Hunter, I.Q., 8, 11, 15, 37
Hyams, Peter. *See 2010: The Year We Make Contact,* 5, 8

I
IBM, 155, 209–210, 212
I, Robot, 123
Immersive Cocoon, 158
Interstellar, 153, 160–161

J
Jenkins, Greg, 10
Johnson, Brian, 10
Jones, Duncan. *See Moon,* 153, 159
Journey Beyond the Stars, 6, 23, 30, 67, 206–208
Jung, Carl, 38–39

K
Kant, Immanuel, 185, 187, 191, 193–194
Kaplan, Mike, 8
Kaufmann, Stanley, 35
Kennedy, John F. *See* Apollo Program, 3, 6
Killer's Kiss, 6, 20, 103, 178
The Killing, 6, 103–104, 110
King Kong, 65
King, Stephen, 15
Kirby, Jack. *See* Marvel Comics, 15, 47–57
Kolditz, Gottfried, 159

Kolker, Robert, 9, 10, 35, 47, 97, 165
Kramer, Peter, 6, 8–10, 16, 29, 65, 183
Kuberski, Phillip, 84
Kubrick, Christiane, 28–29, 219
Kubrick, Katharina, 178
Kubrick, Stanley
   adaptation, 8, 10, 15–16, 35–36, 44, 47–48, 50, 52–58, 131, 184
   aliens, 3, 19–20, 23–24, 27–29, 39, 44, 53–54, 140, 149, 209, 215, 219
   as auteur, 50, 65, 140, 199, 222–223
   attitude to science fiction, 20, 27–28, 30, 203
   childhood, 6, 28, 49
   as collaborator, 25, 47, 65, 67, 70, 135, 137, 157, 199, 203, 222–223
   control, 10, 50, 209, 212, 214, 221, 223
   D.W. Griffith Lifetime Achievement Award, 110
   early career, 6, 7, 11, 20, 140
   interest in extraterrestrials, 19–20, 28–29, 203–205, 209
   interest in social issues, 23–24, 27–31, 138, 157
   Kubrickian, 165–166
   photography, 6, 97, 165, 169–173, 175–179
   political views, 25, 138
   as producer, 66, 199
   production process, 19, 203
   reputation, 7, 9–10, 19, 214
   satire, 140, 142
   unmade projects, 20–22, 24–25, 58
Kubrick Studies, 7, 9–10, 15, 61, 166

L
La Belle et la Bete, 67
La Dolce Vita, 179
Lange, Harry. *See* Ordway, Frederick, 4, 108, 207–210, 212
Lawrence of Arabia, 217
Leakey, Louis. *See* man-apes, 206
Lee, Stan. *See* Marvel Comics, 55
Le Guin, Ursula K., 135
Ligeti, György, 8, 38, 106, 113, 219–221

Index

Lightyear, Buzz, 158
Lockwood, Gary. *See* Poole, Frank, 84, 89, 153, 213, 215, 221
Lolita, 7, 15, 21, 26, 147, 207, 219
Look magazine, 6, 140, 165, 169, 178
Louis XVI bedroom. *See also* Star Gate, 39, 41, 43, 92, 144–145, 157–158, 176–177, 179–180, 194, 206, 219
Lost Worlds of 2001, The. *See* Clarke, Arthur C., 8, 42, 203
Lovejoy, Ray, 208, 218
Low, Colin. *See Universe*, 205
Lucas, George. *See Star Wars*, 7
Luckhurst, Roger. *See The Shining*, 135
Lyndon, Victor, 26, 69–70, 208

M

man-apes
    costumes, 65, 67, 216–217
    Daniel Richter, 66, 70–71, 218
    evolution, 54, 81, 83, 87, 105–106, 175, 178, 207
    extinction, 23, 104, 170, 173
    extraterrestrials, 53
    and mime, 61, 68, 69, 71–76, 84, 89
    monoliths, 38–39, 112, 174, 176, 219
Mankiewicz, Joseph, 24
Marceau, Marcel, 68–70
Marvel Comics. *See* Kirby, Jack, 4–5, 8, 15, 47–52, 55, 57
Masters, Tony, 208, 211, 214, 219, 222
McConaughey, Matthew, 160
McKenna, Richard, 208
Merchandising, 8–9
    Universe (board game), 9
MGM. *See also* O'Brien, Robert, 6–8, 20, 27, 67, 207–210, 213, 215–218, 220–223
Miller, Frank, 85
Mirisch, Walter, 24
modernism, 9, 68, 73, 101, 140–141
monolith
    critical interpretation, 111
    evolution, 23, 57, 105, 170, 195

landscape painting, 192–193
man-apes, 71, 74–75, 81–82, 174–175, 178
phallic symbol, 140, 142–144, 157
planetary alignment, 113
shape of, 53–54, 56, 112, 176, 196, 219
Star Gate, 147, 179, 194
TMA-1, 83, 171–173
2001: A Space Odyssey (novel), 38–39, 43, 141
Moon (2009), 153, 159–161
    Gerty 3000, 160–161
    Sam Bell, 159–160
Moon landings. *See* Apollo Program, 3
Moon-Watcher. *See* man-apes
    Also Sprach Zarathustra, 220
    Daniel Richter, 61, 66, 89
    Encounter in the Dawn, 206
    evolution, 81, 87, 106–107, 119, 211
    jump cut, 23, 107–108, 175, 222
    Marvel Comics, 52, 55
    mime, 69–70, 75–76
    monoliths, 54, 126, 174–175
    2001: A Space Odyssey (novel), 38, 104, 105
    2001: A Space Odyssey (script), 73–74

N

Nabokov, Vladimir. *See Lolita*, 7, 15
Napoleon. *See* Kubrick, Stanley, 58
Naremore, James, 36, 61, 81
    grotesque, 83
NASA, 3–4, 108, 119, 178, 205, 207–208, 210–211
New Film History, 9
Newman, Paul, 24
Nicholson, Jack. *See The Shining*, 110, 177
Nietzsche, Friedrich, 101, 140
Nikon, 176
Nolan, Christopher, 153, 160
    comparisons to Kubrick, 161
North, Alex, 220–221
novelizations, 48–49, 52, 55, 57–58
Novros, Lester, 209–210
Nuclear war, 7, 19, 21–23, 25, 29–30, 119, 203
    on film, 118

Nuclear weapons, 7, 20–21, 23–24, 26, 118
  as phallic symbol, 137

O
O'Brien, Robert. *See also* MGM, 207, 210, 216, 220–221
O'Neal, Ryan. *See Barry Lyndon*, 76
Ordway III, Frederick I. *See* Lange, Harry, 4, 108, 207–212, 216
Orff, Carl, 215, 220
Orion (spacecraft), 136, 209, 213
overpopulation, 22–24

P
Pakula, Alan, 5
paratexts, 8, 15, 49, 58
Paths of Glory, 7, 104
Pederson, Con, 210, 217, 223
Performance Studies, 61, 72–73, 81, 85, 91
Pezzotta, Elisa, 16, 56, 184, 194
Pink Floyd, 5
Planet of the Apes, 65
Plato, 178
Polaris Productions. *See also* Caras, Roger, 9
Poole, Frank. *See* Lockwood, Gary, 84, 86–87, 90, 109–110, 119–121, 131, 153, 155–156, 176, 187
  sexuality, 139, 140, 157
Preminger, Otto, 24

Q
Quatermass and the Pit, 5

R
Rain, Douglas. *See* HAL 9000, 87, 135, 153, 219, 220
Richter, Daniel. *See* man-apes, 61, 66, 69–76, 89, 140, 161, 203, 2016–219, 223
Rocketship X-M, 118
Rockwell, Sam. *See Moon*, 159–160
Romantic movement, 183–186, 189–190, 195
  J.M.W. Turner, 184
  John Martin, 184

Luminism, 190
Rossiter, Leonard, 86, 89

S
Samsung, 155
Sarris, Andrew, 9
Scruton, Roger, 170
Seafarers, The, 6
Sellers, Peter, 25
'The Sentinel' (Clarke), 27, 35, 65, 141, 204–205
Schaller, George. *See* man-apes, 70–71, 76
Schumann, Robert, 220
Schurmann, Gerard, 220
science fiction, 3, 7, 22, 35, 49, 56–57, 121, 135, 141, 144–145, 158–159, 183, 188–189, 195–196
  critical view of films, 5, 28, 159, 204–205
  1950s films, 3, 5
  1960s films, 5
  realism, 5, 10, 28, 30, 81, 135, 155, 178, 186–187, 213
  scientific accuracy, 4, 41–44, 123, 209–210, 212, 215, 223
Scorsese, Martin, 76–77
The Servant, 138
sexual revolution , 136
Shadow on the Sun, 26–28
Shepperton Studios, 212
Shining, The (book), 15
The Shining (film), 61, 97, 104, 110, 144, 177, 179
  Jack Torrance, 179
Signals: A Space Adventure, 158–159
simian cinema. *See* man-apes, 65–66, 75–76
Simondon, Gilbert, 97, 102, 105–108, 110, 112–114
Simpsons, The, 4
Sklar, Robert, 10
slit scan photography, 177, 217
Smyslov, Andrei, 86
Sobchak, Vivian, 35, 154, 186–187, 190
Solaris, 132

Southern, Terry, 21
Space Race, 3–4, 6, 186, 205, 207
Space Station 5 (space craft), 209, 213
Space Station 76, 158
Spartacus. See Douglas, Kirk, 7, 137, 148, 199, 207
Spielberg, Steven, 7, 97
Stanley Kubrick Archive, The, 4, 9–11, 20, 24–25, 117, 124, 165, 177, 199, 203
Star Trek, 5, 119–120
Star Trek: The Motion Picture, 5
Star Wars. See Lucas, George, 7, 31
Star-Child, 5, 38–39, 41, 43, 53, 57, 93, 102, 112, 114, 126, 135, 144–146, 149, 177, 179, 194, 213
Stardust, Ziggy. *See* Bowie, David, 158
Star Gate, 39, 41, 43, 53, 90, 113, 147, 160, 165, 176–177, 179, 184, 189–190, 194, 217
Steckel, Anita, 142
Strasberg, Lee, 68
Strauss, Johann, 4, 38, 136, 220
Strauss, Richard, 38, 160, 220
Supertoys Last All Summer Long, 22, 27, 97
Sylvester, William. *See* Floyd, Heywood, 27, 81, 85–86, 158

T
Tarkovsky, Andrei, 132
Tezuka, Osamu, 207
Thackeray, William Makepeace. *See Barry Lyndon,* 138
Them!, 118–119
3001: The Final Odyssey, 5
Thus Spoke Zarathustra, 38, 107, 144, 160, 220
Time Machine, The, 189
Tintin, 158
TMA-1, 39, 171, 173, 212
To The Moon and Beyond, 209–210
Torgensen, Marilyn, 136
Toy Story, 158
Trumbull, Douglas, 10, 140, 189–190, 192, 196, 210, 214, 217, 219, 223

2001: A Space Odyssey (film)
  Academy Awards, 65–66
  acting, 61, 66, 68, 71, 74–77, 81–87, 89–90, 93, 122, 140
  art cinema, 57
  budget, 10, 207, 211, 213, 216, 220
  communist reaction, 158–159
  critical interpretation, 5, 8–9, 11, 30, 37, 40, 53, 58, 81, 101, 111, 117, 121, 146, 149, 179, 192
  critical reviews, 8, 35, 37, 183, 221–222
  dialogue, 37, 40, 61, 82, 117, 121, 124, 170, 183, 192
  editing, 218, 221–222
  existentialism, 101–102, 183
  fan art, 158
  fandom, 8
  fashion, 131
  formalism, 8, 10, 36, 38, 81, 165, 170–171, 175, 178
  gender, 21, 40, 61, 131–132, 136, 138, 147, 153, 156, 161
  homosexuality, 131, 135, 137–140, 142, 144–146, 157, 159
  influence, 5, 7, 159–161
  intertextuality, 36, 42, 44, 47
  location shooting, 67, 208, 214, 216–217, 219
  nihilism, 97, 101
  parody, 4
  philosophical interpretation, 5, 10, 38, 40, 42–44, 61, 97, 101–102, 111, 114, 170–172, 175–179, 184, 192, 196
  product placement, 209
  prologue, 213–215, 221
  psychoanalysis, 38–40, 68, 73, 75–76, 142, 170
  marketing, 6, 9, 155
  merchandising, 155
  minimalism, 140, 183
  music, 4, 38, 52, 81, 82, 215, 218–222
  reception, 7, 183, 203, 221–222
  release of, 7, 35, 48, 203, 216–218, 220–222

representation of ethnicity, 140
representation of femininity, 132, 135, 137–138, 142, 144, 147, 159
representation of human body, 82–83, 85–89, 92–93
representation of masculinity, 40, 61, 82, 86, 131–132, 137–142, 144, 147–148, 157, 159, 161
representation of space, 10, 28, 30, 38, 40–41, 43, 82, 84, 86, 186–190, 196, 215
representation of technology, 56, 65, 81–84, 86–89, 93, 97–98, 102, 106, 108–110, 113, 117–118, 120–123, 126, 153–155, 170, 172, 178–179, 188, 195, 209–210, 212, 223
semiotics, 10, 36, 40, 85
sexuality, 84–85, 131, 135–136, 145, 149, 157
slowness, 40, 43, 52, 81, 90, 147, 192, 222
special effects, 10, 42, 65, 67, 97–98, 108, 135, 140, 159, 165, 169, 176–177, 183, 186–187, 189–190, 192, 199, 205–217, 219, 221–223
structuralism, 10
sublime, 38, 42, 44, 56, 145, 165, 183–192, 194–195
symbolism, 38, 41, 44, 75
theological interpretation, 5, 38–41, 44, 53, 75, 91, 101, 106, 111, 113, 172
writing of, 23, 27, 35, 42, 47, 65, 70, 73–74, 97, 117, 123–125, 135, 137–139, 142, 147, 157, 174, 193, 203, 205–209, 211–212, 215, 217
2001: A Space Odyssey (novel). *See* Clarke, Arthur C., 5–6, 8, 35, 38, 40–44, 47, 65, 104–106, 111, 117, 135, 139, 141, 144, 147, 157, 172, 178, 193, 211–213

2061: Odyssey Three, 5, 137, 157
2010: Odyssey Two, 5, 42, 47
2010: The Year We Make Contact, 5, 8, 158
Tycho Lunar Crater. *See* TMA-1, 171–172

U

Übermensch. *See* Nietzsche, Friedrich, 140
Ultimate Trip, The. *See also* Kaplan, Mike, 8, 144, 192
United Artists, 6
United Nations, 24–25
Universe. See Low, Colin, 205, 219
Universal Studios, 5
Unsworth, Geoffrey, 66, 216

V

Vadim, Roger, 158
Veevers, Wally, 210, 216, 223

W

Walker, Alexander, 10, 20, 28, 222
Warhol, Andy, 140
Watkins, Carleton, 193
Watson, Ian, 22
Watts, Robert, 169
Wheat, Leonard F., 53, 122
White, Lionel, 6
Whitney Snr, John, 217
Wilde, Oscar, 146
Wilson, Mike. *See* Clarke, Arthur C., 136

Y

Youth culture, 7–8

Z

Zeiss. *See also Barry Lyndo*n, 178